# The Dow Jones–Irwin
## Guide to
# Real Estate Investing
*Revised Edition*

# The Dow Jones–Irwin Guide to Real Estate Investing

*Revised Edition*

## Chris Mader
#### with Jon Bortz

**Dow Jones–Irwin**
Homewood, Illinois   60430

This book is dedicated to Chris Mader, my friend and
husband for twelve very special years. His energy was
unmatched as was his love for life, family, and business.
Chris wanted the life of each person he met to be a little
brighter, more enriched by challenges and as fulfilled as he
felt his was.

Susan Mader

ISBN 0-87094-214-X
Library of Congress Catalog Card No. 82-73928

*Printed in the United States of America*

3 4 5 6 7 8 9 0 K 9 8 7 6 5

# Contents

# Preface

Since 1975, dramatic changes in the real estate industry have necessitated a reassessment of the discussions and conclusions about real estate investing included in the first edition of this book. While many books cover how to select, develop, appraise, finance, improve, operate, and sell real property, few provide insight on how to assess and quantify a property's merits. We have addressed this topic because the answers are too important to oversimplify. Nine out of ten millionaires in this country earned their fortunes by investing in real estate. And in the 1980s, a period already marked by financial and economic volatility—and predicted by many to continue that way—great fortunes will be made and lost by those playing the real estate game.

If you already own real estate, whether it's your home or some other type of property, this book will help you decide whether to hold, sell, or even trade; whether to refinance or add a second mortgage; what impact inflation will have on your investment; and, what risks are associated with each type of property. We examine leverage and tax shelter and discuss sophisticated investment vehicles, such as joint ventures, syndications, and limited partnerships. And we devote an entire chapter to sensitivity, or "what if," analysis: what happens to a property's profitability if our original projections prove wrong.

If you have yet to make the jump into either home ownership or other real estate investments, whether for fear, lack of funds, or lack of knowledge, the authors help you to determine your investing objectives and the types of properties and investments best suited to those objectives. We thoroughly discuss home ownership and its benefits to you, the different types of mortgages and where and on what terms they can be found, and what roles are played by brokers, builders, bankers, and buyers. Shown here are how to compare real estate to other types of investments, such as stocks, bonds, savings accounts, and the like, and how to evaluate and measure the returns from real estate and other investments quickly, accurately, and easily.

Since the death of the principal author, I have received great assistance and encouragement from many people in completing Chris Mader's last written work. Most important, though, are the knowledge, confidence, and kindness passed on to me by Chris Mader, who was not only a brilliant and dynamic individual and educator but also a true friend. All of us who were fortunate enough to come in contact with Chris Mader, whether for a few minutes, hours, or much longer, will surely miss him dearly.

My sincere thanks to Chris's wife Susan, for her confidence in my abilities; to Paul Wilson of the Mader Group, Inc., for permission to use the computer programs and printouts; to my family for their constant support; to Mary Burke for her timely secretarial support; and to the publisher for understanding the importance of this last work of Chris Mader.

Your comments and questions are also welcomed. As Chris Mader noted in the first edition, making correct decisions in real estate investing requires the best in all of us.

November 1982                                              JON BORTZ

# About the Authors

## Dr. Chris Mader

Chris Mader was founder and president of his own company that specialized in executive education. Dr. Mader, creator of the Wharton Management Simulation, pioneered in the development and use of computer simulations to aid in teaching decision making and strategic management. The author of six books on common stocks, computers, strategic management, and real estate, Dr. Mader also served as a senior lecturer at the Wharton School, University of Pennsylvania, where he acted full-time as an assistant professor of management and decision science until he formed his own firm in 1978.

Dr. Mader earned his first degree in engineering at Pennsylvania State University in 1964. He then proceeded to the Wharton School, where he received a master's degree in business administration in 1967 and his doctorate in business and applied economics in 1972. Reknowned as a brilliant and tireless educator, Chris Mader received the Anvil Award for outstanding teaching from Wharton. He taught more than 500 seminars and more than 20,000 executives and students in his 14 years of teaching. On the morning of December 4, 1980, Chris Mader died in a tragic fire in Westchester County, New York, while conducting a seminar in strategic management.

## Jon Bortz

Jon Bortz presently holds a responsible position with a real estate development firm headquartered in Chicago. In that capacity, he is involved with the acquisition, finance, construction, and leasing of commercial real estate. Prior to his present employment, Mr. Bortz was a consultant and seminar leader for the Mader Group, Inc. In his role there, he was involved in seminars in real estate and other subjects for various corporate clients and educational institutions, including the Wharton School. Mr. Bortz currently consults with the Society of Industrial Realtors on the development of various educational programs. He is a certified public accountant and is a graduate of the Wharton School, where he majored in accounting and entrepreneurial management.

# PART I

# Real Estate Investment Analysis

# 1 Real Estate and Inflation

Leverage and tax shelter. These are the often-cited special benefits of real estate investing. But there is another good reason to consider real estate: protection, even profit, from inflation. *Inflation can actually boost your rate of return from real estate investing to 15 percent or even 30 percent compounded annually after tax.*

This book helps you with real estate investing. It includes the profit impact of inflation, which soared in the 1970s and seems embedded for the 1980s. In addition, we analyze such factors as initial costs, mortgage terms, rental income, operating expenses, depreciation, and taxes for their effects on profit and risk.

Part I explains real estate investment analysis using the latest tax laws and most complete techniques. We discuss typical and actual case examples, many from the authors' personal, seminar, and consulting experiences. We also cover who builds and invests, who sells and finances, and how and why. And we help you define what to expect from *your* real estate investing and how to go about it.

Part II then discusses each type of real estate—homes, condominiums, apartments, office buildings, shopping centers, industrial parks, resort property, and land development. The goal is to help you with proper selection and management through analysis of practical examples.

Part III features unique tables that help you make quick, accurate estimates of the profitability and risk of any real estate opportunity.

## Role of leverage, tax shelter, and inflation

Why do real estate investors so often grow wealthy? *Leverage.*
Why do the wealthy so often invest in real estate? *Tax shelter.*
What is the powerful factor propelling these profits? *Inflation.*

*Leverage* means borrowing money to multiply the impact of your own capital. A $200,000 investment can often control a million-dollar property. Even with more modest means, you can buy and mortgage real estate worth four or five times your own investment. Few opportunities have such leverage potential. This is not an unbridled benefit, of course, as the multimillion-dollar difficulties of William Zeckendorf, Sr., several real estate investment trusts (REITs), and, more recently, American Invsco can attest. But legendary fortunes have also been made *and kept* in real estate—ask Gerald Hines, Harry Helmsley, Bob Hope, or Laurence Rockefeller.

*Tax shelter* means the legitimate shielding of income from the government. Various tax laws are designed to encourage investing. Real property, both for housing and commercial purposes, has been deemed a national need and worth stimulating. Federal income tax laws (and most state statutes) offer shelter to the real estate investor. It's one way the wealthy stay wealthy.

*Inflation* is the third and often the most important reason for the success of real estate investors. Inflation causes rents and selling prices to rise for most properties. But sometimes inflation in operating expenses or interest rates can curtail these gains and even produce losses. The analysis and examples in this book can be your guide to profiting from real estate investing by understanding the proper roles of leverage, tax shelter, and inflation.

## Inflation—the dominant factor

During the 1970s, inflation's powerful impact became obvious. Yet even now, in the 1980s, some real estate investors oversimplify their analysis by omitting its complicating effect. This is no longer necessary—and, more importantly, the results are simply wrong if inflation is ignored. Whether you are a professional or part-time investor, we hope to change the way you analyze real estate. We will also provide you with a straightforward way to do it right.

You need only a quick look at the average selling prices of new homes, shown in Figure 1.1, to be convinced of rising prices. The cost of new construction, partially due to enhanced quality, has been inflating strongly for years. During the 1970s, increases in the cost of land, lumber, metals, construction financing, and skilled labor boosted the price of new housing by about 12 percent *each year*—a rate significantly *faster* than overall inflation during that decade.

FIGURE 1.1
Home values 1970–1981
Annual average price of new single-family homes sold, in thousands of dollars.

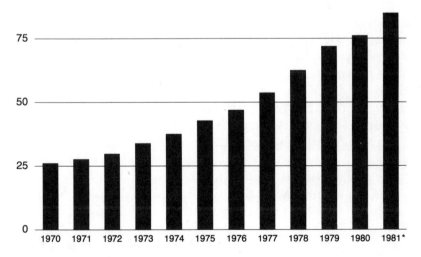

*Through second quarter 1981.
Source: U.S. Census Bureau.

Those who own homes can now, in most cases, take comfort from the inflation-swollen value of those homes. It has become standard practice, in fact, to roll the sales gain from one home into the down payment on a more desirable one. Outsiders watching this escalating merry-go-round now fear being priced out of suitable housing altogether. The cost of buying and financing a dream house has risen faster than savings and income needed to buy and carry it. In fact, a U.S. government study has concluded that only 3 percent of the population can afford to purchase a new home at today's prices and interest rates.

This familiar scenario is recounted to "prove," at a personal and intuitive level, the premise that inflation usually helps real estate investors, while others miss out. In the chapters ahead, we will take a more rigorous look at this and other factors affecting the various types of real estate. But the most important factor—*and the least quantified*—is inflation.

## Why inflation helps real estate investors

While inflation has surged, productivity and real growth have sagged. This "stagflation" is frequently cited as the nation's major economic/political problem. President Ford called inflation "public enemy number one." President Carter's pronouncements listed it as our chief problem. And President Reagan has launched an all-out attack on inflation, citing it as his number one domestic concern. Yet *The Wall Street Journal* has said of inflation, "On no subject around is there more talk and less understanding." The *New York Times* once editorialized that, "Of all the torrent of statistics pouring out of Washington, none exceeds in importance the monthly Consumer Price Index."

The Consumer Price Index (CPI) measures the ever-higher sum needed to buy the typical consumer's market basket of goods. Its escalation from 1967 to 1981 is charted in Figure 1.2. It often seems that the flow of inflation statistics has itself become inflated. We might wryly wonder if inflation troubles us only because we now measure it so much.

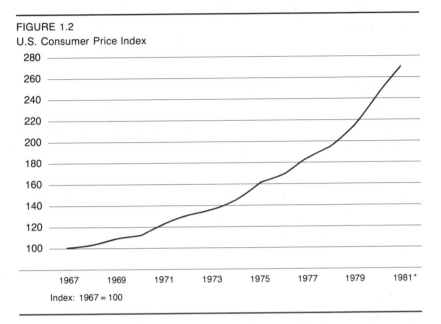

FIGURE 1.2
U.S. Consumer Price Index

Index: 1967 = 100

For those on fixed incomes, eroding purchasing power is no statistical artifact. The value of a constant dollar income, such as from an insurance annuity or debt security, has shrunk dramatically. The seemingly responsible 25-year-old who purchased a whole-life insurance policy in 1940 is now aged 66, and each redeemable dollar has dropped more than 80 percent in purchasing power.

Similarly, the dollars you choose to invest now face an uncertain future if unguarded against inflation. Earning sufficient income to meet rising inflation is a constant concern for most people today. And more than 60 million citizens now have the right to a larger paycheck from time to time just because of inflation, including those receiving Social Security, those covered by certain government and private pension plans, and those under cost-of-living labor contracts. Also, many homeowner's insurance policies now increase coverage (and premiums) automatically to keep current with inflating real estate values. Yet how can the investor seek protection and profit from inflation? How can he or she ensure that purchasing power is preserved and, indeed, possibly expanded?

Real estate, like most other forms of tangible ownership, has historically insulated investors' assets from erosion by inflation. Adequate, attractive, comfortable shelter, be it for residential or commercial purposes, is such a fundamental need that its price has risen along with the average price level. Higher replacement costs and the increasing number of households (though smaller) see to that. Also, higher family incomes (counting multiple wage earners), the fixed supply of land (and development restrictions), and the rising tax brackets brought on by inflation (including housing "shelters" taxes, too) all act to nudge most real estate prices steadily upward.

Appreciation in real estate, both in its rental income and in its market value if sold, can result from factors other than mere price inflation. Tasteful design, regional development, shifting population, good maintenance, selective renovation, or just smart marketing can improve the *real* economic value of a property beyond increases in the Consumer Price Index. Whatever the cause—mere inflation or true appreciation—the profit impact of generally rising rents and selling prices is substantial.

## Analyzing real estate investments

A typical case can show the favorable effects of leverage, tax shelter, and most important, inflation. (This case is analyzed more fully and precisely in Chapter 4.) Suppose that in 1976 you had bought a small suburban medical office building. Its price then was $150,000. How well would you have fared by, say, putting up 25 percent of this price as equity and arranging a 75 percent mortgage for the balance? The financing acts to leverage your own capital.

Assume that each of the four office suites in 1976 rented for $600 per month ($7,200 per year). The total gross income would have been $28,800 annually. It is wise to allow for one suite being vacant three months (an $1,800 loss of rent, or approximately a 6 percent vacancy factor). This would have reduced the theoretical rent roll to $27,000 or what is called *effective gross income,* or what rent you can reasonably expect to collect.

Against this income, you would likely have experienced about $12,000 of operating expenses annually—property taxes, maintenance, utilities paid by the landlord, insurance, supplies, administration, and so on. Deducting these expenses from the actual rents ($27,000 – $12,000) would have left $15,000 of *net operating income.* Compared with the $150,000 total project cost, such income would have constituted a 10 percent annual rate of return. But this common calculation *omits leverage, tax shelter, and inflation.* It is simply incomplete.

Table 1.1 shows the arithmetic for our medical building. It shows a *four-level* analysis of the property, leading to a *total rate of return.* Those key concepts will be used throughout this book. Indeed, the real estate industry has increasingly adopted this viewpoint. Yet one expert recently told me that "perhaps only *one third* of professionals already think this way, and a lesser portion of individual investors. Yet in the 1980s, this four-level analysis will be vital, probably mandatory. Those who don't use it will be left behind."

Let us move beyond Level 1 thinking and the 10 percent return we calculated on that basis. (This rate of return is called the *capitalization rate,* or simply *cap rate.)*

Level 2 shows that by using leverage, you incur the expense of mortgage interest and, usually, you must also make debt repayments, called *amortization.* Here we show a "conventional" mortgage for 25 years at 9 percent interest (remember, this property was bought and financed in 1976).

In this case, annual mortgage payments during the first few years approximate $10,000 annually for interest and $1,250 for loan amortization. Of the $15,000 of net operating income, you are left with $3,750 as your in-pocket cash before taxes. This is called your *spendable* or before-tax *cash flow.* Expressed as a rate of return on equity, it is commonly referred to as a *cash-on-cash return.* Thus, the $3,750 amounts to a 10 percent rate of return on the $37,500 equity invested, as shown in Level 2 of Table 1.1.

TABLE 1.1
Four-level real estate investment analysis: sample real estate investment during inflation

### Suburban medical office building

**LEVEL 1:**   Holding results, before financing and taxes

| | |
|---|---:|
| Gross income .............................. | $28,800 |
| Less: Vacancy............................ | 1,800 |
| Effective gross ........................... | 27,000 |
| Less: Operating expense ................... | 12,000 |
| Net operating income ...................... | 15,000 |

Rate of return on: $\dfrac{\text{Net operating income}}{\text{Total invested}}$ is $\dfrac{\$\ 15,000}{\$150,000}$ = 10%

**LEVEL 2:**   Holding results, after financing and before taxes
Assume: mortgage of 75% ($112,500) at 9% interest for 25 years

| | | |
|---|---|---:|
| Net operating income ................. | (rounded) | $15,000 |
| Less: Mortgage interest ............. | (rounded) | 10,000 |
| Amortization ........................ | | 1,250 |
| Cash flow.................................. | | 3,750 (before tax) |

Rate of return on: $\dfrac{\text{Before-tax cash flow}}{\text{Equity}}$ is $\dfrac{\$\ 3,750}{\$37,500}$ = 10%

**LEVEL 3:**   Holding results, after financing and taxes

| | | |
|---|---|---:|
| Actual gross .............................. | | $27,000 |
| Less: Operating expense ................... | | 12,000 |
| Mortgage interter ............. | (rounded) | 10,000 |
| Depreciation ........................ | | 7,200 |
| Taxable income............................ | | (2,200) |
| Ordinary taxes at 50%................. | | (1,100) |
| Cash flow .......................... | | 4,850 (after tax) |

Rate of return on: $\dfrac{\text{After-tax cash flow}}{\text{Equity}}$ is $\dfrac{\$\ 4,850}{\$37,500}$ = 12.9%

**LEVEL 4:**   Overall results, including sale

| | | |
|---|---|---:|
| Gross sale price ........................... | | $200,000 |
| Less: Selling costs ....................... | | 12,000 |
| Debt repayment ............. | (rounded) | 105,000 |
| Capital gain tax.............. | (rounded) | 16,000 |
| Cash flow................................. | | 67,000 (after sale) |

+ Holding results to date of this sale = Internal rate of return

Level 3 shows that tax shelter is the next benefit. While your $27,000 of effective gross income is all taxable, it is offset by the $12,000 of expenses and the $10,000 of tax-deductible interest payments. (Mortgage amortization constitutes debt repayment and is *not* deductible.) Tax laws also let you depreciate the building, thus recouping its cost untaxed as it wears out over time.

Thus, including depreciation of $7,200, the deductible expenses more than offset your effective gross income. Your $3,750 of before-tax cash flow is completely sheltered. Also, $2,200 of other income is offset by this property's tax deductions. Assuming the owner is in a 50 percent ordinary income tax bracket and has $2,200 of other income to shelter, the tax saved is $1,100. This *after-tax* rate of return on the original equity amounts to 12.9 percent.

The real kicker is inflation. Assume that this property's market value has inflated (or appreciated) at about 6 percent per year, a likely occurrence. By 1981, its market value would be one-third greater, or $200,000. Selling costs for a property of this type and size are about 6 percent of market value. (For smaller properties or land, this percentage is usually higher, counting commissions, taxes, and title and closing costs; for larger properties, transaction costs may be less.) After paying off the remaining mortgage balance and the required capital gains tax, a bonanza still remains. Level 4 of Table 1.1 shows this cash flow from sale to be $67,000.

So what rate of return would we have earned from our 1976 purchase of this medical building? We not only would have made the 12.9 percent annual after-tax return, but we also would nearly have doubled our initial $37,500 stake. And all of this would have been *after taxes.* The capital appreciation alone works out to about 12 percent compounded annually over the five-year holding period. Thus the inflation-swollen sale price produced an annual rate of return practically matching the profits from holding!

Combining these two sources of profit, holding plus sale, produces the Level 4 total rate of return. For this typical property, bought and financed in the past decade, returns were more than 20 percent compounded annually. And this impressive profitability is after all expenses and taxes. In dollar terms, and even in purchasing power, the real estate investor has stayed well ahead of inflation.

## When inflation hurts

During the 1970s, and to a lesser degree in the 1960s, inflation significantly boosted the fortunes of most real estate owners. Rents and selling prices generally increased. But by the 1980s, inflation's pervasive negatives were causing higher and higher operating expenses and financing costs.

Property taxes (depending on location), maintenance, insurance, and especially utilities had all risen faster than inflation. These costs significantly dent rates of return unless recouped in rents, assuming lease terms and market/political conditions permit such rental increases. Ultimately, high expenses can even drive down rentability and resale value. Cities full of vandalized, vacant buildings are mute testimony to this unfortunate effect.

On the financing front, construction loans and permanent mortgages have become enormously more costly. Indeed, by the fall of 1981, mortgage rates nationwide had shot to 17 to 18 percent from just 10 percent two years earlier. And those lenders making mortgage loans were charging origination fees of from 3 to 5 percent of the loan amount just for agreeing to make the loan. Even then, lenders hestitated to make long-term commitments of 25 to 30 years, as had been normal. To some extent, high mortgage rates and short lives reduce the property owner's leverage benefit.

Precisely because these conflicting factors are so difficult to judge, this book provides a way to analyze them easily and accurately. The chapters ahead explain and apply this analysis; the reference tables in Part III then show the differing effects of 10 percent and 15 percent mortgage rates for various rent and expense levels. In addition, they reflect the tax shelter from depreciation allowed on different types of property and the impact of inflation.

Another inflation-related risk can also influence real estate investing. Properties are frequently valued by dividing their annual net operating income (NOI) by some desired rate of return (the cap rate). For example, if we desired a 10 percent return on our medical building having a $15,000 NOI, then a fair price might be $15,000 divided by .10, or $150,000, its actual cost at the time. Until recently, a bank, insurance company, or savings institution would usually loan 75 percent of this valuation on a first mortgage. Thus a cap rate lets you translate from net operating income to an approximate fair market price or collateral value.

What effect does inflation have on the desired rate of return? As interest rates rise to overcome increased inflation, investors may similarly demand higher rates of return from real estate. In 1970 and again in 1974 and 1980–81, both bonds and common stocks fell in price until their interest and dividend yields increased to meet investors' inflation-swollen needs for higher rates of return. Just as bond or stock yields rise and their prices decline in the face of investors' needs to offset inflation, so real estate cap rates may be subject to similar pressures, harming real estate values.

Also, an inflation-triggered recession can depress rental property incomes, especially for commercial property. In New York City in both 1970 and 1974–75, commercial property values declined as a result of inflation-boosted needs for return butting up against recession-weakened commercial demand.

This phenomenon is worldwide. For example, it happened in London during 1974, as shown in Figure 1.3. Amid the emerging energy and inflation crises of that time, interest rates in London soared, and required property yields rose in tandem. This depressed property prices, and many real estate values in that city tumbled by 30 percent.

In Figure 1.3 it is also important to note that, while interest rates and property yields tend to rise and fall together, *the interest rates are higher.* Markets are not dumb. So there must be a reason why supposedly low-risk government bonds are priced by the market to provide higher yields than real estate.

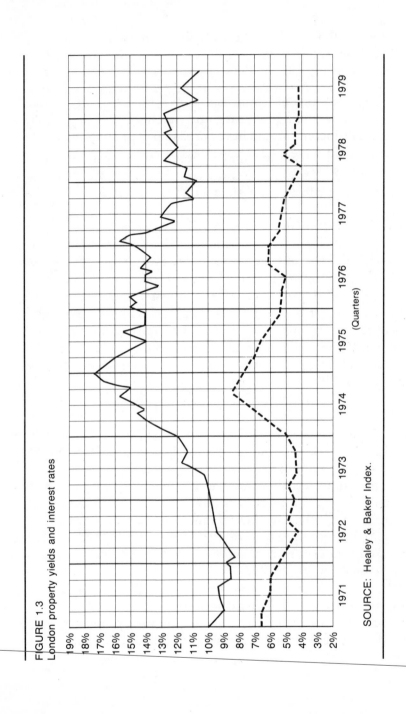

FIGURE 1.3
London property yields and interest rates

SOURCE: Healey & Baker Index.

That reason is *inflation.* The bond income will remain constant over time, but rents will rise due to inflation.

Suppose that, during the distress of 1974, you had bought a London property then yielding 8 percent versus the bond's 16 percent. By 1981 its rent would easily have doubled (and its price *tripled*). Thus, within a few years, and probably ever thereafter, the property's income would have surpassed the bond's income— plus you would have had a huge capital gain!

Property *should* logically yield less than bonds during inflation, *because inflation boosts rents.* Future rent yields improve compared with the property's original cost. By contrast, inflation does *not* boost the interest received from owning an already-issued bond. In fact, rising inflation and interest rates further depress the bond's selling price.

Notice also from Figure 1.3 that the *yield spread* between bonds and prime property widened as the 1970s wore on. This reflects not only inflation (which explains the spread) but also *rising* inflation (which caused the *widening* spread). Thus, rising inflation and interest rates can temporarily hurt property values, just as they depress stock and bond prices. The conclusion: During inflation you should own real estate; during *rising* inflation you should *definitely* own real estate but should *time* your purchases accordingly.

## What has the inflation rate been?

The many statistics leave no uncertainty on this question. Figure 1.2 shows the continuing upward thrust of the U.S. Consumer Price Index. Figure 1.4 shows the *annual* inflation rate. As you can see, the inflation trend line is definitely rising.

Figure 1.5 shows the interest rate on U.S. government short-term and long-term debt. The shaded periods represent recessions, which seem to cause short-term interest rates to fall and long-term interest rates to stabilize temporarily.

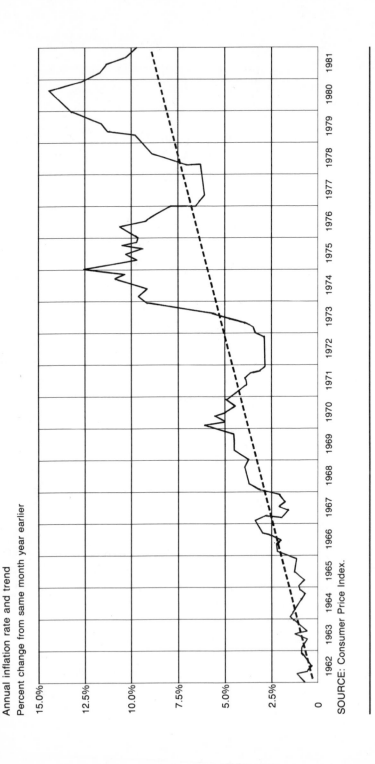

FIGURE 1.4
Annual inflation rate and trend
Percent change from same month year earlier

SOURCE: Consumer Price Index.

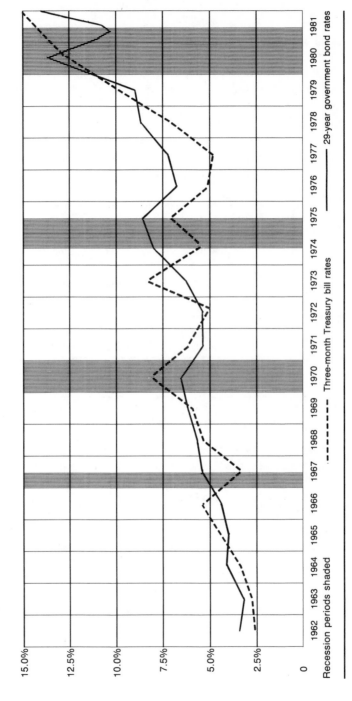

FIGURE 1.5
U.S. government short-term and long-term interest rates

Recession periods shaded

– – – – – – Three-month Treasury bill rates

——————— 29-year government bond rates

## Why inflation will continue

Rising inflation, with interest rates rising in sympathy, reflects our central economic problem—*faltering productivity*. U.S. productivity growth (output per employee) has not kept pace with that of Japan or West Germany, for example, or the United Kingdom. The problem is broadly international, with productivity faltering more as the 1970s passed. Table 1.2 confirms the United States' last-place ranking and this deteriorating worldwide trend.

TABLE 1.2
Annual productivity growth, real GNP per employed worker

| Country | 1963–73 | 1973–79 |
|---|---|---|
| Japan | 8.7% | 3.4% |
| Germany | 4.6% | 3.2% |
| France | 4.6% | 2.7% |
| Italy | 5.4% | 1.6% |
| Canada | 2.4% | 0.4% |
| United Kingdom | 3.0% | 0.3% |
| United States | 1.9% | 0.1% |

SOURCE: Economic Report of the President, January 1980, p. 85, O.E.C.D. data.

As stated in *The Wall Street Journal*, Table 1.2

. . . ought to be writ large, framed and hung conspicuously in the offices of all with responsibilities for economic policy.

The U.S. economy is the weakest of the seven major economies in the industrial world in its capability to generate economic progress, gains in real income, and productivity (these all fundamentally being synonyms for each other). While the stronger capability of the German and Japanese economies to deliver gains in productivity is no surprise, how many informed Americans have embedded in their thinking that we are at the bottom of the list, with even the U.K. ahead of us?

An economy achieving negligible gains in productivity is an economy in for serious trouble as it confronts the major burdens and adjustments being imposed on it for the 1980s.

The watershed year, 1973, of course marked the turning point in the world's continuing energy crisis. That oil is limited and more costly is reality. But for 200 years we have relied on cheap energy to power productivity. Now energy has gone on strike.

By that, we mean that we accept individuals' rights to withhold their labor if they don't like the deal they are offered. To have it otherwise would be slavery. When individuals act together, as in a union, withholding their labor while negotiating terms constitutes a *strike*. In essence, then, the owners of oil resources— the members of the Oganization of Petroleum Exporting Countries (OPEC)—went on strike. They withheld oil, achieving their demands for a higher price.

Now, as the 1980s unfold, capital has also gone on strike. That's right; the owners of capital—those with money to invest to finance productivity improvement—have said they won't invest unless *they* are paid more. After all, they reason, inflation is up, interest rates are up, and energy costs are up—why not returns on capital?

In less than 10 years, and after 200 years of productivity progress, *both energy and capital have gone on strike.* Now where will we get the resources to power and finance productivity? It's as if both our right and left arms have been cut off. We all want 10 percent (or more) pay boosts, it's just more money chasing the same amount of goods—it's inflation. Solving the productivity and wage escalation problem will, in our opinion, take at least a decade. So we expect that inflation will remain embedded in our system, although *temporary* rate declines may occur. As individuals, we must adapt to and even seek advantage from it.

## Summary

The inflation trend line in Figure 1.4 suggests that double-digit inflation annually is a likely prospect. However, reduced inflation, as occurred in 1970-71 and 1975-76, *is* possible. But interest rates on government bonds of 12 percent certainly imply expectations of about 10 percent ongoing annual inflation. In the twisted logic of an inflationary era, the old saying becomes, "Never a lender, but a borrower be."

The examples and tables in this book assume that inflation *must* be analyzed as part of real estate investing. What do *you* think the inflation rate will be? If your answer is *other than zero percent,* then the discussion ahead may change your mind about real estate investing and change the way you analyze such opportunities.

# 2 Real Estate versus Other Investments

Real estate competes with other investments just as surely as one property competes with another. So if you invest, real estate belongs on your list of alternatives. But should it then leap from this list of maybes into your investment portfolio? To answer this issue, frank consideration must be given to:

1. Your investment objectives.
2. How the competing opportunities (such as real estate, stocks, bonds, and commodities) are likely to perform toward meeting those objectives.
3. Whether real estate should therefore be in *your* asset mix.

Our device for helping you decide is a discussion of investment objectives followed by a ranking of various investment opportunities according to those objectives. This Objectives–Opportunities Table is then personalized to your specific desires.

## Why invest?

Perhaps your most important personal resources are health, happiness, time, and money—but only money can be stored and, to a degree, exchanged for the others. Most of us feel we should invest to gain the satisfaction and security of knowing that this one resource will be available in times of want or need. Yet saving and investing continually compete with desires to spend now.

To attain the financial base that most people profess to want, our advice is *insure, invest, and spend the rest.*[1] This priority assures, first, income despite adversity and, second, income for the future before the daily thrust for consumption. How much you should set aside regularly depends on your current assets, your goals, the time remaining to reach them, and your comparative investment success. But you cannot profit at all from real estate, or any of the other competing opportunities, unless you first *decide to invest* some of your resources—time and usually money.

## Your investment objectives

It might seem obvious that *profit,* usually measured as an investment rate of return, is your number one investment objective. You might also say it's the *only* objective (within legal and moral bounds) and, in retrospect, be correct. But investments are commitments to an uncertain future. Their after-the-fact profitability simply is not known at the time of investing. Investors must rely on foresight rather than hindsight. The 3,000-plus investors with whom we've conducted investing seminars acknowledge having the following eight objectives.

### 1. Investment rate of return

This first objective is the primary focus of this book—enabling you to forecast real estate rates of return. We will develop an evaluation procedure that translates your judgments of property costs, rents, mortgage terms, inflation rates, taxes, and other factors into a quantitative, consistent, and comparable measure of profitability. This analysis method is applicable to any property you might consider.

Investment rate of return is the *total return* from owning an investment. It includes both income and capital gains (or losses).

The profitability of a savings account, for example, is easy to compute. The only cash inflows are the fixed, periodic interest payments with no change in the principal (unless interest income is reinvested). For assets with fluctuating prices, such as real estate or common stocks, the total return concept includes both the current income from holding *and* any capital gains (or losses) upon sale.

This principle is well accepted by stock and bond market investors, who look at more than just the current yield. The effects of sale—such as changed market value, selling expenses, and taxes due—are also relevant in real estate analysis, though often overlooked or oversimplified. The evaluation approach used here computes not only the current return from holding, both before and after taxes, but also the overall, total return including the effects of sale.

## 2. Low risk

Our evaluation method can also be used to assess risk, defined as adverse results from unforecasted events. Investors' willingness and ability to accept risk varies with such factors as age, net worth, salary, and psychological temperament. For some, safety of capital rivals rate of return in importance. Others are more willing to gamble, hoping that good fluctuations will overcome the bad and produce total returns higher than those from more conservative investments.

Empirical evidence only partially supports the widely held belief that high return accompanies high risk. Comprehensive stock market research, for example, has shown that medium-risk investments offer somewhat more total return than low-risk investments. However, still higher levels of risk actually provide *lower* overall returns.

This paradoxical result extends also to the bond markets, where medium-grade bonds pay significantly more interest than the highest-quality bonds—more so than is warranted by their only slightly higher default probability. But extremely speculative bonds have not done so well. Horse-race fans also overbet both the favorites and the long-shots, decreasing their relative returns.

There are two explanations for this seemingly irrational risk-taking behavior. First, investors tend to underestimate risk. In relying on foresight, they may have incomplete or unequal information about the potential investment. Second, people like to insure *and* gamble, even though these activities yield an expected loss (the insurer's or casino's expenses plus profit).

Individuals consistently choose the small but certain cost of insurance premiums rather than face large but unlikely losses. By contrast, state lotteries allow a cheap shot at a big payoff, though the odds are slim. The apparent demand for catastrophe avoidance on the one hand and workless wealth on the other allows insurance and gambling to flourish, though neither offers positive expected returns. Applying these phenomena to investing means that the very safe and very risky investments are overvalued by the "insure" and "gamble" instincts in each of us.

## 3. Leverage

This investment objective has a direct and dramatic influence on profitability and risk. By borrowing, as in mortgaging a property, the capital of others magnifies the results achieved on your own money. For example, a project that returns 12 percent annually on the total invested (without considering tax and inflation effects) can be levered favorably by borrowing at 10 percent but is levered unfavorably with a mortgage interest rate of 15 percent.

Leverage magnifies the owner's rate of return on equity when the borrowed capital makes more than it costs. Naturally, a fall-off in earning can reverse the direction of this leverage, magnifying losses. Leverage, more common in real estate than in other investments, serves to increase not only the investor's rate of return but also the risk.

## 4. Liquidity

Investors also strive for the availability, or liquidity, of their principal along with high return, low risk, and sometimes leverage. To a degree, these objectives are again in conflict. For example, before regulations were revised, savings accounts paid only 5 or 6 percent annual interest, while time deposits paid 10 to 15 percent. Thus liquidity could be sacrificed to bolster return but with "substantial penalities for early withdrawal." The zooming popularity of money market funds was due precisely to their liquidity *and* high return on savings-type accounts.

The liquidity of real estate is also limited, seemingly a key drawback. To sell, one must find a qualified and willing buyer and then induce him or her to act. That often takes time, effort, and expense. Liquidity can be hastened through a distress sale or auction, but the selling price (and thus the capital gain and total return) usually suffers.

## 5. Low expenses

Investors typically are concerned with their *net* income from investing after deducting such expenses as *transaction costs, holding costs,* and *management fees.* The levels of these expenses vary from one type of investment to another. In real estate they are rather high. Transaction costs for executing a buy or a sell can easily include a broker's fee of 6 percent, financing fees of 1 to 3 percent (called *points*), legal, title insurance, and closing costs of another 1 or 2 percent, and possibly taxes. Total in-and-out costs, especially for smaller properties, may be 8 to 10 percent or more of the property's value. The impact of transaction costs can be softened by holding the investment at least a few years, but this further sacrifices liquidity.

Holding costs include deductions from income for operating expenses (e.g., property taxes, maintenance, utilities, insurance, and the like) and for interest on capital borrowed for leverage. Depreciation expenses (the accounting deductions allowed as a wearing out of the property over some allowable time period) are not a cash cost. However, they are deductible as an expense for tax purposes, thus sheltering net operating income (or other income) from taxation.

Management fees for hiring a professional property manager may approximate 5 percent of gross income plus a surcharge for finding tenants. By comparison, the expenses for transactions, holding, and management of a securities portfolio tend to be less than in real estate (with such notable exceptions as mutual fund sales loads, over-the-counter stocks with wide dealer spreads, round-trip commissions on small investments, and high portfolio turnover).

### 6. Tax shelter

Investors seek *after-tax* returns and usually invest accordingly. As shown in Table 2.1, Your Objectives–Opportunities Table, various investments have different tax-shelter characteristics. Tax-exempt bonds and specialized oil/leasing/farming tax shelters are rated highest, along with various types of real estate.

As mentioned previously, depreciation "expenses" shelter much or all of a property's cash flow, especially in a new project's early years. Interest costs for leverage and other holding costs or management fees are also deductible from ordinary income. Any profits from sale (after transaction costs) are typically taxed at long-term capital gains rates.

For homeowners, while depreciation is not allowed, any gains on sale go untaxed if reinvested in another residence (of equal or greater cost) within 24 months. Furthermore, such postponed capital gains go untaxed under a one-time exemption, up to $125,000, if the home seller is age 55 or older.

*Refinancing* (analyzed in detail in Chapter 11) provides another way to shelter real estate returns from taxation. In this case, the property is not sold, but rather remortgaged based on the collateral value of several years of mortgage amortization and/or property appreciation. The additional debt proceeds are nontaxable, being a loan to the owner rather than income. However,

TABLE 2.1
Your Objectives–Opportunities Table

| Investment Objectives | Real Estate | | | Savings | | | Bonds | | | Stocks | | | Tangibles | | |
|---|---|---|---|---|---|---|---|---|---|---|---|---|---|---|---|
| | Home Owner-ship | Income Property | Develop-ment Property | Cash | Checking or Savings Accounts | Certifi-cates of Deposit | Straight Bonds | Tax-exempt Bonds | Convert-ible Bonds | Option Writing Hedges | Common Stock | Option Buying | Commod-ities | Oil, Leasing, Farming Shelters | Art, Antiques, Gems, Stamps, Coins |
| 1. Rate of return | + | + | + | – | – | + | | | | + | | | | + | |
| 2. Low risk | + | + | – | + | + | + | | | | | – | – | – | – | |
| 3. Leverage | + | + | + | | | | + | | | | + | + | + | | – |
| 4. Liquidity | – | – | – | + | + | – | + | + | + | | | | + | – | – |
| 5. Low expense | – | – | – | + | + | + | + | + | + | | | | | | – |
| 6. Tax shelter | + | + | + | – | – | – | – | + | | | | | | | |
| 7. Inflation protection | + | + | + | – | – | – | – | – | | | | | + | + | + |
| 8. Personal satisfaction | + | | | + | – | – | | | | | | | | + | + |

interest must be paid on the higher debt balance resulting from such a refinancing. *Property trading* (also discussed in Chapter 11) can also defer the realization of capital gains for tax purposes. And finally, an individual (or his estate) pays no capital gains taxes at death, as property is "stepped up" to market value at death. (But we're not suggesting that avoiding capital gains taxes is a very good reason for dying prematurely.)

### 7. Inflation protection

Continuing inflation has raised investors' consciousness concerning this objective. History has shown, and this book seeks to prove, that real estate investing offers one of the best ways to protect your assets from inflation. In fact, gains in real estate, particularly with proper leverage, often outrun increases in the cost of living. Thus you can achieve not only protection but also *profit* from inflation.

By contrast, a savings account involves a fixed, guaranteed rate of return. But, upon return, that money has lost purchasing power during inflation. For example, $1,000 invested at 5 percent becomes $1,050 at year end (or $1,051.30 with daily compounding). If inflation during the year increases prices by 10 percent, the saver is behind in terms of real goods his or her money can buy. Furthermore, interest income is currently taxable as ordinary, *unearned* income (although Congress is pressing to revise this treatment), with a top bracket of 70 percent. On an after-tax basis, one might need 15 to 30 percent interest income or more just to break even with 10 percent inflation.[2]

### 8. Personal satisfaction

Since money is only one of your resources, making it should not be the sole objective of investing. True, money can be used to buy time for leisure or retirement (health and longevity permitting), but if you don't enjoy investing, why bother? An investment in a personal home (or vacation property) is perhaps most satisfying. Next come such appreciating—and appreciable—

collectibles as art, antiques, gems, stamps, and coins (especially gold ones). Among the least satisfying, especially during recent recurrent bear markets, is ownership of intangible securities such as bonds or common stock. Real estate, in general, provides the security and enjoyment of tangibility, creative development, and even personal use. But in this, as with each objective, you should decide what is important to *you*.

## Comparing opportunities

After assessing your personal objectives, you can judge the suitability of various opportunities and then decide which specific ones to pursue. The major categories include such real estate investments as your own home, income property, and development property. In addition to real estate (the largest of all investment markets), there are common stocks (having better liquidity but higher risk), bonds (featuring low expenses but sacrificing inflation protection), commodities (greater leverage potential), and so forth. Each opportunity tends to have different characteristics with regard to the various objectives.

Real estate, for example, traditionally offers a comparatively high rate of return at moderate risk (except for development property, which rates a minus for the objective of low risk). Its leverage potential is large, but liquidity is restricted. Unfortunately, expenses—for transactions, operations, and supervision—are high compared with other investments. On the plus side again, real estate's tax shelter and inflation protection are almost unmatched and personal satisfaction is often achieved.

By comparison, art/antiques/gems/stamps/coins tend to provide a moderate rate of return, again with modest risk, but allow little leverage, are terribly illiquid, and are expensive to buy, hold, and sell. They typically provide great personal satisfaction and excellent inflation protection based on tangibility and rarity; (genuine) sets of circa 1740 Queen Anne walnut side chairs simply aren't being made any more.

## Your Objectives-Opportunities Table

Table 2.1, "Your Objectives–Opportunities Table" (the O-O Table), rates these different investment opportunities for performance in regard to each of our eight objectives. The plus signs indicate a high expected ability to fulfill that objective. The minus signs indicate weakness in that performance dimension. A blank represents a medium, or neutral, expectation. The O-O Table can help you judge which types of investments best suit *your* needs.

The first horizontal row shows that the *Real Estate* category as well as "Option Writing Hedges" and "Oil, Leasing, Farming Shelters" score well on rate of return. The latter two are sophisticated money-management vehicles. However, each has serious drawbacks in comparison with other investment objectives. Option writing hedges typically offer little tax-shelter or inflation protection. The oil/leasing/farming deals are often very risky and usually illiquid.

The low-risk objective is rated in row two of the O-O Table. The plus rating goes to the *Savings* category. The most risky opportunities are "Development Property," "Common Stock," "Option Buying," "Commodities," and "Oil, Leasing, Farming Shelters." Thus, when read row by row, the O-O Table shows which investment opportunities most or least fulfill a particular objective.

By looking down a column, you can judge a particular type of investment. For example, "Income Property" rates a plus on rate of return, leverage, tax shelter, and inflation protection. It rates average (blank) on risk and personal satisfaction. It ranks poor (minus) in liquidity (often taking months to sell) and expense (rather high for transactions, holding, and management).

These ratings, it should be noted, are *not* subjective. Rather, they reflect investment characteristics that are inherent in these different types of opportunities. Naturally, not all income property will provide a high rate of return—such opportunities do entail some risk. Similarly, not all commodities provide inflation protection—some go down in price, not up. But an objective consensus of experience and opinion indicates that the ratings assigned are those that all investors can typically expect from each type of opportunity.

## Does real estate belong in your portfolio?

Many experts feel that decisions regarding the *types* of assets and their relative *proportions* in your portfolio are even more important than decisions on individual investments. For example: How much should you invest? At what overall risk level (or what portions at different risk levels)? How diversified should you be? How leveraged? How liquid? What is your present and projected tax bracket? Are you on fixed income or will your salary probably rise with inflation? Does your personal satisfaction come from blowing money or building financial security?

In short, you should invest in light of your own objectives. The O-O Table allows you to decide in a consistent, unemotional way what types of opportunities suit you. Table 2.2 omits the rating entries and has an extra column for you to rate your own objectives. Fill out this column by assigning your most important objectives a + rating. The least important ones earn a −. The moderately important ones stay blank. This completed column describes an *objectives profile* that is uniquely yours.

For example, the stereotyped "wealthy young bachelor" might score rate of return and leverage as a plus, while low risk and liquidity rate a minus for their unimportance to him. Expenses, tax shelter, inflation protection, and personal satisfaction might all rate a neutral blank. A far different set of objectives would be expected for an eldely retiree dependent on investment income or for a growing family of limited means and a need for liquidity.

Next, you can rate the various opportunites for suitability. You do this by comparing your objectives chart with each opportunity rating in Table 2.1. If either your objective or the opportunity rates minus, score "zero." If either your objective or the opportunity is a +, score 1; if both objective and opportunity are +,

TABLE 2.2
Your Objectives–Opportunities Table

| Investment Objectives | Your Objectives Profile | Real Estate | | | Savings | | | Bonds | | | Stocks | | | Tangibles | |
|---|---|---|---|---|---|---|---|---|---|---|---|---|---|---|---|
| | | Home Ownership | Income Property | Development Property | Cash | Checking or Savings Accounts | Certificates of Deposit | Straight Bonds | Tax-exempt Bonds | Convertible Bonds | Option Writing Hedges | Common Stock | Option Buying | Commodities | Oil, Leasing, Farming Shelters | Art, Antiques, Gems, Stamps, Coins |
| 1. Rate of return | | | | | | | | | | | | | | | | |
| 2. Low risk | | | | | | | | | | | | | | | | |
| 3. Leverage | | | | | | | | | | | | | | | | |
| 4. Liquidity | | | | | | | | | | | | | | | | |
| 5. Low expense | | | | | | | | | | | | | | | | |
| 6. Tax shelter | | | | | | | | | | | | | | | | |
| 7. Inflation protection | | | | | | | | | | | | | | | | |
| 8. Personal satisfaction | | | | | | | | | | | | | | | | |
| Column totals | | | | | | | | | | | | | | | | |

score 2. Record this score in that row and column of Table 2.2. Then sum each column.

Cash is an easy opportunity with which to begin. It is listed in the *Savings* category. However, cash provides no rate of return, tax shelter, or inflation protection and rates a minus for those objectives. So, no matter what your objectives profile is, cash provides no benefits along these dimensions and scores zero. Cash scores points if you favor such objectives as low risk, liquidity, low expense, and personal satisfaction, where it rates a plus because most people still like to have cash around, despite its deficiencies! After scoring cash along each of *your* objectives, total its scores and write the sum at the bottom of that column.

If your objectives lean toward a high rate of return, leverage, tax shelter, and inflation protection, and can tolerate some risk and illiquidity, you will find from Table 2.2 that real estate is a high-scoring investment opportunity. It need not be this way. For example, those investors foregoing rate of return, leverage, tax shelter, and inflation protection in favor of low risk and liquidity would find that savings or checking accounts, money market funds, or straight bonds score high. The question is, which opportunities are best for you?

## The record on your investment opportunities

Although real estate is the largest investment market—exceeding the value of savings, bonds, stocks, and tangibles—each property is unique, with consistent, comparable data on profitability and risk scarce. Therefore, real estate investing has been the subject of less research and analysis than the stock or bond markets, for example.

By contrast, during the 20 years since computer-readable stock price files were first compiled, thousands of studies have enumerated the oscillating rate of return of stocks and bonds, as well as their risk, liquidity, expenses, and so on. Also, the remaining opportunity category—*Tangibles* or collectibles—seems to have fared well during the 1970s, as Table 2.3 makes clear.

TABLE 2.3
1970s annual price increase of selected assets

|  | Last 10 Years | Last 5 Years | Last 1 Year |
|---|---|---|---|
| Gold . . . . . . . . . . . | 32% | 28% | 104% |
| Oil . . . . . . . . . . . . | 32 | 18 | 92 |
| Silver . . . . . . . . . . | 24 | 27 | 77 |
| Stamps . . . . . . . . | 22 | 31 | 43 |
| Diamonds . . . . . . . | 15 | 18 | 25 |
| Paintings . . . . . . . . | 13 | 15 | 17 |
| Farmland . . . . . . . . | 13 | 13 | 14 |
| Housing . . . . . . . . . | 10 | 12 | 10 |
| Bonds . . . . . . . . . | 6 | 5 | 3 |
| Stocks . . . . . . . . . | 4 | 15 | 5 |
| CPI . . . . . . . . . . . . | 8 | 9 | 14 |

But remember, gold and most tangibles provide no income (and cost money to store and insure). Real estate usually provides income *and* leveraging potential, augmenting its annual rate of price increase.

Real estate investors seem to have enjoyed decades of relatively unscrutinized but profitable anonymity—bringing to mind the story about the unspectacular student who returned to his class reunion as a very successful restaurateur. When asked how he had made out so well, he replied, "I buy steaks for one dollar each and sell them for three dollars, so I make two percent on every one."

Something had made his business profitable, but it certainly wasn't his analysis. (And inflation has turned those steak prices into hamburger.) Real estate investors have had a similar kind of undocumented success. Over all, their record was aptly described by our niece writing home from summer camp one year. She said, "We are all having fun here, but we don't know how much."

Which opportunity will prove best during the 1980s? The successes of the past did not have to contend with all the problems in real estate today: 13 to 18 percent mortgage rates, 15 to 20 percent land acquisition and construction loan interest, double-digit inflation, zoning restrictions, shortages, environmental impact studies, rent controls, shifting population demographics and mores, zooming energy costs, and altered transportation patterns.

Investors have had to rely heavily on knowledge, experience, and judgment, and they still will. But, increasingly, both professionals and part-timers are seeking a better approach to real estate investment analysis.

## Summary

Depending on the amount of your investible funds, it is wise to diversify into a few different investment opportunities. We have already spoken of an insurance need (before investing). Minimal needs for some low-risk liquid assets probably also dictate a role for some form of savings or money market fund. Next, home ownership may be justified by personal satisfaction (not to mention the favorable rate of return shown in Chapter 7).

What should you invest in next? This chapter has structured investors' eight objectives and their range of opportunities. With your ratings from the Objectives–Opportunities Table, and your ranking of your own objectives, a tally of investment desirability is possible. For those who seek a high rate of return, leverage, tax shelter, and inflation protection—and don't *you?*—the answer is real estate.

## Notes

1. *The Dow Jones-Irwin Guide to Common Stocks* (Homewood, Ill.: Dow Jones-Irwin, 1976), authored by Chris Mader, discusses personal investment objectives and the amount of ongoing investment needed to reach a particular financial goal.

2. Legislation temporarily exempting the first $200 of interest or dividends ($400 for a joint return) became effective in 1981.

# 3 The Real Estate Marketplace

Real estate's institutions and techniques often seem forbidding and bewildering to the uninitiated. To help you select, negotiate, finance, purchase, manage, and sell (or trade) property profitably, an overview of the real estate marketplace is helpful.

This chapter first discusses, in alphabetical order, the key participants in this marketplace. They are the bankers (and how property is financed), brokers (and how property is marketed), builders (and what is available), and buyers (you). Second, we review the categories of advisors—accountants, analysts, appraisers, and attorneys. Third, we present the array of investing vehicles—direct ownership, general partnerships, joint ventures, limited partnerships, real estate corporations, real estate investment trusts (REITs), and syndications.

## Bankers

The term *banker,* though simple, is really too narrow to describe the many institutions and individuals involved in financing residential and commercial real estate. This section will discuss:

1. The types of mortgage lenders.
2. The government's role in housing finance.
3. The types of mortgages.
4. Obtaining financing.

Table 3.1 lists the major participants in the mortgage market and their share of mortgage loans held in 1980. The one- to four-family residential loan market is the largest by far—comprising 60 percent of the nearly $1 trillion of mortgage debt now outstanding. Loans on multifamily apartments account for 12 percent of that mortgage loan total, and commercial loans compose 21 percent. (Farm loans constitute the remaining 7 percent.)

TABLE 3.1
The mortgage marketplace

| | Percent of Dollar Amount of Loans Held For: | | |
| Lending Institution | Home Loans (1-4 Families) | Apartment Loans (Multifamily) | Commercial Loans |
|---|---|---|---|
| Savings associations | 50 | 26 | 20 |
| Commercial banks | 17 | 6 | 32 |
| Federal and related agencies | 13 | 13 | 0 |
| Mutual savings banks | 11 | 14 | 10 |
| Life insurance companies | 4 | 21 | 31 |
| Individuals and others | 5 | 20 | 7 |
| | 100% | 100% | 100% |

SOURCE: Maury Seldin, ed., *The Real Estate Handbook* (Homewood, Ill.: Dow Jones-Irwin, 1980), pp. 574, 589.

## 1. The types of mortgage lenders

As Table 3.1 illustrates, savings associations make the bulk of home mortgages. That is, when home mortgages are being made. (Savings-and-loan organizations are often called S&Ls.) This is their charter and, since 1831, they have emphasized thrift and home ownership. In fact, IRS rules provide a tax break for savings associations that hold the bulk of their assets as residential mortgages. However, revisions in bank regulations announced in 1980 now allow S&Ls to diversify their concentration on home mortgages by lending up to 20 percent of their portfolios on commercial and industrial properties. (Mutual savings banks are owned by their *depositors* rather than shareholders.)

Commercial banks are relatively more active in making loans for commercial property – retail stores, offices, and industrial facilities. However, they are primarily short-term lenders – construction loans of one to two years – although their terms are grudgingly lengthening. Long-term loans are usually sold in the secondary market and are usually made to accommodate good clients. Larger metropolitan banks, called *money center banks,* and some of the larger regional banks have curtailed their residential lending in recent years and have shortened loan maturities.

Life insurance companies receive premiums each year greatly in excess of death benefits paid out. They can and must take the long view to meet their promises to policyholders, sometimes 50 years or more later. Mortgages are a natural investment, therefore, and comprise nearly 30 percent of life insurance company assets. Mostly, these are commercial property loans rather than residential. However, with high rates on home loans, some life companies are buying blocks of residential loans from savings and loans and commercial banks.

*Pension funds* are becoming increasingly important in the mortgage lending business for medium to large-size commercial, industrial, and retail projects. With the passage of the Pension Reform Act of 1976, pension funds can now allocate a larger percentage of their assets to real estate loans and investments. Historically, pension funds have invested the majority of their funds in stocks and bonds, with poor results in many cases. Pension funds offer the potential of billions of additional dollars for loans annually. Considering the countless billions that will go into pension funds in the years to come, it is safe to say their effect on the mortgage lending business will be significant.

*Mortgage bankers* originate loans and service them over time. Typically, however, they present and resell these mortgages to larger, nationwide investors, insurance companies, and pension funds. One point, or 1 percent of the loan principal, is the usual originating fee. Servicing the loan – making collections and managing tax and insurance escrows – often commands an annual fee of 3/8 percent. In addition, when a unique loan is sought or the collateral property is nonstandard, the further services of a *mortgage broker* may be helpful to prepare the loan package and match borrower with lender.

Other financing sources include credit unions and commercial credit companies, private investors organized into syndications, and mortgage companies. Often, creative seller financing is the *only* source during tight money periods.

## 2. The government's role in housing finance

To ensure the availability of loans and marketplace stability for the housing needs of its citizens, the government has increased its role. Primarily, the federal role has been in guaranteeing, subsidizing, and arranging for the resale of mortgages. Also, legislation has caused standardized disclosure of loan particulars ("truth in lending"), standardized settlement costs and procedures, and equal access to credit without discrimination.

The Federal Housing Administration (FHA) was created in 1934 to bring rationality to a depressed—and often foreclosed—real estate market. It does not lend money. Rather, it insures loans made by approved and supervised lending sources. FHA-insured mortgages offer the advantage of lower interest rates based on the government's credit rating (provided for a charge of 1/2 percent added on to the mortgage rate). They also feature high loan-to-value ratios, long loan life, monthly self-amortizing payments, and minimum specifications for building standards. By contrast, the Veterans Administration (VA) usually guarantees mortgages, but it also insures them and sometimes makes loans directly. This agency was created by the 1944 GI Bill; veterans of the Korean and Vietnam wars now qualify, too.

Three additional agencies established by the government are becoming increasingly important in real estate finance—Fannie Mae, Freddie Mac, and Ginnie Mae. During the past dozen years, these offspring of Uncle Sam have been given enlarged roles.

Fannie Mae (the Federal National Mortgage Association), now a public company traded on the New York Stock Exchange, buys mortgages. It conducts auctions in which qualified mortgage sellers competitively offer bundles of mortgages priced to provide a stated interest yield. Fannie Mae's management decides which offers to accept. It buys these mortgages with funds raised in the conventional money markets, relying on its government credit rating to keep interest costs down. This process restores funds to institutions originating the mortgages—so they can create loans again. It also adds to the over $50 billion in assets currently owned by Fannie Mae.

Freddie Mac (the Federal Home Loan Mortgage Corporation) was formed in 1970 to buy mortgage loans from federally chartered savings-and-loan associations.

Ginnie Mae (the Government National Mortgage Association) was orginated in 1968, focusing on FHA-VA government-supported loans. Its creation of a "pass-through" security lets investors buy into a pool of mortgages without the bother of collecting and administering them individually.

We should also mention the Farmers Home Administration (FmHA) here. Formed during the Great Depression, this agency guarantees loans for farming, rural housing, and rural business and industry. ("Rural" may now include cities with populations up to 20,000.) Under FmHA's Section 8 program, private owners who build or rehabilitate housing can receive direct subsidies for renting to low-income households.

## 3. The types of mortgages

*Conventional mortgages* are those obtained from nongovernment sources; they usually require constant monthly payments that cover interest *and* retire principal over a long period, such as 25 or 30 years. These self-amortizing, long-term, fixed-payment loans became common about 40 to 50 years ago, when stability was brought to the reorganized housing finance industry.

Today, the problem is not depression (at least not *that* depression) but rather *inflation*. Volatile, inflation-driven interest rates have caused turmoil again in the mortgage marketplace. Also, the construction industry and housing starts get whipsawed. This relationship during the past few economic cycles is shown in Figure 3.1.

---

FIGURE 3.1
Housing starts vs. mortgage rates

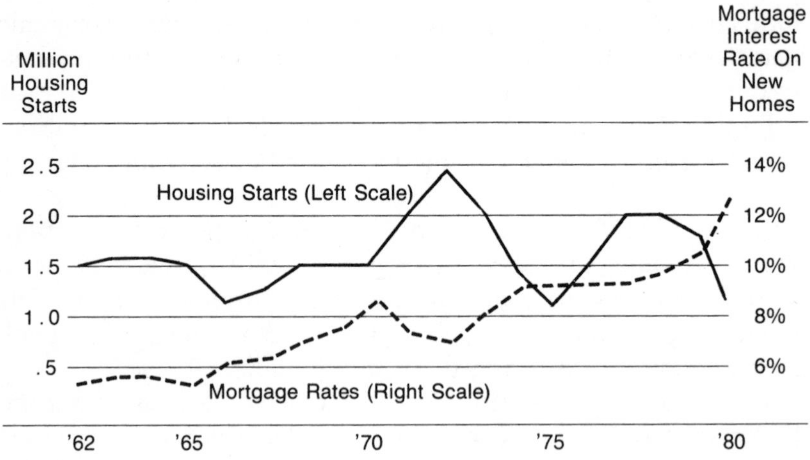

SOURCE: U.S. Census and Federal Housing Administration.

---

Another mortgaging method is the *purchase-money mortgage.* Here the seller extends credit to the buyer. This method of financing becomes much more prevalent during times of tight money, often allowing real estate to be sold when it might not otherwise. This technique may provide tax benefits for the seller, who can report any capital gain stretched out over a period of years. With declining tax rates as promised by the 1981 tax changes, this lowers the effective taxation, with principal payments not taxed until received by the seller.

A *second mortgage* might be used to obtain leverage beyond that granted by a first-mortgage lender. The second loan is junior or subordinated in legal rights to the first. Many mortgages are nonrecourse loans that look only to the property for security, as they are not guaranteed personally by the borrower. Thus the second-mortgage holder takes a greater risk and usually receives a higher interest rate (unless, perhaps, the seller takes back the second mortgage to ensure the sale, in which case a higher rate of interest may be less important).

*Balloon mortgages* feature interest-only payments (or low amortization) with a balloon payment of remaining principal at the end. This improves the buyer's cash flow after debt service (by lowering the amortization component). It is becoming increasingly common since the lender can set a shorter maturity period (10 or 15 years), yet the borrower, during this period, maintains high leverage. Often the property is sold or refinanced prior to mortgage expiration so that the lump sum is actually gotten from the resale or refinancing proceeds.

A *wraparound mortgage* is another technique for achieving or restoring high leverage. If a long-standing, low-interest mortgage exists, then because of amortization and/or appreciation, the property can usually sustain more debt. A second mortgage, for the full leverage sought, can be arranged to "wrap around" this first mortgage. That is, the borrower makes payments only on the new loan, while the lender assumes responsibility for paying off the old one. Lenders are typically happy to do this because they then benefit from the favorable terms of the old mortgage while receiving interest at the current, higher rate.

*Variable-rate mortgages* (VRMs) became common in the latter 1970s, especially in the California housing market. They allow the lender to transfer much of the interest-rate fluctuation risk to the buyer. In short, when rates change, your mortgage payment changes. To remove this risk, many lenders now offer the borrower the alternative of increasing the length of the mortgage rather than the amount of the monthly payments when rates increase. (Limitations on the frequency and amount of mortgage rate change are imposed—semiannual changes of up to 1/2 percent and 2 1/2 percent in total are common—and the rate can not only go up but can also come down, at least in theory!)

*Graduated-payment mortgages,* as advocated by Chris Mader in the January 5, 1976 issue of *U.S. News & World Report,* may now become popular. These mortgages recognize that today's problem is inflation, not imminent foreclosure as with the 1930s short-term, interest-only mortgages. A low initial monthly payment graduates into larger payments in later years. Thus the reality of rising salaries and home values is utilized to provide collateral for long-term financing with lower, more affordable front-end payments.

*Shared-appreciation mortgages* (SAMs) are a most recent phenomenon, introduced initially by the Advance Mortgage Corporation of Chicago. The lender, in exchange for receiving a percentage of the appreciation of the property's value, usually one third, lowers the interest rate on the mortgage one third (normally equal to the same percentage of the appreciation given up). These innovative mortgages allow many potential home buyers to qualify for mortgages for which, given their current income levels and high mortgage interest rates, they otherwise might not qualify. Lenders benefit as the values of homes continue to rise with or even faster than inflation.

Still other responses to inflation are possible. For example, federal regulations now encourage the offering of a new loan form long used in Canada: *rollover mortgages.* These are adjusted in rate every three to five years. That is, maturities are long term, but the interest rate is renegotiated and the remaining principal is "rolled over" periodically.

Looking elsewhere in the world, in England the mortgage amortization period was lengthened, with payments kept constant (until *no* amortization was reached, because interest rates rose so much). Argentina, with *triple*-digit inflation, doesn't have 30-year loans—just 30-*day* ones. The interest rate is adjusted each month. In Brazil, the home mortgage rate is only about 3 percent—unfortunately, the principal is indexed. Thus, if you borrow $100,000 one year and inflation is 40 percent, you owe $140,000, plus 3 percent, of course.

*Buy-down mortgages* are a phenomenon of the early 1980s and provide the buyer of a property (usually a home) with a below-market interest rate for the first several years of the mortgage term. Thereafter, the interest rate on the mortgage reverts to the then-current market interest rate. This type of "creative financing" is made possible by the developer or owner paying a lender a fee that makes up a portion or all of the loss of interest income created by the below-market-rate mortgage. This is obviously costly to the developer or property owner, but it is often neccessary to enable the developer to unload costly inventories of homes being carried at construction loan rates that are significantly higher than mortgage rates.

*Construction mortgages* are of short duration and are meant to finance the risky building and lease-up period. They carry high interest rates, normally floating anywhere from 1 to 4 percentage points over the prime rate, depending on the track record and financial condition of a borrower. Commercial banks, among others, make this type of loan. Often, a prearranged *permanent mortgage,* called a "take-out" mortgage, "kicks in" at completion of construction or a specified occupancy level (often 80 percent) and causes repayment of the construction loan. In fact, construction loans usually require a commitment for permanent funds. However, with the long-term financing market in disarray, some developers and builders are borrowing short-term without take-out commitments, a seemingly riskier strategy.

*Insured mortgages* have principal repayment insured, or guaranteed, totally or in part by a third party. The FHA does this for qualified mortgages (and for a 1/2 percent interest premium). Often only the top 20 percent of principal need be insured, as with such private insurers as Mortgage Guaranty Insurance Corporation (MGIC, pronounced "magic").

The *secondary mortgage market* is the forum for trading mortgages *after* origination by the primary lender. During the 1970s, this form of rechanneling funds surged sixfold, with growth in the private sector outpacing that of the federal credit agencies. Standardized *mortgage-backed securities* have become a staple investment product, along with the stocks, bonds, and commodities that brokers have traditionally offered.

## 4. Obtaining financing

Having reviewed the types of lenders—including the government's role in housing finance—and the various types of mortgages, it's time to get the money. Perhaps working through your real estate or mortgage broker, lenders' current mortgage policies and rates should be screened. Then a *mortgage application* or loan package must be prepared. This specifies the type of loan sought, the property serving as collateral, and the background and financial condition of the borrower. Processing, appraisal, legal, and title report fees are usually charged, along with fees for deed and mortgage registration and, often, property tax escrow. A thorough loan package for an investment property should contain an analysis indicating its financial feasibility and demonstrating the applicant's depth of preparation and planning. Many lenders have said they would rather lend money to someone submitting a well prepared package for a bad property than a bad application for a good property. After submission of your application and approval of your mortgage, money will be furnished at closing.

## Brokers

The most frequently encountered participant in the real estate marketplace and the most numerous, is the broker or real estate salesperson. The latter must pass a state qualifying exam and usually works for a broker. Brokers have additional qualifications and experience. Firms and individuals belonging to the National Association of Realtors® (NAR) may use the registered Realtor® designation. Their compensation is typically on commission, paid by the seller, for transactions arranged. However, a growing innovation is the *discount broker* who (as in stocks) charges less than others or works on a fee basis.

When you buy through a broker, you may be shown a broader list of properties and receive help with the screening and selection process. Usually a broker will also assist in transaction negotiation and in suggesting sources of financing. When you are ready to sell or trade, a broker's existing contacts and marketing capability can again be helpful. Consequently, most properties are sold through brokers.

Real estate marketing begins when an owner desiring to sell lists the property with a broker, often granting exclusive sales agency for 90 days or so. By accepting a listing, the broker commits to use his or her time, effort, money, and experience to seek a buyer. This includes advertising, using a multiple listing service, qualifying prospects, showing the property, communicating offers and counter-offers, generating a signed agreement of sale, and helping the buyer arrange any escrow deposits and financing (or title insurance, zoning, or leasing paperwork) on which the deal may be contingent. In sum, a broker transacts sales frequently, thereby building experience and established contacts and methods, whereas an individual buyer or seller presumably transacts much less often and simply lacks the skills and/or time to market property alone.

Brokers operate their business in a plethora of operational levels and styles (although ultimately it's usually one individual serving one client). The brokerage firm may have only one office, headed by one licensed broker, with perhaps a few salespeople or agents. Larger firms have multiple offices to provide geographic coverage, especially in residential sales. The diversified office may handle many specialties, such as mortgage brokerage, insurance, commercial and industrial sales, leasing, and property management.

Franchised broker networks have grown rapidly, especially in the 1970s. In such networks, a locally owned firm pays annual and ongoing fees to the national franchisor (Century 21 is the largest), thereby benefiting from recognized advertising, established procedures, the availability of sales training, and national referrals.

Broker associations, the largest being NAR, foster professionalism, training, and contacts so brokers can serve clients better. Some special designations include: Certified Property Manager (CPM), Counselor of Real Estate (CRE), Registered Apartment Manager (RAM), Senior Residential Appraiser (SRA), and Member of the Society of Industrial Realtors (SIR).

Locally, most brokers also rely on their multiple listing service (MLS). This body centralizes the listing and data dissemination of offered properties. Increasingly, computerized access helps screen, evaluate, and compare properties, plus capture data on sales levels and price trends by property location and features.

## Builders

Builders and developers create the supply of new housing and investment property. They create their own trade organizations as well, including the National Association of Home Builders, and the Prefabricated Home Manufacturers Institute. The volume of their activity is highly cyclical. It responds significantly to interest rates, which affect both construction loan costs and the mortgage bite sustained by the buyer. Figure 3.1 shows this cyclicality as well as the inverse relationship between new housing starts and mortgage rates.

Other influences on the volume, location, and design of residential construction include vacancy rates, the volume of unsold new construction (or *inventory*), the cost of building materials, population and demographic trends, availability of government assistance programs, zoning controls, rent regulations, energy costs, tax law changes, and so on.

Commercial and industrial buildings are usually larger-scale, longer-term projects. Often land development—zoning, utilities, grading, streets, sewers, etc.—must precede construction. Much of this construction is specialized, literally "built to suit," and owned or leased long-term by the company that will operate the facility. This construction market, though also cyclical and approximately as large as residential construction, follows the somewhat different pattern of the business cycle. Many of these builders of commercial and industrial buildings belong to the National Association of Industrial and Office Parks (NAIOP).

## Buyers

The real estate buyer presumably is *you* (or your client). Your objectives in buying real estate—or deciding not to buy—were discussed in Chapter 2. Most households actually *are* buyers, with two thirds choosing to own their residence. (This still leaves a large market for residential rental property, however, and for condominium conversions.)

Surprisingly, far fewer people also own *investment* real estate. There are an estimated six million owners of income property, with six million more owning land. Taking only the homeowning households, that would mean just one in ten owns rental property, and another one in ten owns land. What's stopping *you* from investing in real estate? If it's whose advice to follow, or the key factors needed for successful investment analysis, then please read on.

## Advisors

Real estate advice comes from all corners – friends at the country club, salespeople, news commentators, workplace colleagues, neighbors, and so on. Their advice may indeed be sound. But mentioned here are four categories of people *paid for their advice*, and generally not on the basis of vested interest, contingent reward, or commissions. These specialists and professionals include: *accountants, analysts, appraisers,* and *attorneys* (and, we're tempted to add, *authors*).

Moneymaking is the primary objective of investing. Accounting, therefore, is the scorekeeping system, and in the United States there are more than 170,000 Certified Public Accountants (CPAs). Also, in the government's employment statistics, there are more than 750,000 other accountants, plus 1.1 million bookkeepers – altogether, more than two million people keeping score!

Analysts and consultants in real estate advise on population and development trends, construction costs and methods, market feasibility, financing and taxes, economic issues, and a host of needed disciplines. This book's major intent is to help you be more knowledgeable and self-sufficient in *investment analysis.*

Appraisers are called on to estimate a property's value to support marketing it, lending on it as collateral, justifying its purchase or basis for income taxation, and tallying net asset and net worth valuations.

Attorneys, of course, are trained and licensed to dispense legal advice, including preparing contracts of sale, financing, leasing, interpreting tax impacts, and litigating disputes. It is likely that attorneys can also advise you on which of the following several *vehicles* to select for owning real estate.

## Vehicles for real estate investing

One key piece of advice you should seek is what vehicle, or legal form, you should select for *your* real estate investing in each case. This section reviews (again in alphabetical order) seven of the most prominent alternatives:

1. Direct ownership.
2. General partnerships.
3. Joint ventures.
4. Limited partnerships.
5. Real estate corporations.
6. Real estate investment trusts (REITs).
7. Syndications.

### 1. Direct ownership

This form of legal ownership (including joint ownership) is most frequent. It allows both income and expenses to be taken directly into one's personal financial statements. Thus losses, as from depreciation, can shelter other income from ordinary taxation. The disadvantage is that the owner is liable to the full extent of his or her (or their) personal net worth. Insurance can protect you against this risk. Also, lenders often require direct owners to sign personally as collateral beyond the property itself.

### 2. General partnerships

General partnerships (as distinguished from limited partnerships, also discussed in this chapter) have the same tax and liability features as direct ownership. That is, the partnership organization itself is untaxed. Rather, it flows income and expense through to the partners, according to their proportionate interests. It is merely a legal, contractual binding of the subscribers to the partnership agreement. Its advantage lies in the pooling of talents and capital combined with the efficiency of segregating responsibilities among the partners as per their expertise.

## 3. Joint ventures

These are a form of general partnership (or joint-direct owner-ship) usually involving *large-scale development* (hence the word *venture*). Typically, one partner provides the labor or develop-ment expertise and the other provides the necessary capital. Often a landowner or developer will agree with an insurance company, pension fund, or other institution to create and finance income property. For putting up the land at cost and for construction know-how, the developer typically winds up owning some por-tion of the project, often half. The institution often owns a first mortgage in the amount of all project costs, which it pays, plus the remaining piece of the deal. These types of arrangements, structured in a multitude of ways, become much more necessary to the *developer* as money costs rise and long-term financing dries up.

## 4. Limited partnerships

The limited partnership is the most frequently used legal entity for group investing in real estate. This form of ownership features a general partner (or partners) who has managerial authority over the property and full financial liability. The *limited* partners, in contrast, are actually restricted from active management of their investment. Otherwise they risk loss of their favored liability status, which limits loss to only their investment. Thus limited partners abdicate management authority for relief from finan-cial liability.

A limited partnership may have any number of limited part-ners. By contrast, a general partnership gets unwieldy if sizable, because one death, for instance, dissolves the partnership. This is not the case if a limited partner dies or becomes insane. Limited partnership interests are considered to be securities and, as such, come under state and federal regulation. However, most states and the federal Securities and Exchange Commission (SEC) ex-empt *small* groups of coinvestors from registration. Unless quali-fying under this special exemption, limited partnership interests sold to the general public must meet stringent and very costly disclosure requirements. Risks and financial history must be spelled out, for example. (See the discussion of "Syndications" later in this chapter.)

Limited partners (like direct owners, general partners, and joint venturers) are also allowed to deduct their allocated share of expenses from their current personal income. In most situations, this can shelter other ordinary income via tax-deductible operating expenses, mortgage loan interest, and depreciation. Thus the total tax deductions may far exceed one's equity investment. In real estate, this is so *even if* the mortgage is collateralized only by the property. Thus deductions can exceed the investor's amount at risk, whereas in other tax-shelter investments the deductions may not exceed the amount at risk.

These tax advantages contribute to total returns, as we will see. Such shelter is especially desirable to investors having high income. In fact, limited partners often have to certify that they have some minimum income and net worth. This provision supposedly ensures that the investment is suitable for that investor and the investor is qualified and sophisticated enough to invest. Two potential disadvantages are that the limited partner lacks control, and that he or she is comparatively illiquid until the partnership terminates.

## 5. Real estate corporations

The advantages of this legal form are those of any corporation, namely:
1. Stockholder liability is limited to the invested amount.
2. Capital raising and liquidity are facilitated by the ability to sell and transfer shares.
3. The entity itself has an indefinite life.

The principal disadvantage is double taxation, first at the corporate level on earnings and then on dividends when distributed to shareholders. In real estate, it is also significant that losses of the corporation cannot be passed through for shareholders to deduct against their other current income (except in Subchapter S corporations, which can't just passively invest anyway). An attorney, tax advisor, or accountant should be consulted for particular rulings on the intricacies of these organizational, tax, and financial issues.

The shares of larger, publicly held real estate corporations are listed on national stock exchanges. They may participate in one or several functions within the real estate marketplace, such as home building, or other construction, development, brokerage, mortgage banking, or property management. Other companies own substantial real estate needed in their businesses, such as forest products, mining, energy, farming and distributing, or retailing operations. Growing recognition of property ownership by major corporations has led to creation of corporate real estate departments. Naturally, there follow associations such as the International Council of Shopping Centers (ICSC) and the National Association of Corporate Real Estate Executives (NACORE).

## 6. Real estate investment trusts (REITs)

REITs are funds pooled for investment in real estate. That is, they sell shares of stock, and often convertible bonds and other debt securities, and then invest the proceeds in real estate. A trust itself does not build or manage property. Rather, by pooling the capital of many, it provides diversification and centralized administration. Most are affiliated with and managed by some large financial institution, such as a bank or insurance company.

REITs receive special tax treatment. Specifically, if they pay out 90 percent or more of their annual income to shareholders, they pay no income taxes, which are instead collected from the shareholder at his or her personal rate. This parallels the functioning of a limited partnership, except that, in this case, a majority vote of shareholders can influence—or remove—the trust's management.

REITs are classified as *mortgage* or *equity* trusts, depending on whether they lend on or own property. A mortgage trust arranges either *short-term* (construction) or *long-term* (permanent) loans. Some trusts, called hybrid trusts, mix these types of assets for diversification beyond that afforded by diverse geography and many deals. But since they employ leverage to a significant degree, earnings are highly dependent on interest rates and the yield curve (i.e., interest rates for various maturity dates). Accordingly, their overall investment performance has been very volatile.

## 7. Syndications

Our final form of real estate investing is really a large, usually registered, widely marketed, limited partnership. Major brokerage houses and investment management firms organize syndications to earn sales and management fees. The proceeds are invested in selected real estate or in properties already bought, subject to the syndicate's financing. Syndications have also become a major source of debt financing for expansions and renovations.

## Summary

Among the many participants in the real estate marketplace, the prime functions accomplished are those of the banker, broker, and builder. As the buyer in this market, your advisors include accountants, analysts, appraisers, and attorneys. Your vehicles for investing span direct ownership, general or limited partnerships, joint ventures, real estate corporations or investment trusts, and syndications.

# 4 The REAL "Total Return" Analysis

Most books on real estate discuss *operating* problems, such as how to develop land, design and construct buildings, or broker, manage, or appraise properties. While we review those topics, this book's main focus is on the most important real estate decision: whether or not to *invest* in a property. The operating problems are important, but they begin—or don't begin—because of an investment commitment. The ensuing operations are then all in an effort to achieve the kinds of investment objectives we have already discussed.

Real estate investing should not *and need not* be based on oversimplified analysis. Our upcoming examples and the reference tables of Part III illustrate a comprehensive evaluation method that is easy to understand and apply. After screening many investment opportunities, negotiating terms, arranging financing, and investing time, money, and skill, why skimp on the analysis? At that point you deserve an accurate, timely method for assessing investment merit, including rate of return, risk, leverage, liquidity, expenses, tax shelter, and inflation protection. The remaining goal, personal satisfaction, is subjective, but a good analysis ought to contribute to that, as well.

## Traditional analysis

Real estate evaluation has been based on a series of methods that approximately compute a property's value. This task requires experience and judgment, since each property is unique. For example, professional appraisers are encouraged to use each of three methods to determine a property's value:

1. The current cost of reproducing the property less depreciation from deterioration and functional and economic obsolescence.
2. The value indicated by recent sales of comparable properties in the market.
3. The value that the property's net earning power will support, based on a capitalization of net income.

These are known as the *cost, market,* and *income* approaches, respectively.

A similar point of view is taken here. The value received from a property is compared to the resources invested. If the property is being developed, the amount invested is its *cost.* If it already exists and is being purchased, the amount invested is its *market* price (including transaction costs). In either case, the investor must determine—in advance—whether the property will produce a sufficient *income* to justify investing this cost or market price.

Too often, property analysis for investment purposes has been, at best, inconsistent, and at worst, incorrect. Does the analysis include the effects of leveraging and, if so, with what financing terms? Some analyses deal with before-tax cash flow, while others present after-tax results. Sometimes a vacancy contingency is omitted. At other times transaction costs are overlooked.

## The four levels of rate of return

To avoid comparing apples and oranges indiscriminately, we have developed a standardized and comprehensive analysis method for determining a property's investment merit. It includes results calculated both in dollars and as percentage rates of return. Four important levels of profitability are presented:

Level 1. Net income to total project cost (before leverage, tax
        shelter, and sale)
Level 2. Cash flow to equity (after leverage)
Level 3. Cash flow to equity (after tax shelter)
Level 4. Overall cash flow to equity (after holding and sale)

## Level 1. Net income to total project cost

This basic computation estimates the property's current rate of
return, before considering the effects of leverage, tax shelter, and
resale during inflation. As such, it is akin to computing a common stock's dividend yield, which also omits the effects of borrowing (called "margin" for stocks), taxation, and stock-price appreciation or decline.

A property's net operating income is found by adjusting its
historical or estimated rent roll for expected vacancy. The result
is called *effective gross income,* or simply *gross income.* From this,
operating expenses must be subtracted. Table 4.1 shows the net
operating income for the suburban medical office building bought
for $150,000 in 1976, as cited in Chapter 1. The *minimum* data
requirements for this computation are:
1. Total project cost.
2. Gross income.
3. Operating expense.

This Level 1 analysis is widely practiced in the real estate field.
It is the essence of the income method of appraisal. The 10 percent figure for rate of return is called the capitalization rate, or
"cap rate." Unfortunately, while easy to compute and widely
used, this method is incomplete.

## Level 2. Cash flow to equity (after leverage)

Since most properties are purchased subject to a mortgage, and
we endorse doing so, the effect of leverage is analyzed next. After
the Great Depression, one fundamental financial reform was a
restructuring of standard mortgage contracts. As discussed in
Chapter 3, rather than calling for the loan principal to be due
in full after only several years, conventional mortgages were

TABLE 4.1
Level of rate of return on suburban medical office building

| Rent roll: | Suite #1 at monthly rental of............ | | $ 600 |
|---|---|---|---|
| | #2 ........................... | | 600 |
| | #3 ........................... | | 600 |
| | #4 ........................... | | 600 |
| | Monthly rent roll..................... | | $ 2,400 |
| | | | × 12 |
| | Annual rent roll...................... | | $28,800 |
| | Less: Vacancy*...................... | | 1,800 |
| | Gross income.................... | | $27,000 |
| Operating expenses: | Property taxes................. | $ 3,300 | |
| | Maintenance.................. | 2,800 | |
| | Utilities (owner's portion)........ | 2,400 | |
| | Supplies..................... | 1,700 | |
| | Management.................. | 1,100 | |
| | Insurance.................... | 700 | |
| | Total........................ | $12,000 | $12,000 |
| Net operating income: | Gross income less operating expenses.................... | | $15,000 |
| Level 1 Rate of return = | $\dfrac{\text{Net operating income}}{\text{Total project cost}}$ is $\dfrac{\$15,000}{\$150,000}$ = 10% | | |

*It should be noted that vacancy can be shown as a deduction before gross income, as above, or as an item of operating expense. In either case the accounting and tax treatment produce an identical result.

designed to be self-amortizing and of longer life. That is, their monthly payments include both interest on the outstanding debt balance and partial repayment of the loan. The monthly payment required to amortize the mortgage when due can be computed from the

1. Mortgage amount.
2. Mortgage interest rate.
3. Mortgage life.

Table 4.2 shows a schedule of mortgage payments due each year for a 10 percent interest rate. For general reference, a $1,000 mortgage amount and 25-year life are shown. For higher interest rates, and for larger mortgages, one can scale up accordingly for an approximation.

Notice that each year's total mortgage payment remains constant. However, the amount required for interest decreases and

TABLE 4.2
Mortgage payment table
Payments per $1,000 of mortgage amount at 10 percent interest for 25 years

| Year | Payment | Interest | Amortization | Loan Balance |
|------|---------|----------|--------------|--------------|
| 1 | $110 | $100 | $10 | $990 |
| 2 | 110 | 99 | 11 | 979 |
| 3 | 110 | 98 | 12 | 967 |
| 4 | 110 | 96 | 14 | 953 |
| 5 | 110 | 94 | 16 | 937 |
| 10 | 110 | 86 | 24 | 844 |
| 25 | 110 | 16 | 104 | 0 |

the portion applicable to amortization increases as the loan balance is paid off. To get dollar amounts for the medical building with 75 percent financing (a $112,500 mortgage), multiply the 9 percent mortgage figures by 112.5. Then we can compute the owner's cash flow, or residual money in-pocket after operating expenses and mortgage payments. This amounts to $3,671 and is often called a *spendable*. As a rate of return, it is 9.8 percent of the $37,500 equity. This Level 2 rate of return relates annual "cash in" to initial "cash out," or equity, and equals the cash-on-cash return.

The effect of leverage here is slightly negative. That is, the 9.8 percent rate of return after financing is somewhat less than the Level 1 return of 10 percent. However, it is important to note that amortization provides a buildup of equity in the property, though this benefit does not yet provide cash in-pocket for the owner. Also, the tax benefits and appreciation potential have not been factored in yet, so our analysis is again incomplete.

## Level 3. Cash flow to equity (after tax shelter)

Since *after-tax* results are sought by investors, and since tax laws can take a significant bite or produce a significant refund, they must be included as relevant to investment analysis. Real estate's vaunted tax shelter stems from three tax law provisions:

1. Expenses incurred for investment purposes are deductible, including (with some limitations) interest expense.
2. Depreciation is allowed, providing a tax-free recovery of the project's total cost (excluding land).
3. Long-term capital gains are not recognized until sale (and can be deferred by trading) and are then usually taxed at a lower rate.

In the early years of an income property, the owner can usually report expenses, including depreciation, that exceed the property's gross income. This loss for tax purposes shelters not only cash flow but other income as well. Over time, however, depreciation and deductible interest expenses usually decline and net income may rise due to rent increases. Then taxes may be due on part or all of the cash flow.

Table 4.3 lists the depreciation allowed each year using the four depreciation methods applicable to buildings built or purchased on or before Dec. 31, 1980 (again per $1,000 over 25-year life). The Year 1 after-tax results from our medical building purchased in 1976 are shown in Table 4.4. Notice that the tax loss causes a tax rebate of $1,137 that actually *increases* our after-tax cash flow from its before-tax level. (This does assume other income to shelter, as a 50 percent tax bracket would imply and as the tax law allows.)

TABLE 4.3
Depreciation schedules per $1,000 of depreciation amount with 25-year life

| Year | Straight Line 100% | 125% | 150% | 200% |
|---|---|---|---|---|
| 1 ............ | $  40 | $  50 | $  60 | $  80 |
| 2 ............ | 40 | 48 | 56 | 74 |
| 3 ............ | 40 | 45 | 53 | 68 |
| 4 ............ | 40 | 43 | 50 | 62 |
| 5 ............ | 40 | 41 | 47 | 57 |
| 10 ............ | 40 | 39 | 36 | 38 |
| 15 ............ | 40 | 39 | 36 | 28 |
| 20 ............ | 40 | 39 | 36 | 28 |
| 25 ............ | 40 | 39 | 36 | 28 |
| Totals ......... | $1,000 | $1,000 | $1,000 | $1,000 |

TABLE 4.4
Cash flow to equity (after tax shelter)

| | | |
|---|---|---:|
| Taxable income | Gross income . . . . . . . . . . . . . . . . . . . . . . . . . . | $27,000 |
| | Less: Operating expense . . . . . . . . . . . . . . . | 12,000 |
| | Mortgage interest . . . . . . . . . . . . . . . . | 10,074 |
| | Depreciation. . . . . . . . . . . . . . . . . . . . . | 7,200 |
| | | $ − 2,274 |
| Income tax = | Taxable income . . . . . . . . . . . . . . . . . . . . . . | $ − 2,274 |
| | × Tax rate. . . . . . . . . . . . . . . . . . . . . . . . . . | × .50 |
| | | $ − 1,137 |
| Cash flow (after tax) = | Cash flow (before tax) . . . . . . . . . . . . . . . . . . | $ 3,671 |
| | Less: Income tax . . . . . . . . . . . . . . . . . . . . . . | + 1,137 |
| | | $ 4,808 |

Level 3
Rate of return = $\dfrac{\text{After-tax cash flow}}{\text{Equity}}$ is $\dfrac{\$4,808}{\$37,500}$ = 12.8%

Accelerated types of depreciation denote write-offs faster than the straight-line method. Under the old depreciation laws, the faster write-off methods generally improved the tax shelter in the early years at the expense of later years. After varying periods, straight-line write-off of the remaining depreciable amount became best for accelerated methods and was adopted, as is done in Table 4.3. Accelerated depreciation acted to postpone taxes, of course, so Congress limited the depreciation rate allowable for each class of real estate as follows:

200 percent for new residential property only.

150 percent for new commercial property.

125 percent for used residential property having a life of 20 years or more.

100 percent for all other property.

The recently enacted Economic Recovery Tax Act of 1981 allows for a simpler and quicker method of recovering costs of real estate. According to the new legislation, the purpose of the new Accelerated Cost Recovery System (ACRS) is to encourage investment in buildings and other capital assets, increase productivity, and reduce the detrimental effects of inflation on the replacement of capital. The belief was that prior depreciation laws did not adequately provide for the replacement of capital assets as they wore out or became obsolete. In addition, ACRS was written to eliminate disputes between taxpayers and the IRS over proper useful lives, depreciation methods, and salvage values.

Under ACRS, taxpayers are entitled to "recovery deductions" (instead of depreciation deductions) using "recovery rates" (instead of depreciation lives and methods or types). Congress has always liked to use new jargon to make this more complicated! These recovery rates, which are identical for new and used property, are determined using a property classification system. Salvage value is no longer taken into account, as if it ever was previously. There are five property classifications, but only two relate to real estate—"five-year property" and "fifteen-year property." For the purposes of our discussion, five-year property (personal property) includes most machinery and equipment. Fifteen-year property includes both residential and nonresidential real property used in a trade or business. As was the case under the old laws, this class does not include land or personal residences, neither of which are depreciable. Under the prior tax law, taxpayers were required to do the mathematical calculations necessary to determine all depreciation deductions. With ACRS, the IRS now provides tables that have predetermined annual or monthly recovery rates for all types of property. For 1981–82, the recovery rates for five-year property are shown in Table 4.5. To compute the recovery deduction, just apply the recovery percentages in the table against the tax basis of the property. The recovery rates in Table 4.5 approximate a 150 percent declining balance method using a half-year convention in the first year, switching to straight-line in later years when advantageous. Generally, there is no recovery deduction in the year of disposition. After 1984, the recovery rates increase in two steps to eventually approximate the deductions that would be calculated using a 200 percent declining-balance method that switches to the sum-of-the-years digits (SYD) method.

Alternatively, taxpayers may elect to use a method of recovery using one of three straight-line recovery periods for 5-year property—5, 12, or 25 years. Gains or losses are generally recognized upon disposition of recovery property. As under prior law, the portion of the gain on the disposition of personal property that represents recapture of recovery deductions is treated as ordinary income.

TABLE 4.5
ACRS recovery rates for five-year property

| Recovery Year | Recovery Rate |
|:---:|:---:|
| 1 | 15 |
| 2 | 22 |
| 3 | 21 |
| 4 | 21 |
| 5 | 21 |

For real property, other than low-income rental housing, recovery deductions approximate the benefits of using the 175 percent declining-balance method for the early years and the straight-line method in the later years, assuming a 15-year recovery period. The recovery deductions in the taxable years of acquisition and disposition are based on the number of months the property was in service, as opposed to the half-year convention used for personal property. The annual recovery rates for all real property, except low-income housing, are shown in Table 4.6.

The straight-line method may also be used for real property. Unlike the personal property rules, this taxpayer option is allowed on a property-by-property basis. The allowable recovery periods are 15, 35, or 45 years. This alternative may be attractive for taxpayers who wish to reduce depreciation recapture when real property is sold or defer deductions to future years when they would be more beneficial.

Nonresidential property is subject to *full* recovery deduction recapture upon disposition. Therefore, only the gain (if any) in excess of all the recovery deductions taken over the life the asset was held is treated as capital gain. If, on the other hand, the

TABLE 4.6
ACRS recovery rates for all real estate (except low-income housing)

| Recovery Year | Recovery Rate (percent) | | | | | | | | | | | |
|---|---|---|---|---|---|---|---|---|---|---|---|---|
| | 1 | 2 | 3 | 4 | 5 | 6 | 7 | 8 | 9 | 10 | 11 | 12 |
| 1 | 12 | 11 | 10 | 9 | 8 | 7 | 6 | 5 | 4 | 3 | 2 | 1 |
| 2 | 10 | 10 | 11 | 11 | 11 | 11 | 11 | 11 | 11 | 11 | 11 | 12 |
| 3 | 9 | 9 | 9 | 9 | 10 | 10 | 10 | 10 | 10 | 10 | 10 | 10 |
| 4 | 8 | 8 | 8 | 8 | 8 | 8 | 9 | 9 | 9 | 9 | 9 | 9 |
| 5 | 7 | 7 | 7 | 7 | 7 | 7 | 8 | 8 | 8 | 8 | 8 | 8 |
| 6 | 6 | 6 | 6 | 6 | 7 | 7 | 7 | 7 | 7 | 7 | 7 | 7 |
| 7 | 6 | 6 | 6 | 6 | 6 | 6 | 6 | 6 | 6 | 6 | 6 | 6 |
| 8 | 6 | 6 | 6 | 6 | 6 | 6 | 5 | 6 | 6 | 6 | 6 | 6 |
| 9 | 6 | 6 | 6 | 6 | 5 | 6 | 5 | 5 | 5 | 6 | 6 | 6 |
| 10 | 5 | 6 | 5 | 6 | 5 | 5 | 5 | 5 | 5 | 5 | 6 | 5 |
| 11 | 5 | 5 | 5 | 5 | 5 | 5 | 5 | 5 | 5 | 5 | 5 | 5 |
| 12 | 5 | 5 | 5 | 5 | 5 | 5 | 5 | 5 | 5 | 5 | 5 | 5 |
| 13 | 5 | 5 | 5 | 5 | 5 | 5 | 5 | 5 | 5 | 5 | 5 | 5 |
| 14 | 5 | 5 | 5 | 5 | 5 | 5 | 5 | 5 | 5 | 5 | 5 | 5 |
| 15 | 5 | 5 | 5 | 5 | 5 | 5 | 5 | 5 | 5 | 5 | 5 | 5 |
| 16 | — | | 1 | 1 | 2 | 2 | 3 | 3 | 4 | 4 | 4 | 5 |

Use the column for the month of the first year the property is placed in service.

optional straight-line recovery system is used, then the entire amount of the gain is capital gain.

For all residential property, gain on disposition is treated as ordinary income only to the extent that the recovery deductions taken over the life the asset was held exceed those permitted under the straight-line method using a 15-year recovery period. Thus, if the optional straight-line recovery system is used, all gain on disposition is capital gain. These recapture rules for residential property are basically unchanged as compared to the prior law.

Low-income rental housing is allowed recovery deductions roughly equivalent to the 200 percent declining-balance method using a 15-year recovery period with a switch to straight line when beneficial. This advantage, plus other tax law differences that apply to low-income housing are designed to encourage investment in low-income rental housing.

The new rules do not permit the use of component depreciation, as was allowed under prior laws. Therefore, the recovery deduction for an entire building must be computed using one recovery method and one period. Exceptions are provided for personal property and a substantial improvement to the building, which is treated as a separate building. Remember, all buildings purchased or placed in service in 1981 or thereafter are treated under the new tax law. Table 4.7 summarizes the major provisions of the accelerated cost recovery system.

Returning to our medical building example, the factors required to compute this component of our tax-shelter effect, are:
1. Depreciation amount.
2. Depreciation life.
3. Depreciation type.
4. Ordinary income tax rate.

## Level 4. Overall cash flow to equity (after holding and sale)

Measurement of a property's investment merit is not complete until the effects of sale are considered. Even if a near-term sale is not contemplated, amortization continually builds up equity while depreciation deductions tend to create a future tax liability. These countervailing forces, plus the important impact of inflation and transaction costs, make it necessary to compute (rather than guess or ignore) the after-sale results of our investment.

Let us first assume that the property's sale price doesn't change and that selling costs can be overlooked. We will also assume that a 20 percent bracket applies for capital gains taxes. Table 4.5 computes this approximate sale cash flow.

Table 4.5 shows that the owner's initial $37,500 equity is almost fully recovered after sale. But it is wholly inadequate to ignore both inflation and transaction costs in this analysis of the effects of sale. Also, a further tax liability stems from a provision known as *recapture of excess depreciation*. For all buildings purchased or

TABLE 4.7
Summary of accelerated cost recovery
Provisions for property placed in service in 1981–1984

|  | Recovery Period (useful life): A. General rule B. Optional | Methods of Depreciation A. General rule B. Optional |
|---|---|---|
| **Tangible Personal Property** Autos, trucks, R&D equipment and miscellaneous short-lived assets[1] | 3 Years 5 or 12 Years | 150% D.B. or straight line Straight line |
| Other equipment | 5 Years 12 or 25 Years | 150% D.B. or straight line Straight line |
| **Real Estate** Commercial | 15 Years 35 or 45 Years | 175% D.B. or straight line Straight line |
| **Residential** Low-income housing | 15 Years 35 or 45 Years | 200% D.B. or straight line Straight line |
| Other | 15 Years 35 or 45 Years | 175% D.B. or straight line Straight line |

NOTES: 1. Short-lived assets include personal property with a present asset depreciation range midpoint life of 4 years or less.

2. Under prior law, gain on the disposition of commercial property was treated as ordinary income to the extent prior depreciation taken exceeded that which would have been allowable under the straight-line depreciation method. Under the new Act, gain on the dispostion of commercial property is treated as ordinary income to the extent of **all** prior depreciation if the 175% declining-balance method of depreciation is utilized.

3. If applicable, taxpayers are allowed a half-year's depreciation in the year an asset is placed in service (regardless of the exact date the asset is placed in service) and none in the year of sale. All real property is pro-rated monthly based on the month the asset is placed in service.

4. An asset's salvage value at the end of its useful life is ignored in all cases for purposes of computing depreciation.

TABLE 4.7 *(concluded)*
Summary of accelerated cost recovery
Provisions for property placed in service in 1981–1984

| | Depreciation Recaptured as Ordinary Income:<br>A. General Rule<br>B. Optional | Miscellaneous Provisions:<br>Half-year Convention[3]<br>Salvage Value Limitation[4] |
|---|---|---|
| **Tangible Personal Property** | | |
| Autos, trucks, R&D equipment and miscellaneous short-lived assets[1] | All prior depreciation<br>All prior depreciation | Applicable<br>None |
| Other equipment | All prior depreciation<br>All prior depreciation | Applicable<br>None |
| **Real Estate** | | |
| Commercial | All prior depreciation[2]<br>None | N/A<br>None |
| **Residential** | | |
| Low-income housing | Excess over straight line<br>None | N/A<br>None |
| Other | Excess over straight line<br>None | N/A<br>None |

placed in service prior to 1981 where accelerated depreciation has been taken, the law requires that the excess depreciation be taxed at the seller's ordinary bracket when sold. Excess depreciation is calculated as the difference between the amount taken, and that amount that would have been taken if straight line had been used. So three additional factors are necessary to compute an overall, or Level 4, rate of return:

1. Net sale price.
2. Percent annual inflation.
3. Capital gains tax rate.

The first item reflects the transaction costs of selling, namely commissions and closing costs. Suppose these costs equal 6 percent of the property's market value at the time of sale. Then immediate liquidation of our medical building would produce a net sale price of only $141,000, not the $150,000 assumed in Table 4.8.

---

TABLE 4.8
Cash flow from sale at the end of Year 1

---

| | | |
|---|---|---|
| Sale price | $150,000 | |
| Less: Debt repayment | 111,245 | (after $1,255 amortization) |
| Taxes due | 1,440 | (20% of $7,200 depreciated) |
| Sale cash flow | $ 37,315 | |

---

With inflation, however, we get a counterbalancing benefit. That is, we would expect the net sale price to rise over time. At 6 percent annual inflation, in one year the price gain would practically pay for the 6 percent transaction costs. After five or ten years, a worthwhile and tempting gain is available. But sale triggers a tax liability due on any gains beyond the property's book value, or *tax basis.* And some taxation may be at the ordinary income rate. By now the analysis is getting too tedious for hand calculation, so we'll bring in bigger guns.

## The role of computerized analysis

Computers are really phenomenal tools. They can perform a CPA-day's worth of arithmetic—perfectly accurate and according to the latest depreciation and tax rules—in only a few seconds. In fact, using computers just for accounting has been likened to squirrel hunting with a cannon. Their best use is in aiding decision making and managerial productivity. By analogy, relying on only a pencil to aid in important real estate decisions is like elephant hunting with a peashooter.

Many firms, and increasingly individuals, routinely use computers today for real estate analysis. An increasing number of professional articles have described various approaches and computer programs. In fact, most of this analysis is even possible with the better hand calculators, though still much more time consuming. Certainly today, professionals and individuals alike should use this four-level rate-of-return method to judge for themselves the profit potential of real estate as compared to other types of investments under conditions of uncertainty.

## The REAL analysis

Table 4.9 is the first of many similar tables in this book that result from using a computer program called REAL.[1] The name REAL could stand for Real Estate Analysis Liberator—a concise and fashionable description, but contrived. The program also could be called REAP, presumably suggesting Real Estate Analysis Profits. But let's stick with REAL, which simply stands for "real"—as in the real, accurate truth about analyzing real estate—really.

Table 4.9 contains the analysis of our suburban medical office building. The first report section, titled "Key Operating Factors Are..." lists the values of the items already noted as necessary for a thorough investment analysis. They are grouped at the top of the report into five categories:

1. Total project cost.
2. Mortgage terms.
3. Operating and inflation assumptions.
4. Depreciation.
5. Tax rates.

The next report section lists a "Pre-operating Summary," containing facts that are easily derived from the key operating factors. For example, since the medical building's total cost was $150,000 and $112,500 was mortgaged, the equity amount required is shown as $37,500, and the mortgage is 75 percent of the total project cost. Further to the right, the "% Net Resale to Cost" shows that we expect 94 percent back on sale, after allowing 6 percent of our total project cost for transaction costs.

The next category, labeled "% Income to Cost," equals 18 percent—meaning that gross income in the first year is 18 percent of the original total project cost. With no income fluctuations, in 5 years we would collect rent equal to five times 18 percent, or 90 percent of the total cost. In 5.6 years we would reach

# TABLE 4.9
## REAL analysis for the suburban medical office building—base case

KEY OPERATING FACTORS ARE ---

| TOTAL PROJECT COST | MORTGAGE TERMS | | | OPERATING & INFLATION ASSUMPTIONS | | | | | | DEPRECIATION | | | TAX RATES | |
|---|---|---|---|---|---|---|---|---|---|---|---|---|---|---|
| | AMOUNT | % INTR | LIFE | NET RESALE PRICE | % INFL | GROSS INCOME | % INFL | OPERATING EXPENSE | % INFL | AMOUNT | LIFE | RATE | INCOME | CAP GAIN |
| 150000 | 112500 | 9.00 | 25 | 141000 | 0 | 27000 | 0 | 12000 | 0 | 120000 | 25 | 150% | 50% | 20% |

PRE-OPERATING SUMMARY ---

| EQUITY AMOUNT | MORTGAGE TERMS | | | % NET RESALE TO COST | % INCOME TO COST | GROSS RENT MULT | % EXPENSE TO INCOME | % NOI TO COST | % DEPREC TO COST |
|---|---|---|---|---|---|---|---|---|---|
| | % DEBT | MONTHLY | YEARLY | | | | | | |
| 37500 | 75.00 | 944 | 11329 | 94.0 | 18.0 | 5.6 | 44.4 | 10.0 | 80.0 |

OPERATING RESULTS ---

| | HOLDING RESULTS BEFORE INCOME TAXES | | | | | | HOLDING RESULTS AFTER TAXES | | | | | OVERALL RESULTS IF SOLD AT YEAR END | | | | | |
|---|---|---|---|---|---|---|---|---|---|---|---|---|---|---|---|---|---|
| YR | GROSS INCOME | OPERATE EXPENSE | MORTGAGE INTR | MORTGAGE AMORT | CASH FLOW | % RE TURN | DEPREC IATION | TAXABLE INCOME | TAXES DUE | CASH FLOW | % RE TURN | SALE PRICE | DEBT REPAY | TAXES DUE | CASH FLOW | TOTAL PROFIT | % IRR |
| 1 | 27000 | 12000 | 10074 | 1255 | 3671 | 9.8 | 7200 | -2274 | -1137 | 4808 | 12.8 | 141000 | 111245 | -360 | 30115 | -2577 | -6.9 |
| 2 | 27000 | 12000 | 9956 | 1373 | 3671 | 9.8 | 6768 | -1724 | -862 | 4533 | 12.1 | 141000 | 109872 | 2304 | 28824 | 665 | 0.9 |
| 3 | 27000 | 12000 | 9828 | 1502 | 3671 | 9.8 | 6362 | -1189 | -595 | 4266 | 11.4 | 141000 | 108371 | 4045 | 28585 | 4691 | 4.5 |
| 4 | 27000 | 12000 | 9687 | 1642 | 3671 | 9.8 | 5980 | -667 | -333 | 4004 | 10.7 | 141000 | 106728 | 5595 | 28677 | 8788 | 6.5 |
| 5 | 27000 | 12000 | 9533 | 1797 | 3671 | 9.8 | 5621 | -154 | -77 | 3748 | 10.0 | 141000 | 104932 | 6966 | 29103 | 12961 | 7.7 |
| 6 | 27000 | 12000 | 9364 | 1965 | 3671 | 9.8 | 5284 | 352 | 176 | 3495 | 9.3 | 141000 | 102967 | 8168 | 29866 | 17219 | 8.5 |
| 7 | 27000 | 12000 | 9180 | 2149 | 3671 | 9.8 | 4967 | 853 | 427 | 3244 | 8.7 | 141000 | 100817 | 9211 | 30972 | 21569 | 9.1 |
| 8 | 27000 | 12000 | 8978 | 2351 | 3671 | 9.8 | 4669 | 1353 | 676 | 2994 | 8.0 | 141000 | 98466 | 10106 | 32428 | 26020 | 9.5 |
| 9 | 27000 | 12000 | 8758 | 2572 | 3671 | 9.8 | 4389 | 1854 | 927 | 2744 | 7.3 | 141000 | 95895 | 10860 | 34245 | 30582 | 9.8 |
| 10 | 27000 | 12000 | 8516 | 2813 | 3671 | 9.8 | 4297 | 2186 | 1093 | 2578 | 6.9 | 141000 | 93082 | 11569 | 36349 | 35263 | 10.0 |

*payback*—100 percent of our investment returned to us as gross rent. This is commonly referred to as the *gross rent multiplier,* which is shown in the next column. It is the reciprocal of .18, or the 18 percent income-to-cost figure. This statistic, often used, omits expenses, not to mention leverage, tax shelter, and inflation. (We call the gross rent multiplier our Level 0.) The "% NOI to Cost" is Level 1—the rate of return found by comparing net operating income (income less expenses) to the total project cost.

The next section of the report, titled "Operating Results," takes all the vital issues into account. It shows a year-by-year investment analysis of the property before tax, after tax, and after sale. Thus this report format parallels the four-level analysis we showed already for Year 1 of our medical building.

The columns on the far left show the property's year-by-year $27,000 annual gross income. Next is listed the $12,000 annual operating expense, followed by an accurate calculation, using a monthly amortization schedule, of the amount of mortgage interest and amortization during each year. This gross income, less expense and mortgage payments, produces a before-tax cash flow of $3,671.[2] As shown, this represents a 9.8 percent return on the $37,500 equity. The Level 2 rate of return holds constant at 9.8 percent over time and is very close to the 10 percent shown as Level 1. You might reasonably ask, therefore, why bother with Level 2, since it's practically the same as Level 1?

The after-tax results of holding the investment are presented in the middle third of the report. Allowable depreciation is $7,200 in Year 1 but then drops as time marches on. Taxable income— which is gross income less operating expense, interest, and depreciation—is computed to be *minus* $2,274. Thus this property shelters the before-tax cash flow completely and can still offset some other income, as well.

Let's assume the owner faces a 50 percent ordinary income tax bracket. This results in "Taxes Due" of minus $1,137, really a refund of this amount (or, in reality, that much less tax the owner sends the IRS). The after-tax cash flow for Year 1 is therefore boosted to $4,808, a 12.8 percent rate of return on the original $37,500 of equity. This second "% Return" column is the Level 3 rate of return. Notice that by Year 5 it is 10 percent and that over the first ten years it averages about 10 percent—the same result as from the Level 1 calculation! (Again, you ask, why bother going beyond the simplicity of Level 1?)

The rightmost third of the analysis shows the effects of selling the property after holding it for any number of years. The "Sale Price," which is net of 6 percent for transaction costs, is $141,000. The "Debt Repay" column shows the mortgage balance due at any year end. The "Taxes Due," based on the federal legislation applicable to pre-1981 buildings, deducted from the net sale price in arriving at the "Cash Flow" figures: $30,115 in Year 1.

What is our *total return* after taxes, including both holding results and capital gain or loss? The rightmost two columns list these overall results. "Total Profit" is the sum of all after-tax cash flows from holding year by year and then selling at a particular year end, less recovery of the original equity. With sale at the end of Year 1, a $2,577 loss results. Why? Because transaction costs are not overcome by net rental income or sale price gains in this example. To be profitable, the property must be held longer, be sold without commissions and other costs, or appreciate, if only due to inflation.

By contrast, the Year 3 total profit is $4,691. It is the sum of $4,808, $4,533, and $4,266—the yearly holding cash flows after taxes—plus the $28,585 sale cash flow after three years, less recouping the original $37,500 equity. This sequence of after-tax cash flows, for sale at the end of Year 3, produces a slight but inadequate profit. When distilled to a total rate of return, shown in the rightmost column as "% IRR," an unexciting 4.5 percent is the answer.[3] If the building is held for longer holding periods, however, this Level 4 rate of return rises. In fact, for a sale at Year 10, the overall return is 10 percent—the same as we figured at Level 1! (Maybe I shouldn't have been so critical.)

## The inflation factor

Table 4.9 lists among its key factors an annual inflation assumption of 0 percent. This applies equally to the net sale price, the gross income, and the operating expense. Do you believe that? If not, we can change the inflation factor's value, as shown in Table 4.10. The form in Table 4.10 is crucial to our analysis. It

**TABLE 4.10**
Key factors for suburban medical office building

### Real Estate Investment Analysis Form—Thirteen Key Factors

Client _____    Phone # _____

Address _____    Project title _____

_____    Years of analysis _____

| 1. Total project cost | $150,000 | |
|---|---|---|

**Mortgage Terms**

| 2. Mortgage amount (show either $ or %) | $112,500 | or _____% of total project cost |
|---|---|---|
| 3. Interest rate | 9% annually | |
| 4. Mortgage life | 25 years | |

**Operating & Inflation Assumptions**

| 5. Net resale price (today, before inflation, net of transaction costs) | $141,000 | or _____% of total project cost |
|---|---|---|
| 6. Gross income (annually, before inflation, net of vacancy) | $ 27,000 | or _____% of total project cost |
| 7. Operating expense (annually, before inflation) | $ 12,000 | or _____% of gross income |
| 8. Annual inflation (resale price, income, expense) | 6%   6%   6% <br> resale   income   expense | |

**Depreciation**

| 9. Total depreciable base (not annual amount) | $120,000 | or _____% of total project cost |
|---|---|---|
| 10. Depreciable life | 25 years | 200% for low-income housing |
| 11. Depreciable rate (percent of straight line) | 150%‡ | 175% for most real estate* <br> 150% for tangible personal property <br> 100% for all other† |

**Tax Rates**

| 12. Ordinary income | 50% |
|---|---|
| 13. Capital gains | 20% |

SOURCE: The Mader Group, Inc.
*Usually preferable for nonresidential property.
†Usually preferable for commercial property only because of ERTA recapture provisions.
‡150 percent of straight-line depreciation is used here because this property was built prior to 1981 and therefore subject to pre-1981 depreciation rules for new commercial property.

specifies the 13 key operating factors—*including* inflation. Notice that we will now assume a modest 6 percent annual inflation rate to be applied to the property's net sale price, gross income, and operating expense. For a hand-calculated analysis, it would be a loathsome task to refigure all the cash flows, taxes, and so on. But a brief burst of computer power produces the revised results shown in Table 4.11.

Your trained and curious glance should immediately drift to the rightmost column of the report. There we see the overall or total rate of return (Level 4). This rate of return includes all the effects of leverage, tax shelter, and sale with inflation; it presents an accurate, REAListic picture of the property's investment merit. In all, this report quantifies seven of our eight investment objectives: rate of return, risk (by comparing tables using varying key factor values), leverage, liquidity, expenses, tax shelter, and inflation protection. Personal satisfaction is still for you to judge.

The no-inflation analysis may be interesting, and it held sway in real estate circles for decades, but the 1970s made it obsolete. The impact of rising rents and sale prices is absolutely dynamite. And for the 1980s, our 6 percent annual inflation assumption probably seems conservative. It is certainly closer to the truth than assuming *no* inflation. Yet that degree of inflation (6 percent) *boosts the overall rate of return to more than double the no-inflation levels.*

Figure 4.1 graphically compares the rightmost columns of Tables 4.9 and 4.11. The inflation-swollen rate of return is nothing less than excellent. After-tax returns of 20 percent or more compounded annually are attainable. But the property must be held at least a few years, thereby mitigating the effects of transaction costs. To provide comparable results, a bond, for example, would have to pay a 40 percent or higher interest rate, because its income is fully taxable. Clearly, real estate can be the key to profiting from inflation.

## Summary

An analysis method has been developed that includes only the *minimum* number of key factors—13 in all—needed for a thorough, accurate real estate investment analysis. You can use it to com-

## TABLE 4.11
### REAL analysis for the suburban medical office building—6% inflation

KEY OPERATING FACTORS ARE ---

| TOTAL PROJECT COST | ---MORTGAGE TERMS--- AMOUNT | % INTR | LIFE | ----OPERATING NET RESALE PRICE | % INFL | ----OPERATING & INFLATION ASSUMPTIONS---- GROSS INCOME | % INFL | OPERATING EXPENSE | % INFL | ---TAX RATES--- INCOME | CAP GAIN |
|---|---|---|---|---|---|---|---|---|---|---|---|
| 150000 | 112500 | 9.00 | 25 | 141000 | 6 | 27000 | 6 | 12000 | 6 | 50% | 20% |

| ----DEPRECIATION---- AMOUNT | LIFE | RATE |
|---|---|---|
| 120000 | 25 | 150% |

PRE-OPERATING SUMMARY ---

| EQUITY AMOUNT | ---MORTGAGE TERMS--- % DEBT | MONTHLY | YEARLY | % NET RESALE TO COST | % INCOME TO COST | GROSS RENT MULT | % EXPENSE TO INCOME | % NOI TO COST | % DEPREC TO COST |
|---|---|---|---|---|---|---|---|---|---|
| 37500 | 75.00 | 944 | 11329 | 94.0 | 18.0 | 5.6 | 44.4 | 10.0 | 80.0 |

OPERATING RESULTS ---

| YR | ---HOLDING RESULTS BEFORE INCOME TAXES--- GROSS INCOME | OPERATE EXPENSE | --MORTGAGE-- INTR | AMORT | CASH FLOW | % RE TURN | ---HOLDING RESULTS AFTER TAXES--- DEPREC IATION | TAXABLE INCOME | TAXES DUE | CASH FLOW | % RE TURN | ---OVERALL RESULTS IF SOLD AT YEAR END--- SALE PRICE | DEBT REPAY | TAXES DUE | CASH FLOW | TOTAL PROFIT | % IRR |
|---|---|---|---|---|---|---|---|---|---|---|---|---|---|---|---|---|---|
| 1 | 27000 | 12000 | 10074 | 1255 | 3671 | 9.8 | 7200 | -2274 | -1137 | 4808 | 12.8 | 149460 | 111245 | 2052 | 36163 | 3471 | 9.3 |
| 2 | 28620 | 12720 | 9956 | 1373 | 4571 | 12.2 | 6768 | -824 | -412 | 4983 | 13.3 | 158428 | 109872 | 5790 | 42766 | 15057 | 19.4 |
| 3 | 30337 | 13483 | 9828 | 1502 | 5525 | 14.7 | 6362 | 665 | 332 | 5193 | 13.8 | 167933 | 108371 | 9432 | 50131 | 27615 | 22.3 |
| 4 | 32157 | 14292 | 9687 | 1642 | 6536 | 17.4 | 5980 | 2198 | 1099 | 5437 | 14.5 | 178009 | 106728 | 12997 | 58284 | 41205 | 23.3 |
| 5 | 34087 | 15150 | 9533 | 1797 | 7608 | 20.3 | 5621 | 3783 | 1892 | 5716 | 15.2 | 188690 | 104932 | 16504 | 67255 | 55891 | 23.6 |
| 6 | 36132 | 16059 | 9364 | 1965 | 8744 | 23.3 | 5284 | 5425 | 2713 | 6032 | 16.1 | 200011 | 102967 | 19970 | 77075 | 71743 | 23.6 |
| 7 | 38300 | 17022 | 9180 | 2149 | 9949 | 26.5 | 4967 | 7131 | 3565 | 6383 | 17.0 | 212012 | 100817 | 23414 | 87781 | 88833 | 23.5 |
| 8 | 40598 | 18044 | 8978 | 2351 | 11225 | 29.9 | 4669 | 8907 | 4454 | 6772 | 18.1 | 224733 | 98466 | 26852 | 99414 | 107237 | 23.2 |
| 9 | 43034 | 19126 | 8758 | 2572 | 12579 | 33.5 | 4389 | 10761 | 5381 | 7198 | 19.2 | 238217 | 95895 | 30304 | 112018 | 127040 | 23.0 |
| 10 | 45616 | 20274 | 8516 | 2813 | 14013 | 37.4 | 297 | 12528 | 6264 | 7749 | 20.7 | 252510 | 93082 | 33871 | 125557 | 148327 | 22.7 |

Reprinted with the permission of The Mader Group, Inc., Narberth, PA.

FIGURE 4.1
Total return for 0% inflation and 6% inflation

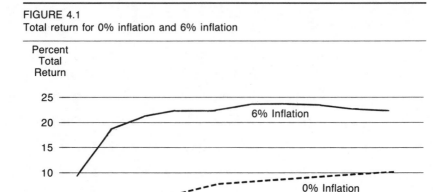

pute consistent, correct rates of return. Level 1 considers the property's rate of return before financing. Level 2 then includes the effects of leverage; Level 3 is after tax shelter; and Level 4 shows resale after inflation or appreciation. The results of our medical-building analysis indicate that real estate is illiquid and, if sold prematurely, can produce a loss. But the good news is that *inflation can double the total rate of return available from real estate.*

# Technical
# Appendix


This book attempts to present quantified, state-of-the-art analysis of real estate investing *and to do so in an appealing, digestible way.* We rely on nothing more than basic arithmetic and actual case examples to provide experience and show application. But the first edition of this book, published in 1975, produced so many inquiries on *exactly* how to derive and interpret each number in the REAL table, that we've added this technical appendix. Skip it if you already know about internal rates of return (IRR)—or don't care to—or if you completely followed the item-by-item explanation just presented in Chapter 4. (The best use of this appendix is to refer to it months or years from now, whenever you have a particular analysis in hand that you wish to review or explain to someone else.)


## Internal rate of return

This is the generally accepted calculation for reducing *to one number* the rate of return inherent, or "internal," in a series of cash flows. Most investments involve an initial cash outflow, hopefully followed by sufficiently pleasing and long-lasting cash inflows. Let us use our medical building again as an example.

# TABLE 4.12
## REAL analysis for the suburban medical office building—base case with key

KEY OPERATING FACTORS ARE ---

| TOTAL PROJECT COST | --MORTGAGE TERMS--- AMOUNT | % INTR | LIFE | NET RESALE PRICE | ----OPERATING & INFLATION ASSUMPTIONS---- % INFL | GROSS INCOME | % INFL | % OPERATING EXPENSE | % INFL | ----DEPRECIATION-- AMOUNT | LIFE | RATE | ---TAX RATES--- INCOME | CAP GAIN |
|---|---|---|---|---|---|---|---|---|---|---|---|---|---|---|
| (A) 150000 | 112500 | 9.00 | 25 | 141000 | 0 | 27000 | 0 | 12000 | 0 | 120000 | 25 | 150% | 50% | 20% |

PRE-OPERATING SUMMARY ---

| EQUITY AMOUNT | --MORTGAGE TERMS--- % DEBT | MONTHLY | YEARLY | % NET RESALE TO COST | % INCOME TO COST | GROSS RENT MULT | % EXPENSE TO INCOME | % NOI TO COST | % DEPREC TO COST |
|---|---|---|---|---|---|---|---|---|---|
| (B) 37500 | 75.00 | 944 | 11329 | 94.0 | 18.0 | 5.6 | 44.4 | (C) 10.0 | 80.0 |

OPERATING RESULTS ---

| | ----HOLDING RESULTS BEFORE INCOME TAXES--- | | | | | | ----HOLDING RESULTS AFTER TAXES--- | | | | |
|---|---|---|---|---|---|---|---|---|---|---|---|
| YR | GROSS INCOME | OPERATE EXPENSE | --MORTGAGE-- INTR | AMORT | CASH FLOW | % RE TURN (E) | DEPREC IATION | TAXABLE INCOME | TAXES DUE | CASH FLOW | % RE TURN (F) |
| (D) 1 | 27000 | 12000 | 10074 | 1255 | 3671 | 9.8 | 7200 | -2274 | -1137 | 4808 | 12.8 |
| 2 | 27000 | 12000 | 9956 | 1373 | 3671 | 9.8 | 6768 | -1724 | -862 | 4533 | 12.1 |
| 3 | 27000 | 12000 | 9828 | 1502 | 3671 | 9.8 | 6362 | -1189 | -595 | 4266 | 11.4 |
| 4 | 27000 | 12000 | 9687 | 1642 | 3671 | 9.8 | 5980 | -667 | -333 | 4004 | 10.7 |
| 5 | 27000 | 12000 | 9533 | 1797 | 3671 | 9.8 | 5621 | -154 | -77 | 3748 | 10.0 |
| 6 | 27000 | 12000 | 9364 | 1965 | 3671 | 9.8 | 5284 | 352 | 176 | 3495 | 9.3 |
| 7 | 27000 | 12000 | 9180 | 2149 | 3671 | 9.8 | 4967 | 853 | 427 | 3244 | 8.7 |
| 8 | 27000 | 12000 | 8978 | 2351 | 3671 | 9.8 | 4669 | 1353 | 676 | 2994 | 8.0 |
| 9 | 27000 | 12000 | 8758 | 2572 | 3671 | 9.8 | 4389 | 1854 | 927 | 2744 | 7.3 |
| 10 | 27000 | 12000 | 8516 | 2813 | 3671 | 9.8 | 4297 | 2186 | 1093 | 2578 | 6.9 |
| | H | I | J | K | L | M | N | O | P | Q | R |

| | ----OVERALL RESULTS IF SOLD AT YEAR END----(G) | | | | | |
|---|---|---|---|---|---|---|
| | SALE PRICE | DEBT REPAY | TAXES DUE | CASH FLOW | TOTAL PROFIT | % IRR |
| 1 | 141000 | 111245 | -360 | 30115 | -2577 | -6.9 |
| 2 | 141000 | 109872 | 2304 | 28824 | 665 | 0.9 |
| 3 | 141000 | 108371 | 4045 | 28585 | 4691 | 4.5 |
| 4 | 141000 | 106728 | 5595 | 28677 | 8788 | 6.5 |
| 5 | 141000 | 104932 | 6966 | 29103 | 12961 | 7.7 |
| 6 | 141000 | 102967 | 8168 | 29866 | 17219 | 8.5 |
| 7 | 141000 | 100817 | 9211 | 30972 | 21569 | 9.1 |
| 8 | 141000 | 98466 | 10106 | 32428 | 26020 | 9.5 |
| 9 | 141000 | 95895 | 10860 | 34245 | 30582 | 9.8 |
| 10 | 141000 | 93082 | 11569 | 36349 | 35263 | 10.0 |
| | S | T | U | V | W | X |

Reprinted with the permission of The Mader Group, Inc., Narberth, PA.

TABLE 4.12 (concluded)
REAL analysis for the suburban medical office building—key

A *13 key factors.* Values to be judged by the analyst

B *Computed summary.* Shows equity amount, Level 1 rate of return and other results

C *Level 1.* Net operating income divided by the total project cost, expressed in percent

D *Year 1 results.* The year's cash flows, income, taxes, profits, and percent return results

E *Level 2.* Cash flow (after expenses and mortgage payments), divided by the original equity

F *Level 3.* Cash flow (after depreciation and taxes), divided by the original equity

G *Level 4.* Overall (internal) rate of return found by discounting the holding results after taxes (Column Q) through year of sale, plus the "Sale cash flow" (Column V) for the year of sale, against the original equity

H *Gross income.* Key factor value, possibly increasing annually by a specified inflation factor

I *Operating expense.* Key factor value, possibly increasing annually by a specified inflation factor

J *Mortgage interest.* Interest on a mortgage for the year shown

K *Mortgage amortization.* Payments on a mortgage going for debt reduction

L *Cash flow.* Spendable, or cash left over from operations but before income taxes

M *Percent return.* The Level 2 rate of return as defined above

N *Depreciation.* Expense allowed for tax purposes but not requiring cash

O *Taxable income.* Gross income less operating expenses, interest, and depreciation (Column H minus Columns I, J, and N)

P *Taxes due.* Income taxes due (Column O times income tax rate)

Q *Cash flow.* Cash from holding after income taxes (Column L minus Column P)

R *Percent return.* The Level 3 rate of return as defined above

S *Sale price.* Market value at indicated year end, after transaction cost allowance

T *Debt repayment.* Mortgage balance remaining at year end, after cumulative amortization payments to date

U *Tax due.* Capital gain tax due upon sale at the specified year end, based on book value and recapture rules

V *Sale cash flow.* Sale proceeds from net resale price after debt repayment and payment of tax due (Column S minus Columns T and U)

W *Total profit.* Cumulative after-tax cash flow from holding (Column Q) through the year of sale, plus the sale cash flow (Column V) for the year of sale, less recovery of the original equity

X *IRR.* Total or internal rate of return, compounded annually after tax. This is the Level 4 rate of return and it includes the effects of leverage, tax shelter, and inflation.

(See Table 4.12, which is simply Table 4.9 labeled alphabetically for ease of definition and discussion.)

Note at Point B that invested equity of $37,500 is a cash outflow. The mortgage wasn't the *owner's* outflow, so it doesn't count yet. The successive annual inflows—after expenses, mortgage payments, and taxes—are shown in Column Q. Then upon sale of the property, the additional after-tax inflow to the owner is reported in Column V. Figuring Level 4 rates of return is now like reading a Chinese menu—pick as many from Column Q as you like, plus one from Column V, as shown in Table 4.13.

TABLE 4.13

| Time | Owner's Cash Flow |
|------|------------------|
| Year (0) | – $37,500 initial equity |
| Year 1 | + 4,808 holding, after tax, for 1 or several years |
| Year 2 | + 4,533 |
| Year 3 | + 4,266 |
| Year 3 | + 28,585 sale cash flow, after tax |

Now we must use discounting to compute a rate of return that takes into account this *timing* of money, as well as the *amount* of money. This is known as recognizing the *time value of money.* By this we mean that money today is worth more than the same nominal amount of money in the future. This is because if we had it today, we could invest it and hopefully have a greater sum at some point in the future. If we don't have it today, we give up this *opportunity.* So comparing money in the future with money today would be like comparing apples and oranges, or in an inflationary period, grapes and raisins. We must *discount* future cash flows to the present, to take into account this lost opportunity. The *ratio of discount* is determined by using the following formula:

$$PV = \frac{CF_1}{1+i} + \frac{CF_2}{(1+i)^2} + \frac{CF_3}{(1+i)^3} + \ldots$$

PV stands for "present value," $CF_1$ is the cash flow in Year 1, $CF_2$ is the cash flow in Year 2, and so on. Then $i$ is the annual rate of return, or discounting factor which reflects the time value of money. Cash flow received in future years has a lesser *present* value. The IRR is that *i* that causes PV to be equal to the owner's initial equity outflow. Thus the year-by-year returns, when discounted for delay, justify the up-front investment by providing the stated internal rate of return. In order to solve for *i,* you need to use a computer or calculator that has this capability. Our computer determined that .045 (4.5 percent) was the answer. So if

$$\$37,500 = \frac{4,808}{1.045} + \frac{4,533}{(1.045)^2} + \frac{4,266}{(1.045)^3} + \frac{28,585}{(1.045)^3}$$

we replace every *i* in our equation (as is done above) with .045, we can prove that the computer was correct. Thus, the IRR, or Level 4 rate of return of this investment is 4.5 percent. This compound annual rate of return on our medical building reflects holding for three years and then selling, assuming the key factors as specified. (And if you don't want a 4.5 percent total return – and if you don't think inflation will be zero – then keep reading!)

## Notes

1. The REAL computer program, originally written by Chris Mader and recently updated by Jay Stevenson, is now the property of The Mader Group, Inc. It has been used for ten years in consulting to real estate professionals and private investors.

2. Computers, like accountants, round off results for reporting purposes. Annual reports no longer carry figures out to pennies; large companies usually round off to the nearest $1,000 and General Motors to the nearest $100,000! Unlike accountants, however, computers don't have the common sense to always arrange the rounding properly. Because each number is correctly but *separately* reported to the nearest dollar, an occasional sum might seem to be one dollar off. This is no cause for concern, especially when you recall that the purpose of the analysis is to estimate the future and not to account for the past. Besides, each individual number is represented as accurately as possible.

3. This IRR, standing for the *internal rate of return* or total rate of return (or Level 4), equalizes future cash flows to the intial cash outlay by considering

TABLE 4.14
Income tax calculation upon sale of property

| Year 1 | | |
|---|---|---|
| 1. Net sale price | $141,000 | |
| 2. Tax basis | | |
| (cost less accumulated depreciation) | $150,000 | Cost basis |
| Less: | 7,000 | Year 1 depreciaton |
| | $142,800 | Tax basis |
| 3. Taxable gain upon sale | $141,000 | Net sale price |
| Less: | 142,800 | Tax basis |
| | $ −1,800 | Taxable gain (minus for loss) |
| 4. Capital gain tax calculation | $ −1,800 | Taxable gain |
| | × 20% | Long-term capital gain tax rate |
| | $ −360 | |

| Year 2 | | |
|---|---|---|
| 1. Net sale price | $141,000 | |
| 2. Tax basis | | |
| (cost less accumulated depreciation) | $150,000 | Cost basis |
| | 7,200 | Year 1 depreciation |
| Less: | 6,768 | Year 2 depreciation |
| | $136,032 | |
| 3. Taxable gain upon sale | $141,000 | Net sale price |
| Less: | 136,032 | Tax basis |
| | $ 4,968 | Taxable gain |
| 4. Capital gain tax calculation | | |
| (recover excess depreciation) | $ 4,800 | Straight-line depreciation |
| $7,200 − $4,800 = | $2,400 | Year 1 excess depreciation |
| $6,768 − $4,800 = | 1,968 | Year 2 excess depreciation |
| | 4,368 | Recaptured at ordinary rate |
| | × 50% | Tax rate |
| | $ 2,184 | |
| | $ 4,968 | Taxable gain |
| | $ 4,368 | Excess recaptured |
| | $ 600 | Subject to capital gain |
| | × 20% | Tax rate |
| | $ 120 | |
| Total tax: | $ 2,184 | Recapture |
| | 120 | Capital gains |
| | $ 2,304 | Tax due |

their timing. For example, receiving $1.12 one year hence implies a 12 percent annual return if $1.00 must be invested today to get it. Both the timing and the amount of future cash flows are taken into account by this internal rate of return computation. Also, for greatest simplicity and consistency, the cash inflows are assumed to occur at year end. To the extent that net income is actually received during the year and can draw interest, extra profits and slightly higher rates of return can be achieved.

# 5 Two Case Examples—1970s versus 1980s

This chapter illustrates two case examples using the REAL analysis developed in Chapter 4. Both are investments that were actually made. Each reflects its own era—the 1970s versus the 1980s. This chapter also discusses getting started in investment real estate and the steps toward successful buying, operating, and cashing in.

## Getting started

The best initiation into real estate is home ownership. While noneconomic considerations usually take precedence in this decision, the investment aspects are also important. (The special features of this situation are analyzed in Chapter 7.) Furthermore, home ownership provides firsthand experience in selecting, financing, closing on, and operating a property, as well as insight into its tax and appreciation benefits. For those of you who have already purchased a home, we'll help explain why you've probably been financially successful. For those of you looking to jump in for the first time, this typical "starter" real estate investment may be very similar to your present choices.

The first prerequisite is *attitude*. You must be ready to invest, be willing to stay invested, and be able to accept occasional operating responsibilities. Real estate does not have the safety and liquidity of savings, for example, or the liquidity and passive participation of mutual funds. The insecure should note that a property's price is not quoted daily in newspaper financial pages and that arranging rentals or a sale may require some marketing *savoir faire*. It also helps if you get personal satisfaction from the tangibility, uniqueness, and control of your property.

Next comes *knowledge*. Each real estate property is unique. The selling price is a negotiated, private, mutual decision, not a finely adjusted balance of many publicized transactions, as is the case with national stock exchanges. Differential knowledge—such as understanding zoning possibilities or analyzing new highway plans—can lead to revised values that both parties may not be equally aware of. Even with the same knowledge of the property and of its "highest and best use," investors vary in their objectives and their analysis ability. As this book should demonstrate, the exact effects of leverage, tax shelter, inflation, and other factors are not intuitively obvious. Analyzing these factors rapidly and accurately provides an advantage, even with comparable information.

Third, you need *capital*, usually including some of your own. How much depends on the types of properties and degree of diversification you seek. At the minimum, you should plan on having equity of 20 to 25 percent of the total project cost. For a building lot or a few acres of undeveloped country land, equity of $5,000 might do. For a median-priced rental house, plan on needing equity of $10,000 to $15,000. Grander designs—such as a duplex, a several-unit apartment building, or diversification into two or three small properties—typically require at least $20,000 of investable funds. Furthermore, if your annual family income is $25,000 or more, real estate's tax shelter becomes relatively beneficial compared to most investments.

Fourth, you must *invest*. Not a nickel is earned from investing until you buy something. Your attitude, knowledge, and capital must be galvanized into action. And your commitment cannot be easily undone, given the time spent selecting and financing property, coupled with its high transaction costs and resale illiquidity. Getting started is a gutsy decision we urge *you* to make.

## Choosing your first investment property

Exuberant speakers and journalists often extoll the virtues of:
Country land
Waterfront property
Expanding suburbs
Reviving cities
New highway intersections
Resort second homes
The growing South
The growing West
The growing Southwest
And so on.

Legend has it that *location* is the first, second, and third most important factor in real estate. But no investing formula suits everyone. For your first property, choose something within your means, in a familiar location, and within your ability to oversee. Buying an existing income-producing property is less risky than buying development property or holding raw land while waiting for its ultimate user to enter the picture. Check the seller's credentials and verify the property's purported financial statements. Retain experts, but plan to study their methods and documents— your goal is an independent ability to evaluate property and negotiate terms.

Seek and shop for *leverage.* When possible, include necessary appliances, repairs, fixtures, and closing costs in the purchase price, because that price is the main basis for setting the mortgage amount. With existing income property in a stable or upgrading location, your risk of not having rents meet the mortgage is slight. Naturally, smaller units or a single-family house suffer proportionately more if a vacancy persists.

Assume any existing, below-the-market mortgage. A *nonrecourse* loan limits your risk to the equity amount invested. Avoid prepayment penalty clauses. Remember, you will probably sell or refinance after several years. Make sure the seller is willing to pay any mortgage points demanded by the lender. (Points amount to prepaid, extra interest; each point is 1 percent of the loan amount.) See if a second mortgage can be arranged with the seller, although this may stiffen the negotiable selling price.

Above all, choose a property for its *appreciation* potential. View income as a means of paying the mortgage. Tax benefits should still provide an acceptable after-tax rate of return on your down payment. The upside play is a capital gain from resale or a tax-free refinancing or trade. This gain on your first property can then become the cornerstone for your real estate pyramid. Beware, however, the long easy slide down from a pyramid's precarious pinnacle. In short, get carried, not buried, by your first investment.

For subsequent investments, these guidelines change. You can then more knowledgeably diversify or venture into development situations or more remote locations—again selecting properties for their appreciation potential. Look for factors like expanding development, population growth or shift, new infrastructure (roads, utilities, schools, and shopping), and increasing status attached to the area. Remember that inflation works on all property, so try to find the extra advantage that real appreciation provides. For example, selective repairs to older properties can lead to both increased income and capital gains. In general, however, quality in location and construction appreciates the most.

## The investment analysis

Having selected opportunities according to the qualitative guidelines above, a REAL analysis can be extremely useful. Our examples and the tables in Part III let you do this analysis easily. With the quantitative results you obtain, you can discover the investment characteristics of each property and then compare them. Additionally, you can investigate various possible terms, such as a 16 percent mortgage interest rate for 80 percent of the purchase price versus a 15 percent rate for only 70 percent financing. This sharpens your ability to make moneymaking and money-saving decisions.

A thorough investment analysis begins with a *base case*. This is a set of "best guesstimate" values for our 13 key factors. The REAL analysis is then your mechanism for translating these judgments into measures of investment performance. Next, as is done in Chapter 6, you can selectively vary the values of key factors to determine their individual impact on overall results. This is called a *sensitivity analysis* and it provides great insight into the sources and degree of risk.

## Base case—1970s

This actual investment involved a middle-class, desirable-suburb, residential property, which fits our guidelines for your initial real estate investment. Its traditional four-bedroom-plus-family-room design made this property easily marketable. In addition, its quiet street location bordered on a secluded town park. Its appeal was further enhanced by the local school district's fine reputation— important because the largest percentage growth in any age group during 1975–80 was among the 30- to 35-year-olds. This maturing post–World War II baby-boom group then needed such family-oriented, metropolitan housing.

The brick-and-stone construction (20 years old) kept maintenance down. Additionally, by being relatively near the city center and mass transit, this location would benefit from the changing economics of transportation. For these reasons—and because the prior owners were named Devine—we called it "the Devine property."

Before negotiating purchase and mortgage, we performed several variations of the REAL analysis based on comparable sales, rentals, expenses, and available mortgage terms. Many key factors can be determined accurately, such as the depreciation and tax factors. Other factor values, such as rental rates and mortgage terms, are under your control or subject to known market conditions. The total project cost is the major issue for negotiation. That leaves the net resale price, operating expense, and percent of annual inflation as most in doubt—and hence worth analyzing for their impact on profit and risk. Table 5.1 shows the actual key factors applicable to this property. Table 5.2 then shows the REAL report, as projected at the time of purchase in 1973.

Note that the top section of Table 5.2 repeats the 13 key factor values. The next section computes some easily derived amounts and percentages. Then follows the year-by-year display of investment results derived from the key factor values.

Using applicable accounting, depreciation, and tax rules, profitability results are computed on a before-tax, after-tax, and after-sale basis. As discussed, the most crucial answers are at the far right—the total rate of return. This is the compound annual, after-tax rate of return on equity for each holding period shown: one through ten years. This base case suggested that our property would indeed be "divine." For example, the total return ranges from 25 percent to 20 percent compounded annually after tax.[1]

The "Total Profit" column (next-to-rightmost column) shows the cumulative dollar profit from holding the property and then selling it at the end of the indicated year. As of Year 5, profits were projected to total $13,270, in large measure due to inflation working for us. Furthermore, some of these dollars come in interim years and can be invested elsewhere before Year 5.

How much would we profit before sale? The left-of-center columns labeled "Cash Flow" and "% Return" reveal the before-tax cash flow from holding in dollars and as a percentage return on the original equity. In this example, the results are not spectacular: $326 in cash flow (gross income, less operating expense and mortgage payments). As a percent of the $9,000 equity, that provides only a 3.6 percent return. Clearly, this cash-on-cash return is only part of the property's investment merit.

Looking now at the columns labeled "Cash Flow" and "% Return," under "Holding Results After Taxes," we see the full profit from holding, counting tax shelter. It is $833 in the first

**TABLE 5.1**
1970s example: the Divine property—5% inflation

### Real Estate Investment Analysis Form—Thirteen Key Factors

Client_____   Phone # _____

Address_____   Project title _____

_____   Years of analysis _____

| | | | |
|---|---|---|---|
| 1. | Total project cost | $37,800 | |

**Mortgage Terms**

| | | | |
|---|---|---|---|
| 2. | Mortgage amount (show either $ or %) | $28,800 | or _____% of total project cost |
| 3. | Interest rate | 7.5% annually | |
| 4. | Mortgage life | 25 years | |

**Operating & Inflation Assumptions**

| | | | |
|---|---|---|---|
| 5. | Net resale price (today, before inflation, net of transaction costs) | $37,800 | or _____% of total project cost |
| 6. | Gross income (annually, before inflation, net of vacancy) | $ 4,080 | or _____% of total project cost |
| 7. | Operating expense (annually, before inflation) | $ 1,200 | or _____% of gross income |
| 8. | Annual inflation (resale price, income, expense) | 5%  5%  5% <br> resale  income  expense | |

**Depreciation**

| | | | |
|---|---|---|---|
| 9. | Total depreciable base (not annual amount) | $32,000 | or _____% of total project cost |
| 10. | Depreciable life | 25 years | 200% for low-income housing |
| 11. | Depreciable rate (percent of straight line) | 125%‡ | 175% for most real estate* <br> 150% for tangible personal property <br> 100% for all other† |

**Tax Rates**

| | | |
|---|---|---|
| 12. | Ordinary income | 40% |
| 13. | Capital gains | 20% |

SOURCE: The Mader Group, Inc.
*Usually preferable for nonresidential property.
†Usually preferable for commercial property only because of ERTA recapture provisions.
‡125 percent of straight-line depreciation is used here because this property was purchased prior to 1981 and therefore subject to pre-1981 depreciation rules for used residential property.

## TABLE 5.2
## 1970s example: the Divine property—5% inflation

KEY OPERATING FACTORS ARE ---

| TOTAL PROJECT COST | ---MORTGAGE TERMS--- AMOUNT | % INTR | LIFE | NET RESALE PRICE | -----OPERATING & INFLATION ASSUMPTIONS----- % RESALE INFL | GROSS INCOME | % INCOME INFL | OPERATING EXPENSE | % EXPENSE INFL | ----TAX RATES--- INCOME | CAP GAIN | ----DEPRECIATION-- AMOUNT | LIFE | RATE |
|---|---|---|---|---|---|---|---|---|---|---|---|---|---|---|
| 37800 | 28800 | 7.50 | 25 | 37800 | 5 | 4080 | 5 | 1200 | 5 | 40% | 20% | 32000 | 20 | 125% |

PRE-OPERATING SUMMARY ---

| EQUITY AMOUNT | ---MORTGAGE TERMS---- % DEBT | MONTHLY | YEARLY | % NET RESALE TO COST | % INCOME TO COST | GROSS RENT MULT | % EXPENSE TO INCOME | % NOI TO COST | % DEPREC TO COST |
|---|---|---|---|---|---|---|---|---|---|
| 9000 | 76.19 | 213 | 2554 | 100.0 | 10.8 | 9.3 | 29.4 | 7.6 | 84.7 |

OPERATING RESULTS ---

| YR | ---HOLDING RESULTS BEFORE INCOME TAXES--- GROSS INCOME | OPERATE EXPENSE | --MORTGAGE-- INTR | AMORT | CASH FLOW | % RE TURN | ---HOLDING RESULTS AFTER TAXES-- DEPREC IATION | TAXABLE INCOME | TAXES DUE | CASH FLOW | % RE TURN | ---OVERALL RESULTS IF SOLD AT YEAR END--- SALE PRICE | DEBT REPAY | TAXES DUE | CASH FLOW | TOTAL PROFIT | % IRR |
|---|---|---|---|---|---|---|---|---|---|---|---|---|---|---|---|---|---|
| 1 | 4080 | 1200 | 2146 | 408 | 326 | 3.6 | 2000 | -1266 | -506 | 833 | 9.3 | 39690 | 28392 | 858 | 10440 | 2272 | 25.2 |
| 2 | 4284 | 1260 | 2115 | 439 | 470 | 5.2 | 1875 | -966 | -386 | 856 | 9.5 | 41675 | 27953 | 1685 | 12037 | 4726 | 24.4 |
| 3 | 4498 | 1323 | 2080 | 474 | 621 | 6.9 | 1758 | -663 | -265 | 886 | 9.8 | 43758 | 27479 | 2485 | 13794 | 7369 | 23.6 |
| 4 | 4723 | 1389 | 2044 | 510 | 780 | 8.7 | 1648 | -358 | -143 | 923 | 10.3 | 45946 | 26969 | 3262 | 15716 | 10214 | 23.0 |
| 5 | 4959 | 1459 | 2004 | 550 | 947 | 10.5 | 1545 | -48 | -19 | 966 | 10.7 | 48243 | 26419 | 4019 | 17805 | 13270 | 22.3 |
| 6 | 5207 | 1532 | 1961 | 593 | 1122 | 12.5 | 1545 | 169 | 68 | 1054 | 11.7 | 50656 | 25826 | 4799 | 20030 | 16548 | 21.8 |
| 7 | 5468 | 1608 | 1915 | 639 | 1306 | 14.5 | 1545 | 399 | 160 | 1146 | 12.7 | 53188 | 25188 | 5604 | 22397 | 20061 | 21.3 |
| 8 | 5741 | 1689 | 1866 | 688 | 1498 | 16.6 | 1545 | 642 | 257 | 1242 | 13.8 | 55848 | 24500 | 6434 | 24915 | 23820 | 20.8 |
| 9 | 6028 | 1773 | 1812 | 742 | 1701 | 18.9 | 1545 | 898 | 359 | 1342 | 14.9 | 58640 | 23758 | 7290 | 27592 | 27840 | 20.4 |
| 10 | 6329 | 1862 | 1755 | 799 | 1914 | 21.3 | 1545 | 1168 | 467 | 1447 | 16.1 | 61572 | 22959 | 8175 | 30439 | 32133 | 20.0 |

Reprinted with the permission of The Mader Group, Inc., Narberth, PA.

year (9.3 percent return on the initial equity) and rises slightly thereafter. But notice that the after-sale "% IRR" is much higher: 25.2 percent for a one-year holding period. Inflation, it was projected, would produce a significant capital gain. In this case, the total return remains high but tapers off for longer holding periods because the leverage and tax-shelter benefits begin to dissipate.

### Arranging financing

We were satisfied the Devine property would meet our investment objectives and arranged to buy it. We have suggested that you seek substantial leverage, especially for your earlier projects, when capital building (rather than safety or liquidity) is probably the key goal. Several phone calls and a few visits to mortgage lenders informed us about the availability and cost of mortgage financing, including points, prepayment penalties, and insurance premiums, as well as application, appraisal, and attorney's fees. (Be prepared to disclose your personal financial status—a net-worth statement is usually required.)

Mortgage rates are largely dictated by national money market conditions. Still, mortgage terms may vary from lender to lender at any particular time, so it pays to shop around. However, on specialized deals or when enlisting a professional mortgage broker to obtain financing, "shopping a deal" may be a poor practice. After drumming up alternatives, your major decision is probably choosing between various interest rates and mortgage amounts, often expressed as a *loan-to-value ratio.*

Which should you choose? A REAL analysis of each situation allows a dollar-by-dollar comparison. Usually—if you can stand the added risk—the larger mortgage boosts the rate of return, partly because less equity is required. Is a large mortgage worth it, despite your intuition to rebel against current high interest rates? You have to decide, but at least you can use more than the seat of your pants as a "base" for decision making.

### Negotiating purchase terms

Armed with assurances of acceptable financing, we negotiated terms with the seller. In addition to the purchase price, you should consider what appurtenances are included—the closing date, the form and timing of payment, any conditions to the sale, and access to the property or financial records prior to closing. Each party to the negotiation seeks varying objectives, ultimately concluding in a voluntary deal that, by definition, is advantageous to both.

Recognizing your adversary's position and desires has been called the first step toward successful bargaining. Then have good reasons why you are a qualified, interested, and desirable buyer—but explain why you feel the asking price is too high. Be prepared to raise your own initial offer if you expect the seller to change his. You can yield most favorably on those factors having greater importance to the seller, while insisting on terms you deem necessary. By offering compromise and articulating reasons for your firmer positions, a note of fairness and a chord of acquiescence may be struck.

Such negotiation ends successfully with the signing of an *agreement of sale*. This legal binder states what is being sold and for what consideration, subject to stated conditions. Signing is usually accompanied by a deposit toward the purchase price. If the proposed buyer defaults on the agreement, then the deposit can often be retained by the seller as liquidated damages and/or the buyer can be sued for *specific performance* of the sale contract. Consequently, the agreement of sale should be made subject to suitable financing and to any other conditions that might cause noncompliance.

## Closing the deal

The deal is not done, as they say, until checks have been deposited *and have cleared*. Closing is the event that transfers ownership, where old and new mortgage and tax accounts are consummated, and where professionals such as brokers, attorneys, and title insurers get paid. (Of course, some expenses are incurred whether or not closing takes place.) The process involves meeting to execute and confirm the purchase arithmetic, sign appropriate documents, and deliver usually certified payment.

## Renting the property

Sunday newspapers and broker listings are the standard means for reaching tenant prospects for any vacancies. Selection of prospects should be made only after reviewing the full response to your marketing effort. Payment dependability, probable care for the property, and lease starting date and duration are factors to judge. One guideline is that housing—excluding utilities—averages about one fourth of a renter's gross income. (For a large or low-income family, with greater housing needs and lesser taxes, the guideline is one third.) You can use this rule to judge the income level required of prospective tenants. Collecting the first and last month's rent in advance, plus a security deposit of one month, is advisable. But remember, rent received in advance is taxable as income.

## Operating guidelines

Either you or someone hired as your agent will have to act as the property manager. Professional property managers charge around 5 percent of gross income for residential properties, but higher rates apply to smaller properties or single units. For short-term resort property bookings, the commission for rental and upkeep can run to 50 percent. Management of commercial and industrial facilities may be obtained for less than 5 percent, usually between 3 and 4 percent of gross income.

The manager's functions—whether performed by you or another—include:

1. Establishing rental rates.
2. Marketing the available space.
3. Qualifying and investigating tenants' credit.
4. Preparing and executing leases.
5. Collecting rents.
6. Supervising maintenance and repairs.
7. Directing purchasing.
8. Auditing and paying bills.
9. Preparing and paying taxes.
10. Maintaining proper records and reporting to the owner.

In addition to these mechanistic responsibilities of the property manager, creative policies can also help you toward your financial goals: increased rent, decreased operating expenses, and assured appreciation. For example, broad marketing can increase the flow and quality of tenant applicants. A target tenant profile can be sought by such tactics as property design (e.g., high-security areas for upper-income or retired prospects), decoration, appurtenances, athletic facilities, social activities, and the like. Regular and prompt maintenance tends to gain tenant respect and restrain repair costs. Periodic rental adjustments tracking inflation and market trends are vital. This can be accomplished by short-term lease contracts (if vacancy is not a problem) or by rent-escalator clauses.

## Cashing in

Beyond seeking a suitable holding profit, capital appreciation is the main reason to invest in real estate during times of inflation. You have three ways to cash in on such inflation/appreciation: Sell, refinance, or trade. Selling is most common but has the least favorable tax consequences and transaction costs. By referring to Table 5.2, our base case, we can study the projected results of selling at any year end. (Refinancing and trading properties are analyzed in Chapter 11.)

Sale at the end of Year 1 should produce a net sale price of $39,690. This stems from the initial net sale price ($37,800) plus the 5 percent inflation assumed in our base case. From the sale proceeds, the mortgage balance due would be $28,392 (after $408 of amortization during Year 1). Taxes due reflect the difference between the net sale price and book value (cost less cumulative depreciation—here, $37,800 less $2,000, or $35,800). Including recapture, the projected tax due from sale is $858.[2]

## When to sell

To recover equity—to become liquid again—we may wish to sell. But how long is the ideal holding period? The REAL report can shed light here, too. Look at the sale "Cash Flow" column of the report in Table 5.2. It shows your *liquid value equity*—that is, the amount *you* could extract from the property by the act of sale. This is, therefore, the amount that you choose to parlay when you choose *not* to sell. For the end of Year 1, holding means leaving $10,440 of otherwise liquid funds invested in the property.

What do you gain by holding? Each year produces an after-tax cash flow from holding (Level 3 return) and a changed sale cash flow. The "Total Profit" column combines these two sources of return. To find the benefits of holding one more year, subtract the prior year's total profit from this year's to find the *incremental profits*.

For example, *not* selling at the end of Year 1 provides the $856 after-tax cash flow of holding for Year 2. Also, the sale cash flow increases from $10,440 in Year 1 to $12,037, a difference of $1,597. This holding gain ($856) plus sale gain ($1,597) add up to $2,453 of incremental profit. This can be verified by taking the Year 2 total profit ($4,726) and subtracting Year 1's figure ($2,272). Within a dollar of round-off, we can again see that holding beyond Year 1, through Year 2, brings $2,453 of incremental profit. This incremental profitability from holding another year is quite satisfactory ($2,453 ÷ $10,440, or 23.5 percent).

In the 1970s, inflation was even higher than our REAL projection assumed. Instead of appreciating at 5 percent per year, the Devine property went up 12 percent per year. We sold in 28 months for a 28-percent gain in net sale price (to $46,700). This was sufficient to *double* our equity in less than two and a half years, plus provide interim tax-sheltered cash flow, resulting in a total return of over *30 percent compounded annually after tax.*

## Base case—1980s

By the early 1980s, soaring inflation had made a shambles of the long-term mortgage and bond markets. Every mortgage obtained in the 1970s—*just as in the 1960s and 1950s*—turned out to be a bargain! Lenders repeatedly took it on the chin. Now borrowers must pay for high inflation because it's *already in the mortgage rate.*

Figure 5.1
Estimated population growth, 1970–1980

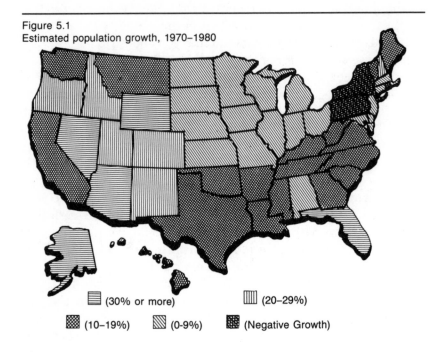

Source: U.S. Bureau of the Census

Does this mean you should no longer invest? Is the 30-year real estate boom, financed cheaply and whipped up by inflation, finally over? We think not. True, current interest rates—*having reached voting age*—do take time to get used to. But let's quantify the effect of historically high interest rates, taking note of their accompanying cause: *historically high inflation rates!*

Our base case for the 1980s is again an actual investment. We followed a Sun Belt strategy this time. As Figure 5.1 verifies, Florida population growth and property potential are among the best in the United States. Table 5.3 shows the REAL analysis for a Florida condominium bought in early 1980 with a 13 percent mortgage.

## TABLE 5.3
### 1980s example: Florida condominium—10% inflation

KEY OPERATING FACTORS ARE ---

| TOTAL PROJECT COST | ---MORTGAGE TERMS--- | | | ----OPERATING & INFLATION ASSUMPTIONS----- | | | | | | ---TAX RATES--- | |
|---|---|---|---|---|---|---|---|---|---|---|---|
| | AMOUNT | % INTR | LIFE | NET RESALE PRICE, % INFL | GROSS INCOME | % INFL | OPERATING EXPENSE | % INFL | | INCOME | CAP GAIN |
| 53300 | 40300 | 13.00 | 30 | 50102  10 | 5100 | 10 | 1500 | 10 | | 50% | 20% |

| ----DEPRECIATION---- | | |
|---|---|---|
| AMOUNT | LIFE | RATE |
| 45000 | 30 | 200% |

PRE-OPERATING SUMMARY ---

| EQUITY AMOUNT | ---MORTGAGE TERMS--- | | | % NET RESALE TO COST | % INCOME TO COST | GROSS RENT MULT | % EXPENSE TO INCOME | % NOI TO COST | % DEPREC TO COST |
|---|---|---|---|---|---|---|---|---|---|
| | % DEBT | MONTHLY | YEARLY | | | | | | |
| 13000 | 75.61 | 446 | 5350 | 94.0 | 9.6 | 10.5 | 29.4 | 6.8 | 84.4 |

OPERATING RESULTS ---

| YR | GROSS INCOME | OPERATE EXPENSE | ---MORTGAGE-- INTR | AMORT | CASH FLOW | % RE TURN | DEPREC IATION | TAXABLE INCOME | TAXES DUE | CASH FLOW | % RE TURN | SALE PRICE | DEBT REPAY | TAXES DUE | CASH FLOW | TOTAL PROFIT | % IRR |
|---|---|---|---|---|---|---|---|---|---|---|---|---|---|---|---|---|---|
| 1 | 5100 | 1500 | 5232 | 117 | -1750 | -13.5 | 3000 | -4632 | -2316 | 567 | 4.4 | 55112 | 40183 | 1412 | 13517 | 1084 | 8.3 |
| 2 | 5610 | 1650 | 5216 | 134 | -1390 | -10.7 | 2800 | -4056 | -2028 | 638 | 4.9 | 60623 | 40049 | 3465 | 17110 | 5315 | 19.0 |
| 3 | 6171 | 1815 | 5198 | 152 | -994 | -7.6 | 2613 | -3455 | -1727 | 734 | 5.6 | 66686 | 39897 | 5534 | 21255 | 10194 | 22.0 |
| 4 | 6788 | 1996 | 5177 | 173 | -558 | -4.3 | 2439 | -2824 | -1412 | 854 | 6.6 | 73354 | 39724 | 7637 | 25993 | 15786 | 23.0 |
| 5 | 7467 | 2196 | 5153 | 197 | -79 | -0.6 | 2277 | -2158 | -1079 | 1000 | 7.7 | 80690 | 39527 | 9792 | 31370 | 22164 | 23.3 |
| 6 | 8214 | 2416 | 5125 | 224 | 448 | 3.4 | 2125 | -1452 | -726 | 1174 | 9.0 | 88759 | 39303 | 12019 | 37437 | 29405 | 23.3 |
| 7 | 9035 | 2657 | 5095 | 255 | 1028 | 7.9 | 1983 | -700 | -350 | 1378 | 10.6 | 97635 | 39048 | 14335 | 44252 | 37597 | 23.1 |
| 8 | 9938 | 2923 | 5059 | 290 | 1666 | 12.8 | 1851 | 105 | 53 | 1613 | 12.4 | 107398 | 38757 | 16763 | 51877 | 46836 | 22.8 |
| 9 | 10932 | 3215 | 5019 | 330 | 2367 | 18.2 | 1727 | 970 | 485 | 1882 | 14.5 | 118138 | 38427 | 19325 | 60386 | 57227 | 22.6 |
| 10 | 12026 | 3537 | 4974 | 376 | 3139 | 24.1 | 1612 | 1903 | 951 | 2188 | 16.8 | 129952 | 38051 | 22044 | 69856 | 68885 | 22.3 |

Section headers across the operating results:
- ---HOLDING RESULTS BEFORE INCOME TAXES--- (CASH FLOW, % RE TURN)
- ---HOLDING RESULTS AFTER TAXES-- (DEPRECIATION, TAXABLE INCOME, TAXES DUE, CASH FLOW, % RE TURN)
- ---OVERALL RESULTS IF SOLD AT YEAR END---- (SALE PRICE, DEBT REPAY, TAXES DUE, CASH FLOW, TOTAL PROFIT, % IRR)

Reprinted with the permission of The Mader Group, Inc., Narberth, PA.

It is important to note that cash flow after financing but before taxes (Level 2) is *negative* for the first five years on this property. High interest rates are the cause. Conventional thinking would rule out buying this property, or building new ones like it, based on current rents. Yet if no one builds, what will happen to rents? With lack of new supply, and with comparable costs rising with inflation, rents will rise along with inflated salaries, or more. If rents rise, net operating income improves, and what will happen to resale values? All things being equal, they should rise.

Simply put, a four-level, total return analysis is required. If we assume 10 percent annual inflation, then rent, expense, and resale escalation still produce a healthy after-tax, after-sale rate of return—despite high mortgage rates.

The shock of expensive mortgage financing and the collapsing debt markets have resulted in a sharp drop in both demand and housing starts. Coupled with used-house resales and an increasing number of condominium conversions, we have greatly reduced supply, have bottlenecked demand, and now, have produced the best buying opportunity since the mid-1970s. The message of the first edition of this book was true in 1975 and will be true again in the 1980s: *Inflation boosts real estate profits.*

## Summary

A base case analysis provides a quick, convenient, accurate projection of a proposed opportunity's investment merits. It should be an early step in checking out any property situation.

For getting started, we recommend used residential income property near where you live—for stability, familiarity, and convenience. If your investment analysis looks favorable, you must arrange financing, negotiate terms, close the deal, manage the property, and some day cash in. You should have the right attitude, knowledge, and capital, but you *must act.*

The REAL analysis quantifies several important but often overlooked variables, such as transaction costs, equity buildup through mortgage amortization, and tax liability upon sale. It can also be used to help decide optimal mortgage terms and holding periods. Perhaps most important, it underscores—even for the 1980s—the dramatic *profit impact of inflation.*

## Notes

1. As the next chapter's risk analysis will show, this high return is principally dependent on two assumptions: that the property was bought cheaply, enabling it to be resold with no loss despite transaction costs; and that inflation would boost income, expenses, and resale price at 5 percent per year. These assumptions were borne out. Furthermore, the mortgage proved to be attractive relative to more recent interest rates.

2. *Recapture* means that, under certain conditions, the taxes postponed by accelerated depreciation are "recaptured" by taxing some profits at the ordinary tax rate. Here, straight-line depreciation of $32,000 for 20 years implies a $1,600 deduction per year. However, 125 percent of that amount ($2,000) was taken as allowed by tax rules. Thus, $400 of that $2,000 deduction is considered excess depreciation and is subject to recapture. Hence, a 40 percent ordinary tax rate is applied to $400 of the $3,890 taxable gain. This yields $160 in tax due. The 20 percent capital gain rate applies to the remaining $3,490 gain, here yielding a $698 tax liability. In total, the taxes due for sale at the end of Year 1 are $858, as shown in Table 5.2. Remember, these recapture rules apply to pre-1981 buildings. Real property bought or placed in service after 1980 falls under the recently passed 1981 tax law, as discussed in Chapter 4.

# 6 Risk Analysis— What If?

After performing a base-case REAL analysis, it is helpful to evaluate *risk*—the results of adverse changes from the base case. For example, what would be the effect on rate of return if the total project cost ran over budget by 2 percent, 5 percent, or 10 percent? What if the project could be swung for 5 percent less cost than assumed in the base case? What is the risk from higher than anticipated mortgage rates? From high vacancy? And so on.

To answer such questions, a risk analysis asks a series of "what if?" questions. In this chapter, changing each of the 13 key factors is discussed briefly and the impact summarized. The most significant results are also graphically displayed for quick comprehension. This analysis of variations from the base case leads to practical decision-making guidelines for investors.

## What if—

Mortgage interest rates climb over 16 percent?
Utility costs go up 50 percent in one year?
Rent controls are imposed in some locations?
Foreign investors pay prices yielding zero cash flow?
Ordinary income and capital gain taxes (and the California property tax) are lowered?

Each of these events *did* happen since the first edition of this book, unimaginable as that would have seemed in 1975. That ought to justify a chapter on risk analysis! This analysis is useful precisely because no one can research, judge, or contract with certainty all thirteen key factors.

First, we will update our medical-building example. This analysis was previewed in Chapter 1 and detailed in Chapter 4. So far, we have analyzed the original owner's position—including a 9 percent mortgage rate. Remember, that "high" rate seemed scary in 1976, yet inflation made it pay off handsomely.

What now? Will real estate again pay off, despite mortgage rates in the teens? We've asked that question at seminars in numerous cities since interest rates zoomed. "The Quizzical Client Case," as we call it, asks about the economics of buying that 1976 vintage medical building in the 1980s marketplace. The case write-up is shown in Table 6.1.

The survey results are shown in Table 6.2, listed by date taken and location. Compared with similar surveys done years ago, the interest rate has risen sharply. Even within the six months shown, rates soared. Also significant, the mortgage amount and life have both decreased. The income and expense estimates, to a degree, reflect regional differences. Taking the overall survey average, should you buy such a property today? Can you still profit from inflation with current mortgage terms?

Our analysis for the medical building, now for the 1980s buyer, assumes the following key factor values:

1. Total project cost (per case statement) = $200,000

2-4. Mortgage terms = survey average

5. Net sale price = 94 percent of market value (6 percent selling expense)

6-7. Gross income and operating expense = survey average

8. Inflation of 0 percent and 5-10-15 percent (see Tables 6.3 and 6.4)

9-11. Depreciation = 80 percent (building), with 25-year life,[1] straight line

12-13. Tax rates = 50 percent and 20 percent brackets (equals approximately a $50,000 per year taxable income)

TABLE 6.1

The quizzical client case

A four-office suburban medical building has just come on the market. In 1975, its total project cost was $150,000. The owner will now sell for $200,000. The brick two-story structure has 5,000 square feet of rental space. The one-acre site features attractive landscaping and parking for 40 cars.

As a prospective buyer, you might ask, "How would it work out if I bought it with a mortgage obtainable in today's market and held for up to ten years?"

You know that financial information is obtainable from the seller, but you want a quick investment estimate. Assuming the $200,000 figure is your total project cost, please jot down below a reasonable, likely value for each key factor in this case.

| | |
|---|---|
| Total project cost | $200,000 |

Mortgage terms

      Mortgage amount                $ _____

      Mortgage interest rate            _____ % per annum

      Mortgage life                     _____ Years

Operating assumptions

      Annual gross income            $ _____
      (after vacancy allowance)

      Annual operating expense        _____
      (includes maintenance, property taxes,
      utilities, insurance, and all
      miscellaneous, but excludes financing
      costs)

We will at first assume no inflation. Since that seems unlikely, we will next assume that rent increases at 10 percent annually, but expenses escalate at 15 percent per year. This would act to increase net operating income somewhat, allowing some resale value growth. A 5 percent annual rate of appreciation is realistic and allows for an aging building. The full REAL results for 0 percent inflation are listed in Table 6.3. Then, assuming 10 percent inflation of rents, faster 15 percent escalation of expenses, and slower 5 percent resale growth, revised results are shown in Table 6.4. This tabulation illustrates the real power of a model—analyze the base case, then revise it to answer the "what ifs(?)."

## TABLE 6.2
### The quizzical client case—survey average

The opinions tabulated below were provided by seminar participants on the dates and at the locations shown. They were asked to judge the probable mortgage terms, gross income, and operating expenses for a $200,000 suburban medical office building having 5,000 square feet of rental space.

The *average value* of each key factor is listed below.

| Date | Location | Number of Responses | Mortgage Amount | Mortgage Interest Rate | Mortgage Life | Annual Gross Income | Operating Expenses |
|---|---|---|---|---|---|---|---|
| 12/79 | Palm Beach | 66 | $150,000 | 12.7% | 18.5 Yrs. | $42,159 | $19,544 |
| 1/80 | Houston | 66 | 152,040 | 12.5 | 18.3 | 43,850 | 17,221 |
| 2/80 | Chicago | 45 | 149,000 | 12.1 | 23.5 | 40,234 | 17,289 |
| 3/80 | San Francisco | 62 | 144,000 | 17.0 | 22.3 | 40,846 | 25,008 |
| 4/80 | Philadelphia | 31 | 145,000 | 17.4 | 24.5 | 56,180 | 29,480 |
| 5/80 | Chicago | 55 | 149,000 | 14.9 | 12.2 | 50,430 | 24,606 |
| | Survey Average | 286 | $148,000 | 14.5% | 20.7 Yrs. | $44,842 | $22,205 |

A REAL analysis was run using the Total Survey Average value for mortgage terms, income, and expense. Reasonable fixed data values were assigned to the other key factors: selling costs, depreciation terms, and tax rates. Two versions of this analysis are graphed: Table 6.3 shows no inflation/appreciation in income, expense, and selling price, and Table 6.4 shows increases in these factors.

On average, the survey estimates translate into a profitable investment. Notice, however, the strong impact of rising rents and selling prices. The Year 5 total return without inflation is 1.8% compounded annually after taxes. With inflation, this return jumps to 16%—an effect too strong to ignore.

## TABLE 6.3
### 1980s medical building—survey average—no inflation

KEY OPERATING FACTORS ARE ---

| TOTAL PROJECT COST | ---MORTGAGE TERMS--- AMOUNT | % INTR | LIFE | ----OPERATING & INFLATION ASSUMPTIONS---- NET RESALE PRICE | % INFL | GROSS INCOME | % INFL | OPERATING EXPENSE | % INFL | ----DEPRECIATION---- AMOUNT | LIFE | RATE | ---TAX RATES--- INCOME | CAP GAIN |
|---|---|---|---|---|---|---|---|---|---|---|---|---|---|---|
| 200000 | 148000 | 14.45 | 21 | 188000 | 0 | 44841 | 0 | 22205 | 0 | 160000 | 25 | 100% | 50% | 20% |

PRE-OPERATING SUMMARY ---

| EQUITY AMOUNT | ---MORTGAGE TERMS--- % DEBT | MONTHLY | YEARLY | % NET RESALE TO COST | % INCOME TO COST | GROSS RENT MULT | % EXPENSE TO INCOME | % NOI TO COST | % DEPREC TO COST |
|---|---|---|---|---|---|---|---|---|---|
| 52000 | 74.00 | 1874 | 22487 | 94.0 | 22.4 | 4.5 | 49.5 | 11.3 | 80.0 |

OPERATING RESULTS ---

| | ---HOLDING RESULTS BEFORE INCOME TAXES--- | | -MORTGAGE- | | | | ---HOLDING RESULTS AFTER TAXES--- | | | | | ---OVERALL RESULTS IF SOLD AT YEAR END--- | | | | | |
|---|---|---|---|---|---|---|---|---|---|---|---|---|---|---|---|---|---|
| YR | GROSS INCOME | OPERATE EXPENSE | INTR | AMORT | CASH FLOW | % RE TURN | DEPREC IATION | TAXABLE INCOME | TAXES DUE | CASH FLOW | % RE TURN | SALE PRICE | DEBT REPAY | TAXES DUE | CASH FLOW | TOTAL PROFIT | % IRR |
| 1 | 44841 | 22205 | 21310 | 1177 | 149 | 0.3 | 6400 | -5074 | -2537 | 2686 | 5.2 | 188000 | 146823 | -1120 | 42297 | -7017 | -13.5 |
| 2 | 44841 | 22205 | 21128 | 1359 | 149 | 0.3 | 6400 | -4892 | -2446 | 2595 | 5.0 | 188000 | 145463 | 160 | 42377 | -4343 | -4.4 |
| 3 | 44841 | 22205 | 20918 | 1569 | 149 | 0.3 | 6400 | -4682 | -2341 | 2490 | 4.8 | 188000 | 143894 | 1440 | 42666 | -1564 | -1.1 |
| 4 | 44841 | 22205 | 20676 | 1812 | 149 | 0.3 | 6400 | -4440 | -2220 | 2369 | 4.6 | 188000 | 142083 | 2720 | 43197 | 1336 | 0.7 |
| 5 | 44841 | 22205 | 20396 | 2091 | 149 | 0.3 | 6400 | -4160 | -2080 | 2229 | 4.3 | 188000 | 139991 | 4000 | 44009 | 4376 | 1.8 |
| 6 | 44841 | 22205 | 20073 | 2414 | 149 | 0.3 | 6400 | -3837 | -1918 | 2067 | 4.0 | 188000 | 137577 | 5280 | 45143 | 7577 | 2.6 |
| 7 | 44841 | 22205 | 19700 | 2787 | 149 | 0.3 | 6400 | -3464 | -1732 | 1881 | 3.6 | 188000 | 134790 | 6560 | 46650 | 10965 | 3.2 |
| 8 | 44841 | 22205 | 19269 | 3218 | 149 | 0.3 | 6400 | -3033 | -1517 | 1665 | 3.2 | 188000 | 131572 | 7840 | 48588 | 14569 | 3.7 |
| 9 | 44841 | 22205 | 18772 | 3715 | 149 | 0.3 | 6400 | -2536 | -1268 | 1417 | 2.7 | 188000 | 127857 | 9120 | 51023 | 18420 | 4.0 |
| 10 | 44841 | 22205 | 18199 | 4289 | 149 | 0.3 | 6400 | -1963 | -981 | 1130 | 2.2 | 188000 | 123568 | 10400 | 54032 | 22559 | 4.4 |

## TABLE 6.4
### 1980s medical building—survey average—5/10/15% inflation

KEY OPERATING FACTORS ARE ---

| TOTAL PROJECT COST | ---MORTGAGE TERMS--- | | | ---OPERATING & | | NET RESALE PRICE | RESALE % INFL | OPERATING & INFLATION ASSUMPTIONS----- | | | ---DEPRECIATION--- | | | ---TAX RATES--- | |
|---|---|---|---|---|---|---|---|---|---|---|---|---|---|---|---|
| | AMOUNT | % INTR | LIFE | | | | | GROSS INCOME INFL | % OPERATING EXPENSE | % INFL | AMOUNT | LIFE | RATE | INCOME | CAP GAIN |
| 200000 | 148000 | 14.45 | 21 | | | 188000 | 5 | 44841 | 22205 | 15 | 160000 | 25 | 100% | 50% | 20% |

PRE-OPERATING SUMMARY ---

| EQUITY AMOUNT | ---MORTGAGE TERMS--- | | | % NET RESALE TO COST | % INCOME TO COST | GROSS RENT MULT | % EXPENSE TO INCOME | % NOI TO COST | % DEPREC TO COST |
|---|---|---|---|---|---|---|---|---|---|
| | % DEBT | MONTHLY | YEARLY | | | | | | |
| 52000 | 74.00 | 1874 | 22487 | 94.0 | 22.4 | 4.5 | 49.5 | 11.3 | 80.0 |

OPERATING RESULTS ---

| YR | ---HOLDING RESULTS BEFORE INCOME TAXES--- | | | | | | ---HOLDING RESULTS AFTER TAXES-- | | | | | ---OVERALL RESULTS IF SOLD AT YEAR END---- | | | | | |
|---|---|---|---|---|---|---|---|---|---|---|---|---|---|---|---|---|---|
| | GROSS INCOME | OPERATE EXPENSE | --MORTGAGE-- INTR | AMORT | CASH FLOW | % RE TURN | DEPREC IATION | TAXABLE INCOME | TAXES DUE | CASH FLOW | % RE TURN | SALE PRICE | DEBT REPAY | TAXES DUE | CASH FLOW | TOTAL PROFIT | % IRR |
| 1 | 44841 | 22205 | 21310 | 1177 | 149 | 0.3 | 6400 | -5074 | -2537 | 2686 | 5.2 | 197400 | 146823 | 760 | 49817 | 503 | 1.0 |
| 2 | 49325 | 25536 | 21128 | 1359 | 1302 | 2.5 | 6400 | -3739 | -1869 | 3171 | 6.1 | 207270 | 145463 | 4014 | 57793 | 11650 | 10.9 |
| 3 | 54258 | 29366 | 20918 | 1569 | 2404 | 4.6 | 6400 | -2427 | -1213 | 3617 | 7.0 | 217634 | 143894 | 7367 | 66373 | 23847 | 14.0 |
| 4 | 59683 | 33771 | 20676 | 1812 | 3425 | 6.6 | 6400 | -1164 | -582 | 4007 | 7.7 | 228515 | 142083 | 10823 | 75609 | 37091 | 15.4 |
| 5 | 65652 | 38837 | 20396 | 2091 | 4328 | 8.3 | 6400 | 19 | 9 | 4318 | 8.3 | 239941 | 139991 | 14388 | 85561 | 51361 | 16.0 |
| 6 | 72217 | 44662 | 20073 | 2414 | 5067 | 9.7 | 6400 | 1082 | 541 | 4526 | 8.7 | 251938 | 137577 | 18068 | 96294 | 66619 | 16.3 |
| 7 | 79439 | 51362 | 19700 | 2787 | 5590 | 10.7 | 6400 | 1977 | 989 | 4601 | 8.8 | 264535 | 134790 | 21867 | 107878 | 82805 | 16.3 |
| 8 | 87382 | 59066 | 19269 | 3218 | 5829 | 11.2 | 6400 | 2647 | 1324 | 4506 | 8.7 | 277762 | 131572 | 25792 | 120398 | 99830 | 16.3 |
| 9 | 96121 | 67926 | 18772 | 3715 | 5708 | 11.0 | 6400 | 3023 | 1511 | 4196 | 8.1 | 291650 | 127857 | 29850 | 133943 | 117572 | 16.1 |
| 10 | 105733 | 78114 | 18199 | 4289 | 5131 | 9.9 | 6400 | 3020 | 1510 | 3621 | 7.0 | 306232 | 123568 | 34046 | 148618 | 135868 | 15.9 |

Reprinted with the permission of The Mader Group, Inc., Narberth, PA.

## Sensitivity analysis

Table 6.4 shows results for differing rates of change in the property's key operating factors. This quantifies risk—itself an important investment objective, second only to rate of return. In buying General Motors stock or AT&T, *you* can't control the risk; company management does that for you, like it or not. But by being aware of the sources and magnitudes of real estate risk, *you can manage and control them.*

Rather than select particular risks for which to recompute returns, you may wish to review *all* risks. A full and automatic risk analysis is built into the REAL program. It involves changing *each key factor value individually.* This is called a *sensitivity analysis.*

For example, we might ask how much total return would change if each key factor were individually 10 percent higher than assumed in the base case. The sensitivity analysis results shown in Table 6.5 list the revised key factor values as column headings. Notice that each value represents a 10 percent change (top half 10 percent higher, bottom half 10 percent lower) from the base case (Table 6.4). Table 6.5 then shows the *revised* total returns, given each single key factor change of 10 percent. (Remember, total return means Level 4—the overall, compound annual, after-tax rate of return—the internal rate of return, or IRR.)

Next, Table 6.6 (top half 10 percent higher, bottom half 10 percent lower) shows the *change* in IRR from the base case. It is the base-case overall result for each year (rightmost column of Table 6.4) compared to the revised results from the sensitivity analysis of each factor (see Table 6.5). Thus Table 6.6 shows the *change* in total return due solely to the *change* in each key factor.

To understand this powerful analysis—and to draw conclusions—in Figure 6.1 we have graphed these changes in total return caused by the 10 percent increase in each key factor. Notice that for some key factors, a +10 percent change *decreases* return. For example, a 10 percent overrun in "Total Project Cost"—taken with other key factors unchanged—worsens total return significantly. Increased "Operating Expense," when not matched by rental increases, also decreases total return.

# TABLE 6.5
## Sensitivity analysis results

REVISED KEY FACTOR VALUE AT END OF YEAR AND RESULTING IRR DUE TO CHANGE OF 10%

| TOTAL PROJECT COST | --MORTGAGE TERMS-- AMOUNT | % INTR | LIFE | NET RESALE PRICE | --OPERATING ASSUMPTIONS-- GROSS INCOME | OPERATING EXPENSE | --DEPRECIATION-- AMOUNT | LIFE | TYPE | --TAX RATES-- INCOME | CAP GAIN |
|---|---|---|---|---|---|---|---|---|---|---|---|
| 220000. | 162800. | 15.89 | 23.1 | 217140. | 49325. | 24425. | 176000. | 27.5 | 110.00 | 55.0 | 22.0 |
| 1 -21.5 | -1.5 | -1.1 | 0.9 | 31.3 | 5.3 | -1.2 | 1.3 | 0.6 | 1.0 | 1.4 | 0.8 |
| 2 -3.1 | 12.3 | 8.9 | 10.9 | 24.7 | 15.3 | 8.7 | 11.3 | 10.6 | 10.9 | 11.3 | 10.5 |
| 3 3.6 | 16.4 | 12.2 | 14.0 | 22.4 | 18.4 | 11.8 | 14.4 | 13.7 | 14.1 | 14.4 | 13.6 |
| 4 7.0 | 18.1 | 13.6 | 15.4 | 21.1 | 19.7 | 13.1 | 15.7 | 15.0 | 15.4 | 15.7 | 15.0 |
| 5 8.9 | 18.7 | 14.4 | 16.1 | 20.1 | 20.3 | 13.7 | 16.4 | 15.7 | 16.1 | 16.2 | 15.7 |
| 6 10.1 | 18.9 | 14.7 | 16.4 | 19.4 | 20.5 | 13.9 | 16.6 | 15.9 | 16.3 | 16.5 | 16.0 |
| 7 10.8 | 18.8 | 14.9 | 16.4 | 18.8 | 20.6 | 14.0 | 16.7 | 16.0 | 16.4 | 16.5 | 16.1 |
| 8 11.3 | 18.6 | 14.9 | 16.4 | 18.3 | 20.5 | 13.8 | 16.6 | 16.0 | 16.4 | 16.4 | 16.0 |
| 9 11.6 | 18.3 | 14.8 | 16.3 | 17.8 | 20.3 | 13.7 | 16.5 | 15.8 | 16.2 | 16.2 | 15.9 |
| 10 11.7 | 18.0 | 14.7 | 16.1 | 17.4 | 20.2 | 13.4 | 16.3 | 15.6 | 16.0 | 16.0 | 15.7 |

REVISED KEY FACTOR VALUE AT END OF YEAR AND RESULTING IRR DUE TO CHANGE OF -10%

| TOTAL PROJECT COST | --MORTGAGE TERMS-- AMOUNT | % INTR | LIFE | NET RESALE PRICE | --OPERATING ASSUMPTIONS-- GROSS INCOME | OPERATING EXPENSE | --DEPRECIATION-- AMOUNT | LIFE | TYPE | --TAX RATES-- INCOME | CAP GAIN |
|---|---|---|---|---|---|---|---|---|---|---|---|
| 180000. | 133200. | 13.00 | 18.9 | 177660. | 40357. | 19985. | 144000. | 22.5 | 90.00 | 45.0 | 18.0 |
| 1 51.6 | 2.3 | 3.0 | 1.0 | -29.4 | -3.3 | 3.1 | 0.6 | 1.4 | 1.0 | 0.5 | 1.1 |
| 2 37.7 | 10.1 | 12.9 | 10.9 | -5.0 | 6.5 | 13.1 | 10.5 | 11.3 | 10.9 | 10.5 | 11.2 |
| 3 32.8 | 12.6 | 15.9 | 14.0 | 4.2 | 9.7 | 16.3 | 13.7 | 14.4 | 14.0 | 13.7 | 14.4 |
| 4 30.1 | 13.8 | 17.1 | 15.3 | 8.6 | 11.1 | 17.7 | 15.0 | 15.8 | 15.4 | 15.1 | 15.7 |
| 5 28.2 | 14.3 | 17.6 | 15.9 | 11.1 | 11.7 | 18.3 | 15.6 | 16.4 | 16.0 | 15.8 | 16.3 |
| 6 26.8 | 14.6 | 17.8 | 16.1 | 12.5 | 12.0 | 18.6 | 15.9 | 16.7 | 16.3 | 16.1 | 16.6 |
| 7 25.7 | 14.7 | 17.8 | 16.2 | 13.4 | 12.1 | 18.7 | 16.0 | 16.7 | 16.3 | 16.2 | 16.6 |
| 8 24.7 | 14.7 | 17.6 | 16.1 | 13.9 | 12.1 | 18.7 | 15.9 | 16.7 | 16.3 | 16.2 | 16.5 |
| 9 23.8 | 14.7 | 17.4 | 15.9 | 14.2 | 11.9 | 18.6 | 15.8 | 16.5 | 16.1 | 16.0 | 16.4 |
| 10 23.1 | 14.6 | 17.2 | 15.7 | 14.3 | 11.7 | 18.4 | 15.6 | 16.3 | 15.9 | 15.8 | 16.1 |

Reprinted with the permission of The Mader Group, Inc., Narberth, PA.

**TABLE 6.6**
Sensitivity analysis results

CHANGE IN KEY FACTOR VALUE AND RESULTING CHANGE IN IRR (SENSITIVITY MINUS ORIGINAL)

| | TOTAL PROJECT COST | ---MORTGAGE TERMS--- | | | NET RESALE PRICE | ---OPERATING ASSUMPTIONS--- | | ---DEPRECIATION--- | | | ---TAX RATES--- | |
|---|---|---|---|---|---|---|---|---|---|---|---|---|
| | | AMOUNT | % INTR | LIFE | | GROSS INCOME | OPERATING EXPENSE | AMOUNT | LIFE | TYPE | INCOME | CAP GAIN |
| | 20000. | 14800. | 1.44 | 2.1 | 19740. | 4484. | 2220. | 16000. | 2.5 | 10.00 | 5.0 | 2.0 |
| 1 | -22.5 | -2.5 | -2.0 | -0.0 | 30.4 | 4.3 | -2.1 | 0.4 | -0.3 | 0.0 | 0.5 | -0.1 |
| 2 | -14.0 | 1.4 | -2.0 | -0.0 | 13.8 | 4.4 | -2.2 | 0.4 | -0.3 | 0.0 | 0.4 | -0.4 |
| 3 | -10.4 | 2.4 | -1.9 | 0.0 | 8.3 | 4.4 | -2.3 | 0.4 | -0.3 | 0.1 | 0.3 | -0.4 |
| 4 | -8.4 | 2.7 | -1.8 | 0.0 | 5.7 | 4.3 | -2.3 | 0.4 | -0.3 | 0.1 | 0.3 | -0.4 |
| 5 | -7.1 | 2.7 | -1.6 | 0.1 | 4.2 | 4.3 | -2.3 | 0.4 | -0.3 | 0.1 | 0.2 | -0.3 |
| 6 | -6.2 | 2.6 | -1.6 | 0.1 | 3.2 | 4.2 | -2.3 | 0.4 | -0.3 | 0.1 | 0.2 | -0.3 |
| 7 | -5.5 | 2.5 | -1.5 | 0.1 | 2.5 | 4.2 | -2.4 | 0.4 | -0.3 | 0.1 | 0.2 | -0.3 |
| 8 | -5.0 | 2.4 | -1.4 | 0.1 | 2.0 | 4.2 | -2.4 | 0.4 | -0.3 | 0.1 | 0.1 | -0.3 |
| 9 | -4.5 | 2.2 | -1.3 | 0.1 | 1.7 | 4.2 | -2.5 | 0.4 | -0.3 | 0.1 | 0.1 | -0.2 |
| 10 | -4.2 | 2.1 | -1.3 | 0.2 | 1.4 | 4.2 | -2.5 | 0.3 | -0.3 | 0.1 | 0.1 | -0.2 |

CHANGE IN KEY FACTOR VALUE AND RESULTING CHANGE IN IRR (SENSITIVITY MINUS ORIGINAL)

| | TOTAL PROJECT COST | ---MORTGAGE TERMS--- | | | NET RESALE PRICE | ---OPERATING ASSUMPTIONS--- | | ---DEPRECIATION--- | | | ---TAX RATES--- | |
|---|---|---|---|---|---|---|---|---|---|---|---|---|
| | | AMOUNT | % INTR | LIFE | | GROSS INCOME | OPERATING EXPENSE | AMOUNT | LIFE | TYPE | INCOME | CAP GAIN |
| | -20000. | -14800. | -1.45 | -2.1 | -19740. | -4484. | -2221. | -16000. | -2.5 | -10.00 | -5.0 | -2.0 |
| 1 | 50.6 | 1.4 | 2.1 | 0.0 | -30.4 | -4.3 | 2.1 | -0.4 | 0.4 | 0.0 | -0.5 | 0.1 |
| 2 | 26.8 | -0.8 | 2.0 | 0.0 | -15.9 | -4.4 | 2.2 | -0.4 | 0.4 | 0.0 | -0.4 | 0.4 |
| 3 | 18.8 | -1.4 | 1.8 | -0.0 | -9.8 | -4.4 | 2.3 | -0.4 | 0.4 | -0.0 | -0.3 | 0.4 |
| 4 | 14.7 | -1.6 | 1.7 | -0.1 | -6.7 | -4.3 | 2.3 | -0.4 | 0.4 | -0.0 | -0.3 | 0.4 |
| 5 | 12.2 | -1.7 | 1.6 | -0.1 | -4.9 | -4.3 | 2.3 | -0.4 | 0.4 | -0.0 | -0.2 | 0.3 |
| 6 | 10.6 | -1.6 | 1.5 | -0.1 | -3.7 | -4.2 | 2.3 | -0.4 | 0.4 | -0.0 | -0.2 | 0.3 |
| 7 | 9.3 | -1.6 | 1.4 | -0.2 | -2.9 | -4.2 | 2.4 | -0.4 | 0.4 | -0.0 | -0.1 | 0.3 |
| 8 | 8.4 | -1.5 | 1.4 | -0.2 | -2.4 | -4.2 | 2.4 | -0.4 | 0.4 | -0.0 | -0.1 | 0.3 |
| 9 | 7.7 | -1.4 | 1.3 | -0.2 | -1.9 | -4.2 | 2.5 | -0.4 | 0.4 | -0.0 | -0.1 | 0.2 |
| 10 | 7.1 | -1.4 | 1.2 | -0.2 | -1.6 | -4.2 | 2.5 | -0.4 | 0.4 | -0.0 | -0.1 | 0.2 |

Reprinted with the permission of The Mader Group, Inc., Narberth, PA.

FIGURE 6.1
Effects on total return of changing each of the 13 key factors
Comparison of the sensitivity or risk due to 10% increase
Assumes sale at end of Year 5

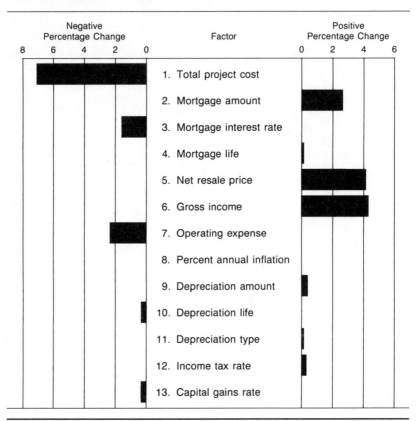

When certain other key factors are changed by + 10 percent, returns *increase*. Higher rents, for example, increase return. Certain results are also dependent on the holding period. (Figure 6.1 shows the sensitivity analysis results for a five-year holding period.) Other results depend on the specific nature of the base case. The following sections discuss each key factor and its *risk* impact.

## 1. Total project cost

As shown in the sensitivity analysis in the bottom half of Table 6.6, or in Figure 6.1, the price you pay for your property is one of the most important factors. Overpaying always hurts your rate of return. But while the risk from mistakenly overpaying is great, you can soften the impact by leveraging more or by holding longer. Suppose, for example, that we had to pay more for our medical building than was assumed in our base case. Adding 10 percent would raise its 1981 price to $220,000. Is paying this much a disastrous blunder?

How much an overpayment hurts the rate of return depends mainly on two issues: how you finance it, and your holding period. Figure 6.2 shows this situation's *risk*—that is, the adverse change in total return. The graph illustrates two financing possibilities (for holding periods ranging from one to ten years):

1. A constant mortgage amount (overpayment financed with equity).
2. A constant mortgage proportion (overpayment financed with debt and equity).

FIGURE 6.2
Risk from overpayment varies with financing and holding period

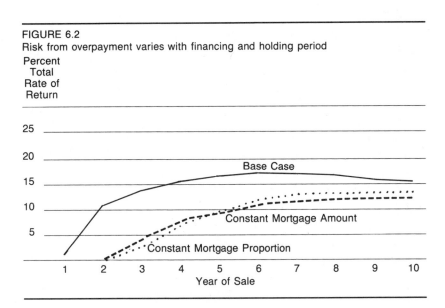

Figure 6.2 reveals that overpayment hurts but less so for longer holding periods. By then, rental income outweighs the relative capital loss experienced from the too-high purchase price. Also, with a constant mortgage proportion (say 75 percent), extra debt covers most of the overpayment. Naturally you pay more interest on the larger mortgage, but a good project's rate of return is improved with leverage, partly because less equity is required. With inflation, and if you hold on for several years, the overpayment risk moderates.

By contrast, with a short holding period (say one or two years) the results are disastrous. This is precisely how many developers go bankrupt. For example, the John Hancock building in Chicago incurred a $5 million cost overrun because of faulty foundation work. Additional equity was needed to complete construction. That led to the eventual financial demise of one of the project's partners, Jerry Wolman, whose highly leveraged $80 million real estate empire tumbled from the lack of staying power to ride out this type of risk.

## 2. Mortgage amount

This second key factor also significantly influences the rate of return. Usually, more leverage makes a good deal better and makes a bad deal worse. And it always increases risk due to potential cost overruns, increased vacancy, rampant expenses, or similar problems. Figure 6.3 shows that an increased mortgage on the medical building generally boosts its rate of return on the lower equity required. For example, if the mortgage amount is increased by 10 percent to $162,800 (81.4 percent of the total project cost), then the annual compounded rate of return for each of the first five years improves from 16 percent to 18.7 percent. That's almost a 17 percent improvement in the returns as a result of only a 10 percent increase in debt.

This extra leverage also increases risk. The investment's merit becomes very sensitive to a shortfall in income, as from low rents or vacancy. A 10 percent drop in gross income has a more adverse impact on rate of return when leverage is high. You must judge

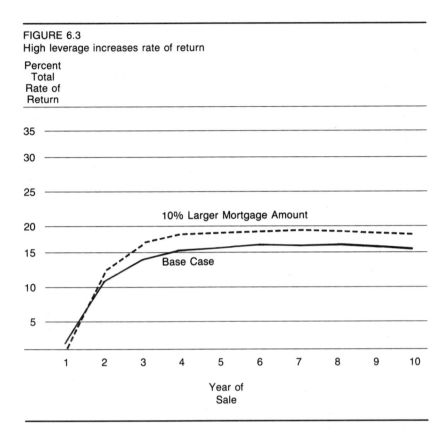

FIGURE 6.3
High leverage increases rate of return

Percent
Total
Rate of
Return

10% Larger Mortgage Amount

Base Case

Year of
Sale

this trade-off of return and risk for yourself. But a general rule is: If the project is worth doing, it is probably safe to borrow about 75 percent of the total project cost.

## 3. Mortgage interest rate

This factor is perhaps the most discussed variable. The 1980 (and 1981) credit crunch propelled residential mortgages well over 15 percent and sharply curtailed home building and resales. Should you invest with such mortgage terms? What would our base case results have been if the interest rate were higher than our survey thought appropriate for the medical building? (Indeed, by the end of our survey, rates had risen.)

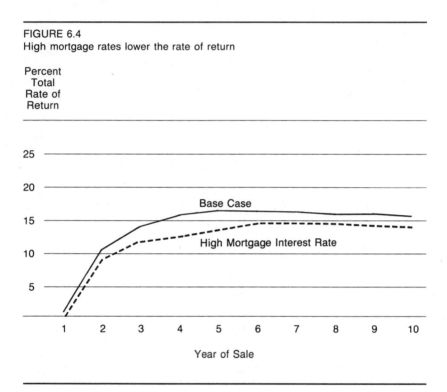

FIGURE 6.4
High mortgage rates lower the rate of return

Percent
Total
Rate of
Return

Base Case

High Mortgage Interest Rate

Year of Sale

Figure 6.4 shows the lower profit profile if the project had to be financed with a 16 percent mortgage (rather than at 14 percent) *and all other factors remain unchanged.* Surprisingly, the REAL analysis suggests that mortgage interest rates are *not* as crucial as widely supposed. This large increase in the mortgage interest rate knocks down the total rate of return by a fairly modest amount. And since inflation has produced a very robust rate of return in the first place, the higher mortgage rate is hardly a death knell. Furthermore, should the higher interest rate be accompanied by higher inflation, then escalating resale prices might more than compensate for the higher mortgage costs. Thus with *higher* inflation, despite the correspondingly higher interest rates, the real estate investor still profits. Our conclusion is that you can afford to pay an inflated mortgage rate *if* you expect ongoing inflation, and more so if you expect increasing inflation.

## 4. Mortgage life

This fourth factor proves to have little impact on your rate of return. (It is necessary for the correct mortgage computations, however). Longer mortgages stretch out amortization payments. This keeps up the owner's cash flow and leverage. For mortgages as long as 25 years, however, a 10 percent lengthening has little significance. For the medical building, a 10 percent *shortening* to an 18.9-year mortgage life (as the survey increasingly thought likely) cuts the annual rate of return by only 0.2 percent and then only for longer holding periods of several years. It is usually more important to negotiate a favorable mortgage amount and interest rate than to be fussy about its duration.

## 5. Net sale price

This key factor shows the impact of selling costs on the real estate investor. The "total project cost" factor includes your buying costs, but these are usually much less than selling costs because commissions are paid by the seller. Thus, to liquidate your investment, sizable transaction costs must be anticipated. "Net sale price" is defined as the proceeds, after commissions and other closing expenses, from immediately reselling your investment. If you expect to encounter 6 percent transaction costs, the "% net sale to total" would be 94 percent. Future sale prices also encounter this same proportionate cost of liquidating. Thus you would recover 94 percent of market value at that future year.

Suppose the property was favorably bought so that it could be immediately resold, if need be, with full recovery of the total project cost. By changing the net sale price to 100 percent of the total project cost, we can gauge the impact of selling costs. Figure 6.5 shows this factor's dramatic impact, especially for short holding periods. Over a decade, however, transaction costs have less of an effect on total annual returns. The risk is in being forced to sell early, possibly because of too little income with too much leverage. Then transaction costs only add to your headaches.

---

FIGURE 6.5
Selling costs decrease the rate of return.

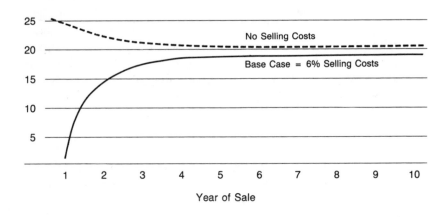

Percent
Total
Rate of
Return

Year of Sale

---

## 6. Gross income

Rental levels have an important influence on the rate of return throughout an investment. Usually, careful attention is paid to this factor because overpricing relative to the market can lead to high turnover and vacancies. Yet too low a rent leaves "money on the table" that could have been earned. Our base case includes $44,842 initial gross income, estimated to inflate at 10 percent annually.

The sensitivity analysis (Tables 6.5 and 6.6) shows that a 10 percent shortfall in gross income lowers total annual return only modestly. However, two other risks stem from an income short-fall. The first is that the property's cash-flow position worsens. While tax rebates from depreciation tend to soften this blow, the owner may still be forced to add to his commitment or to sell prematurely, before expected appreciation can be realized. If so, the second risk is that the net sale price is likely to be lower than originally projected, reflecting the lower-than-expected rents and cash flow. And we have already seen that a lower net sale price substantially cuts total annual return. Although for clarity each key factor is being discussed separately now, *their risks may act in tandem.*

## 7. Operating expense

Operating expenses also act in tandem with rents and resale values to determine return and risk. Expenses, including management fees or the owner's time, often take up to half of gross income. Accordingly, elaborate expense projections typically precede the construction or purchase of an income property. Certain expenses are increasingly being made the tenant's responsibility in order to minimize this risk. Nonetheless, the real estate investor usually finds that operating cost control is his most visible and constant problem. Rental income is pegged for the short run by leases, so any expense bulges are particularly distasteful.

What does sensitivity analysis reveal? Again, this highly visible variable has, like the mortgage rate, received more fanfare than its due. We are not saying to ignore operating costs. But other factors, such as inflation (and appreciation potential), are dramatically underanalyzed by comparison. For our base case, a 10 percent increase above each year's budgeted operating expenses lops only about 2 points off each year's total rate of return.

A much greater risk is escalating expenses coupled with *stagnant rents* (as from a long-term lease or rent controls). With maintenance, taxes, utilities, security, insurance and other costs escalating, a *chronic* reduction in net operating income can result. For older properties held past the point of favorable leverage and tax shelter, the owner may have little incentive to hang on. But this trouble usually takes many years to develop. The conclusion? Be sure that rents can be raised to cover inflating costs and be aware of the political risk of controls forbidding you to do so.

## 8. Percent annual inflation

As you have seen by now, inflation (or appreciation) has a powerful profit impact. Study Figure 6.6 a moment, as it is the major thrust behind this book. During the 1970s, when inflation became a growing and ubiquitous problem, investors were thoroughly disappointed by stocks, bonds, and savings as a means of storing purchasing power. But what happened in real estate? We have witnessed a renewed appreciation in—and appreciation for—real estate values. The *after-tax* total returns shown here are unparalleled by other investment opportunities. And real estate in this country is still undervalued relative to land and building prices in other developed countries. In urban Europe or Japan, for example, comparable housing might cost double what we would expect to pay.

Some year the securities markets will bounce back and some real estate operators will choose unwisely or be unlucky. But as an investor, be your tendencies toward insurance or gambling, you should know the odds. If you believe the odds are that inflation will continue over the long run, and you have enough net worth to tolerate illiquidity and today's lack of cash flow due to high interest rates, and you have enough income to desire its shelter, then Figure 6.6 is your road map to real estate investing.

## 9. Depreciation amount

Depreciation is the main source of real estate's tax shelter capability. Tax policy recognizes that a wearing out of a physical asset occurs across its economic lifetime. Thus a depreciation provision is allowed, providing an untaxed return of the money invested in improvements (not land). However, with rapidly rising replacement costs, merely recouping one's initial investment

FIGURE 6.6
Inflation boosts real estate's total rate of return

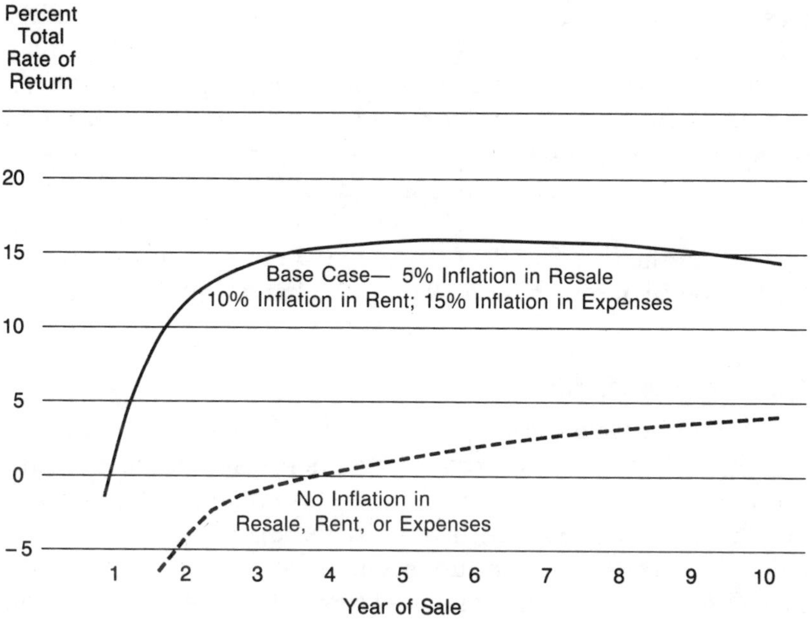

Percent
Total
Rate of
Return

means additional funds are needed to replace a building when it effectively wears out. Thus, the latest tax laws hope to provide additional incentives for investing in property and equipment by reducing their write-off periods to 15 years for buildings and 5 years for equipment. Highly codified standards have typically stipulated the amount, life, and type of such deductions. However, the 1981 tax law has tried to simplify these standards. From the investor's viewpoint, depreciation represents a tax-deductible "expense" that is not a *cash* cost. Indeed, it often generates a rebate on income taxes otherwise due.

In our base case, the depreciation amount is $160,000. The remainder of the $200,000 total project cost is the value of the land, which does not wear out. Suppose the building itself does not wear out as rapidly as it is depreciated. Suppose, in fact, that it actually appreciates/inflates in value, as most properties do, at least until they become hopelessly outdated. This appreciation, coupled with depreciation write-offs, results in a capital gain tax liability upon sale. So, because the tax saving is partly paid back at sale, depreciation's effect on total return is somewhat less dramatic than popularly supposed. For example, as the top half of Table 6.6 shows, boosting our medical building's depreciable amount by 10 percent (to $176,000) increases the annual return for each of the first five years by only 0.4 points—only a 2.5 percent increase in return for a 10 percent change in this key factor.

## 10. Depreciation life

A shorter depreciation life, all other things being equal, fattens the total return. That is because larger depreciation expenses are thereby allowed in the earlier years. This enhances the up-front tax shelter and annual cash flow (Level 3), while the counterbalancing tax recoupment upon sale is deferred and converted to the lower capital gain tax rates (except to the extent recaptured). However, the effect of shortening depreciation life—or the risk from it being longer than anticipated—is modest.[2]

## 11. Depreciation type

Various types of depreciation are now in use—and with the passage of the 1981 Tax Act, we are now subject to a new set of rules. The simplest form of depreciation is the *straight line* method. It deducts expenses for depreciation uniformly over the property's depreciation life. For our base case, with $160,000 depreciable over 25 years, this would result in a $6,400 annual deduction.

Prior to the enactment of the 1981 Tax Act, the tax laws dictated which types of depreciation could be applied to the various classes of investment real estate. These included two basic depreciation methods: *straight line* and *accelerated.* For used residential property with a remaining life of more than 20 years, 125 percent of straight line could be used. New commercial property qualified for 150 percent and new residential for 200 percent of straight line. The property owner could elect either accelerated or straight-line—whichever he thought would be beneficial. Disputes often arose between the IRS and the taxpayer over the depreciable lives elected. The 1981 Tax Act should eliminate most of these disputes. (See Chapter 4 for a more in-depth discussion of the 1981 Tax Act.)

## 12. Ordinary income tax rate and
## 13. Capital gain tax rate

The legends about real estate's tax-shelter potency are true. Regardless of the investor's tax bracket, his or her total return remains practically constant. By contrast, interest from savings instruments and most bonds is fully taxed (subject to a slight exclusion after 1980). For an investor in the 50 percent bracket, only half of such before-tax interest income is preserved after Uncle Sam takes his share. The decision guideline? The higher your tax rate, the greater the comparative attractiveness of real estate investing.

## Comparing key factors

This chapter has systematically analyzed each of our 13 key factors. It is now useful to summarize our sensitivity analysis in a consistent, standardized way. We investigated the changes in total return for selected holding periods caused by a 10 percent increase in selected key factors for our medical building. For example, we first assumed a 10 percent overpayment with all other factors remaining unchanged. As discussed, this drops profitability substantially, especially for short holding periods. This indicates substantial risk if this factor is misestimated, as in a construction cost overrun.

In another example, the mortgage amount column reveals the impact of a 10 percent increase in leverage. Since the base-case investment has a favorable return, this incremental leverage boosts it even higher. While developed from our base case, these conclusions are generally applicable. You can use this sensitivity analysis or multiple projections to judge the relative strength of major key factors and their effect on returns for various holding periods. All investment analysis involves forecasting, but now you can gauge the risk from being wrong.

## Summary

Part I has been concerned with real estate investment analysis. During the 1970s, inflation became such a persistent problem that it is now mandatory to include it in your investment thinking. Indeed, real estate can offer a means of *profit*, as well as protection, from inflation. If your own objectives favor a high rate of return with leverage possibilities and tax shelter, and you can tolerate moderate risk and substantial illiquidity, then real estate probably belongs in your investment portfolio.

The real estate marketplace is a large one. And while each property is unique, there are many professionals who can advise you. With the proper attitude, knowledge, and attention, anyone can profitably pyramid even a small capital base into substantial wealth. But each opportunity should be individually analyzed for its likely rate of return and sources of risk. Generally, we advise beginning with existing residential income properties. They typically offer reasonable safety, leverage, and liquidity, plus protection and profit from inflation.

## Notes

1. Unfortunately, this analysis was done before the 1981 tax law changes were passed. However, our sensitivity analysis is perfect for determining the effect on our rate of return of reducing our depreciable life from 25 years to 15 years, as allowed under the new law. We will continue to use straight-line, since it is advantageous given the substantial increase (1981 Tax Act) in the recapture penalty if the accelerated method is elected.

2. If we were to reduce our depreciable life from 25 years to 15 years as allowed by the 1981 tax changes, we can use our sensitivity analysis in the top half of Table 6.6 to figure out the effect on our total rate of return. Our analysis currently shows us that our rate increases by .4 percent when we reduce the depreciable life by two and a half years. If we reduce its life by ten years, we can just multiply .4 percent by four to get our result—an increase of 1.6 percent in our annual compounded rate of return. This increase probably won't make a bad deal look good, but it does lower our risk by returning our invested capital quicker, without recapture when we sell the property. Certainly it does provide additional incentives for investing in borderline properties.

# PART II

# Property Selection and Management

# 7 Home and Condominium Ownership

We have advocated home (or condominium) ownership as a logical and satisfying way to begin investing in real estate. Fifty million households seem to agree, owning not only single-family homes but also townhouses, condominium apartments, and mobile homes in increasing numbers. Admittedly, the economic aspect is only one of many motivations for home ownership. But for many families the steady increase in their home equity through appreciation and mortgage amortization has made it their best investment. The question remains, "Should *you* own your home?"

## The housing marketplace

The housing marketplace is changing. An increasing portion of households own, as shown in Figure 7.1. However, the traditional single-family detached house is being challenged from two sides. On one side are mobile homes, now accounting for virtually all new homes priced under $25,000.

FIGURE 7.1
Owner-occupied housing trends in the United States

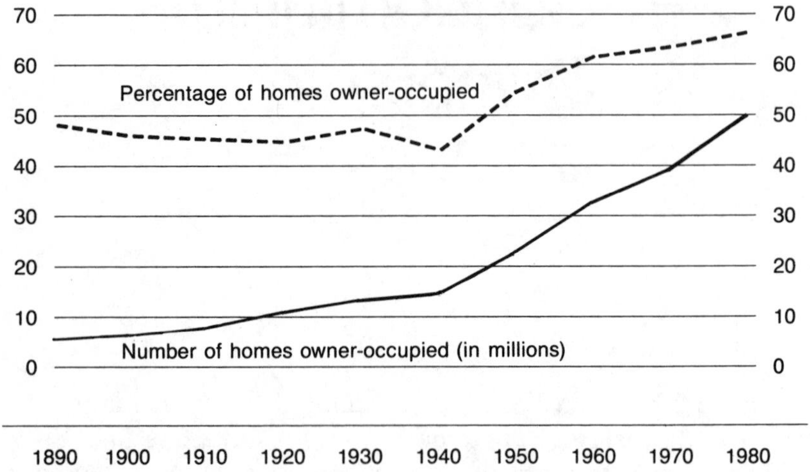

Source: *The Real Estate Handbook* (Homewood, Ill.: *Down Jones-Irwin*, 1980), p. 914.

On the other side, townhouses and condominiums allow a higher density of living units per acre, thus helping dilute the impact of sharply higher land costs on overall home prices. Their common walls also economize on materials and labor and such operating costs as heating and cooling. Thus the condo concept combines the savings of apartment-style construction with the personal and economic benefits of home ownership.

Housing *quality* has generally improved in recent decades, when measured by square footage, number of bathrooms, central climate-control systems, and appliances (dishwasher, garbage disposal, and so forth). For example, during the 1970s, average new-home size grew from 1,400 square feet to 1,600 square feet.

Our prediction is that, while quality will continue to improve, average *size* will reverse trend and begin to decrease. This trend reversal will have three causes:

1. Average household size is decreasing, lowering space demand.
2. Capital is now relatively more expensive, encouraging economizing.
3. Energy is now relatively more expensive, dictating less space to heat/cool (to a degree).

Housing *location* is also subject to change. Our populace is migrating toward the good weather (Arizona, California, and Florida), the good life (Colorado, Oregon, Vermont, and selected resort areas), and the good cities (Dallas, Denver, San Francisco, and Scottsdale, for example). This migration can have dramatic effects on real estate activity and values. For example, Fort Lauderdale alone added more new housing units in the mid-1970s than all of New York City, turning a boom into a glut in the process. Yet that glut was quickly absorbed, and during the latter 1970s, housing prices there strengthened and then rose sharply. For a different reason—the lack of new supply—New York City housing prices also zoomed.

Housing *finance* is also changing. Mortgage innovations, discussed in Chapter 3, will make housing costs more affordable and this is sorely needed. Conventional mortgage costs are shown for the typical home and analyzed later in this chapter.

## The economics of home ownership

Two thirds of households own their home. (The remaining renters form a market analyzed in the next chapter, "Residential Income Property.") Homeowners face a different set of depreciation and tax rules than do investors. Although this book focuses primarily on investment property, this chapter analyzes the economics of home ownership.

First, the rules. You can*not* depreciate your own home. This removes one significant tax shelter. (A neighbor, not aware of this rule, did depreciate his home for tax purposes; a case of ignorance is bliss, if not audited, that is.)

On the other hand, capital gains taxation upon sale of your home is quite favorable. The rule: If you sell your house and

---

TABLE 7.1
Homeowner conventional mortgage costs and qualifying income

---

(Assumes a $50,000, 30-year mortgage)

| Interest Rate | Monthly Payment (Principal & Interest) | Income to Qualify* |
|---|---|---|
| 9% | $402 | $28,800 |
| 10 | 439 | 30,200 |
| 11 | 476 | 31,500 |
| 12 | 514 | 32,900 |
| 13 | 553 | 34,300 |
| 14 | 592 | 35,700 |
| 15 | 632 | 37,200 |
| 16 | 672 | 38,600 |
| 17 | 713 | 40,000 |

*Assumes borrower's monthly fixed costs should not exceed one third of monthly income. A $400/month non-mortgage fixed cost is assumed, covering property taxes, utilities, insurance, and car loans (i.e., other debt costs somewhat raise the income needed to qualify for the mortgage).

---

buy or build and occupy a higher-priced one within 24 months, you can defer paying any capital gains tax. If you are 55 or older, you are eligible for a further, one-time tax break. Gains of up to $125,000 on sale of your principal residence go untaxed. Also, "sweat equity" from your own repair and good maintenance efforts can become capital gains when recovered at sale, thereby constituting tax-favored compensation. The overall result is that home ownership can provide capital appreciation that is significantly if not completely tax sheltered.

An additional feature is the tax deductibility of interest on mortgage money borrowed to finance a home purchase. (On all leveraged investments, except tax-free bonds and the All-Savers Certificate, such interest expenses are deductible from income in figuring ordinary income tax. There is a limitation on deductible interest, however, to the amount of investment income plus $10,000.) Real estate taxes are also deductible. Thus the government pays part of the costs of home ownership.

The surprise, however, results from correctly accounting for the *rent savings* afforded by ownership. We will use an example to prove this great economic benefit.

## Home ownership—an example

A REAL analysis can shed light on the implied profitability of home ownership, as well as that of investment property. We use the term *implied* because homeowners don't actually pay rent to themselves but rather *save* paying that amount. Suppose, for example, that a $70,000 home can be purchased using a $55,000 conventional mortgage at 14 percent for 30 years. Then the market value of comparable housing, if rented, would probably be about $600 per month, for a rent savings of $7,200 per year.

It is important to realize that rent must come from your *after-tax* or take-home pay. You have to earn an even greater sum in salary, which is taxable income. Someone with a 40 percent tax rate would have to earn $12,000 annually just to net the $7,200 needed for rent. In the 50 percent bracket, after-tax consumable cash is only half of gross earnings. Because of income taxes, which Benjamin Franklin did not have to face, this person finds "a penny saved is *two* pennies earned." And with inflation, those pennies had better be dollars by now!

The homeowner's rent savings must be adjusted downward for the maintenance, insurance, supplies, and other expenses that a renter would not have to pay. Also, these upkeep expenses are not tax deductible by the homeowner. Therefore, we must reduce the $600 monthly rental savings by about $100 per month, the assumed outlay for these costs. (Condominium owners, where a paid maintenance staff is employed, might expect these costs to run about $150 per month for a property of this value.) This produces an "implied gross income" of ownership netting to $500 per month (or $450 for our condo). This equals $6,000 annually (or $5,400 of *after-tax* savings).

Only one operating expense is tax deductible for the homeowner—real estate taxes, assumed here at $1,200 per year. Expenses for utilities are assumed to be paid by both the renter and the owner, so they can be excluded from this comparison. Mortgage payments include both interest and debt amortization, with the interest portion tax deductible, as discussed.

Table 7.2 shows an investment analysis of home ownership, including the special no-depreciation and no-capital-gains tax rules. (Note that we have assumed that sale is followed by purchase of a more costly home or that the seller is over age 55 and taking his or her one-time exemption.) For example, because depreciation is not allowed, that column of the analysis shows all zeros, and so does the sale "Taxes Due" column. Since this analysis applies to so many—all homeowners—and the results are so surprising, let us review the Year 1 computation in detail.

The column labeled "Gross Income" represents our $6,000 annual rent savings, after reduction for owner-paid upkeep expenses. This equals the after-tax money that would otherwise have to go to rent a home of equal quality. The "Operate Expense" column includes only property taxes, the one expense item that homeowners can deduct (whereas *all* operating expenses are deductible for investment property).

The next two columns list mortgage interest and amortization. "Cash Flow" is the net rent savings less outlays for property taxes and mortgage payments. The first "% Return" column shows this cash flow as a percentage of the original equity invested of $15,000, the difference between the purchase price of $70,000 and the mortgage of $55,000.

For tax purposes, a homeowner's property generates no income but still provides deductible expenses. The $1,200 of property taxes plus mortgage interest provide sizable tax deductions. This results in taxes due of −$2,665, really a rebate on taxes otherwise payable. The after-tax cash flow of ownership during Year 1 is −$480. This is the sum of the before-tax cash-flow figure and the tax rebate. In the next column, this figure is expressed as a −3.2 percent return on the original equity invested.

## TABLE 7.2
### Home ownership example—no inflation

KEY FACTORS ARE ---

| | ----OPERATING & INFLATION ASSUMPTIONS---- | | | | ----TAX RATES---- | |
|---|---|---|---|---|---|---|

| TOTAL INVESTED | ---MORTGAGE TERMS--- | | | NET SALE PRICE | IMPLIED GROSS INCOME | PROP. TAX OPERATING EXPENSE | % ANNUAL INFLATION | ----DEPRECIATION---- | | | ----TAX RATES---- | |
|---|---|---|---|---|---|---|---|---|---|---|---|---|
| | AMOUNT | % INTR | LIFE | | | | | AMOUNT | LIFE | TYPE | INCOME | CAP GAIN |
| 70000 | 55000 | 14.00 | 25 | 65800 | 6000 | 1200 | 0.0 | 0 | 0 | 0% | 30% | 0% |

COMPUTED SUMMARY ---

| EQUITY AMOUNT | ----MORTGAGE TERMS---- | | | NET SALE TO TOTAL | % INCOME TO TOTAL | % EXPENSE TO INCOME | % NET TO TOTAL | % DEPREC TO TOTAL |
|---|---|---|---|---|---|---|---|---|
| | % DEBT | MONTHLY | YEARLY | | | | | |
| 15000 | 78.6 | 662.07 | 7945 | 94.0 | 8.6 | 20.0 | 6.9 | 0.0 |

COMPUTED RESULTS ---

| YR | ----HOLDING RESULTS BEFORE INCOME TAXES--- | | | | | | ----HOLDING RESULTS AFTER TAXES--- | | | | | ----OVERALL RESULTS WITH SALE AT YEAR END--- | | | | | |
|---|---|---|---|---|---|---|---|---|---|---|---|---|---|---|---|---|---|
| | GROSS INCOME | OPERATE EXPENSE | -MORTGAGE- INTR | AMORT | CASH FLOW | % RE TURN | DEPREC IATION | TAXABLE INCOME | TAXES DUE | CASH FLOW | % RE TURN | SALE PRICE | DEBT REPAY | TAXES DUE | CASH FLOW | TOTAL PROFIT | % IRR |
| 1 | 6000 | 1200 | 7684 | 261 | -3145 | -21.0 | 0 | -8884 | -2665 | -480 | -3.2 | 65800 | 54739 | 0 | 11061 | -4419 | -29.4 |
| 2 | 6000 | 1200 | 7645 | 300 | -3145 | -21.0 | 0 | -8845 | -2653 | -491 | -3.3 | 65800 | 54439 | 0 | 11361 | -4610 | -16.5 |
| 3 | 6000 | 1200 | 7600 | 345 | -3145 | -21.0 | 0 | -8800 | -2640 | -505 | -3.4 | 65800 | 54094 | 0 | 11706 | -4770 | -11.5 |
| 4 | 6000 | 1200 | 7548 | 397 | -3145 | -21.0 | 0 | -8748 | -2624 | -520 | -3.5 | 65800 | 53697 | 0 | 12103 | -4894 | -8.9 |
| 5 | 6000 | 1200 | 7489 | 456 | -3145 | -21.0 | 0 | -8689 | -2607 | -538 | -3.6 | 65800 | 53241 | 0 | 12559 | -4976 | -7.1 |
| 6 | 6000 | 1200 | 7421 | 524 | -3145 | -21.0 | 0 | -8621 | -2586 | -559 | -3.7 | 65800 | 52718 | 0 | 13082 | -5011 | -5.9 |
| 7 | 6000 | 1200 | 7343 | 602 | -3145 | -21.0 | 0 | -8543 | -2563 | -582 | -3.9 | 65800 | 52116 | 0 | 13684 | -4991 | -5.0 |
| 8 | 6000 | 1200 | 7253 | 692 | -3145 | -21.0 | 0 | -8453 | -2536 | -609 | -4.1 | 65800 | 51424 | 0 | 14376 | -4908 | -4.2 |
| 9 | 6000 | 1200 | 7150 | 795 | -3145 | -21.0 | 0 | -8350 | -2505 | -640 | -4.3 | 65800 | 50628 | 0 | 15172 | -4752 | -3.5 |
| 10 | 6000 | 1200 | 7031 | 914 | -3145 | -21.0 | 0 | -8231 | -2469 | -676 | -4.5 | 65800 | 49714 | 0 | 16086 | -4514 | -2.9 |

The rightmost third of the report shows the effects of sale at the end of any particular year. Thus, even though we can't sell our home every year (it's not the Brooklyn Bridge), our REAL report allows us to look at an "if sale" assumption for any year for the next ten years. The "Sale Price" is shown net of assumed selling costs. Here 94 percent of market value (our original purchase price of $70,000) is recouped, allowing 6 percent for commissions and closing costs. "Debt Repay" lists the mortgage balance due upon sale at each year end. "Taxes Due" are zero, as discussed, because of capital gains benefits accorded homeowners. "Cash Flow" is the net proceeds of sale after the mortgage repayment. The "Total Profit" is an implied one, including the effect of rent savings. It tallies the cumulative after-tax cash flows of holding the property through any year, plus the cash flow from sale at that year end, less our original equity investment. The rightmost column, as usual, shows this total profit as a compound annual rate of return.

## Inflation's impact

Few of us really expect a long-term annual inflation rate of 0 percent any more—as Table 7.2 assumes. Let us recompute the investment merit of home ownership including inflation's impact. Suppose your home gains 10 percent annually in resale value and rental equivalent. Table 7.3 shows our homeowner example revised for this effect. Now the story is dramatically different—and better.

The amount saved increases over time as comparable properties command more rent in the marketplace. Maintenance and taxes also rise, but conventional mortgage payments stay fixed. The interest portion slowly decreases, however, reducing our tax deduction. Best of all, the sale price balloons from inflation, even after considering transaction costs. This boosts the total rate of return significantly, as graphed in Figure 7.2. (Isn't it curious that so few homeowners then extend this successful pattern into also owning investment property?)

## TABLE 7.3
## Home ownership example—10/10/10% inflation

KEY FACTORS ARE ---

| TOTAL INVESTED | ---MORTGAGE TERMS--- | | | NET SALE PRICE | IMPLIED PROP. TAX GROSS INCOME | OPERATING EXPENSE | % ANNUAL INFLATION | ---TAX RATES--- | |
|---|---|---|---|---|---|---|---|---|---|
| | AMOUNT | % INTR | LIFE | | | | | INCOME | CAP GAIN |
| 70000 | 55000 | 14.00 | 25 | 65800 | 6000 | 1200 | 10.0 | 30% | 0% |

COMPUTED SUMMARY ---

| EQUITY AMOUNT | ---MORTGAGE TERMS--- | | | % NET SALE TO TOTAL | % INCOME TO TOTAL | % EXPENSE TO INCOME | % NET TO TOTAL | ---DEPRECIATION--- | | | % DEPREC TO TOTAL |
|---|---|---|---|---|---|---|---|---|---|---|---|
| | % DEBT | MONTHLY | YEARLY | | | | | AMOUNT | LIFE | TYPE | |
| 15000 | 78.6 | 662.07 | 7945 | 94.0 | 8.6 | 20.0 | 6.9 | 0 | 0 | 0% | 0.0 |

COMPUTED RESULTS ---

| YR | ---HOLDING RESULTS BEFORE INCOME TAXES--- | | | | | | ---HOLDING RESULTS AFTER TAXES--- | | | | | ---OVERALL RESULTS WITH SALE AT YEAR END--- | | | | | |
|---|---|---|---|---|---|---|---|---|---|---|---|---|---|---|---|---|---|
| | GROSS INCOME | OPERATE EXPENSE | INTR | AMORT | CASH FLOW | % RE TURN | DEPREC IATION | TAXABLE INCOME | TAXES DUE | CASH FLOW | % RE TURN | SALE PRICE | DEBT REPAY | TAXES DUE | CASH FLOW | TOTAL PROFIT | % IRR |
| 1 | 6000 | 1200 | 7684 | 261 | -3145 | -21.0 | 0 | -8884 | -2665 | -480 | -3.2 | 72380 | 54739 | 0 | 17641 | 2161 | 14.4 |
| 2 | 6600 | 1320 | 7645 | 300 | -2665 | -17.8 | 0 | -8965 | -2689 | 25 | 0.2 | 79618 | 54439 | 0 | 25179 | 9724 | 28.0 |
| 3 | 7260 | 1452 | 7600 | 345 | -2137 | -14.2 | 0 | -9052 | -2716 | 579 | 3.9 | 87580 | 54094 | 0 | 33486 | 18610 | 30.4 |
| 4 | 7986 | 1597 | 7548 | 397 | -1556 | -10.4 | 0 | -9146 | -2744 | 1188 | 7.9 | 96338 | 53697 | 0 | 42641 | 28952 | 30.5 |
| 5 | 8785 | 1757 | 7489 | 456 | -917 | -6.1 | 0 | -9246 | -2774 | 1857 | 12.4 | 105972 | 53241 | 0 | 52730 | 40898 | 30.0 |
| 6 | 9663 | 1933 | 7421 | 524 | -214 | -1.4 | 0 | -9354 | -2806 | 2592 | 17.3 | 116569 | 52718 | 0 | 63851 | 54611 | 29.4 |
| 7 | 10629 | 2126 | 7343 | 602 | 559 | 3.7 | 0 | -9469 | -2841 | 3399 | 22.7 | 128226 | 52116 | 0 | 76110 | 70269 | 28.7 |
| 8 | 11692 | 2338 | 7253 | 692 | 1409 | 9.4 | 0 | -9591 | -2877 | 4286 | 28.6 | 141048 | 51424 | 0 | 89624 | 88070 | 28.1 |
| 9 | 12862 | 2572 | 7150 | 795 | 2344 | 15.6 | 0 | -9722 | -2917 | 5261 | 35.1 | 155153 | 50628 | 0 | 104524 | 108231 | 27.6 |
| 10 | 14148 | 2830 | 7031 | 914 | 3373 | 22.5 | 0 | -9860 | -2958 | 6331 | 42.2 | 170668 | 49714 | 0 | 120954 | 130991 | 27.1 |

Reprinted with the permission of The Mader Group, Inc., Narberth, PA.

In Figure 7.2, each curve improves sharply in the early years as the adverse impact of transaction costs gets spread over a longer holding period. But the 10 percent inflation case literally rockets returns to an excellent level. Here the after-tax rate of return, based on rent saved and despite high interest rates, reaches just over *30 percent compounded annually after taxes.* With somewhat faster appreciation, it is even possible that each year's accruing capital gain can equal or exceed your after-tax mortgage and expense outlays. Thus, in the overall sense, *your housing would have been absolutely free!*

## Embedded inflation

Many prospective homeowners now worry if prices *already* reflect inflation, can they still profit from buying at current prices and mortgage interest rates. To address this concern, we prepared a case on resort condominiums for presentation to seminar audiences in Hawaii, including the island of Maui, perhaps the highest-cost U.S. housing marketplace. The results are summarized in Table 7.4, labelled "Maui, Wowie."

First, assume that in 1976 you considered buying the sort of Maui condo unit shown in Figure 7.3. It offers marvelous climate, views, and recreational access. Of course, it's not cheap. In fact, you would never buy it if guided by the conventional yardsticks:

| | |
|---|---|
| Gross rent multiplier (Level 0) | 8.3% |
| Capitalization rate (Level 1) | 9 % |
| Cash-on-cash return (Level 2) | 5 % |

But you think of the tax shelter from losing operations (a rental agent takes *half* of income for short rentals) and depreciation deduction. And mostly you anticipate resale price increases—perhaps 10 percent or even 20 percent a year. If so, Table 7.4 (distilled from our REAL analysis) suggests that total return is quite fantastic—37 to 50 percent—so you buy.

FIGURE 7.2
Rate of return from home ownership—No inflation versus 10% annual inflation

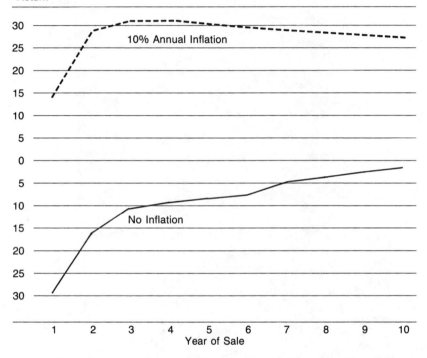

TABLE 7.4
"Maui, Wowie"—results of Hawaii's condo speculation

| | Assumptions | | | Year 1 Results | | | Year 4 Results | | |
|---|---|---|---|---|---|---|---|---|---|
| Purchase Date | Resale Inflation | Level 0 | Level 1 | Level 2 | Level 3 | Level 4 | Level 2 | Level 3 | Level 4 |
| 1976 | 10% | 8.3 | 9% | 5% | 17% | 23% | 20% | 20% | 37% |
| 1976 | 20% | 8.3 | 9 | 5 | 17 | 61 | 20 | 20 | 58 |
| 1980 | 0% | 11.1 | 7 | −17 | 7 | −22 | −6 | 9 | −6 |
| 1980 | 10% | 11.1 | 7 | −17 | 7 | 12 | −6 | 9 | 28 |

FIGURE 7.3
Two-bedroom Maui condominium floor plan

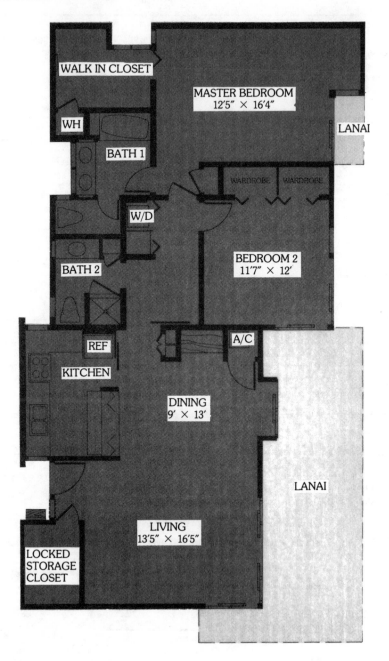

Did resale prices increase? Yes, but not at our projected 10–20 percent a year. In fact, they increased at an unprecedented 40+ percent per year. Values by 1978 doubled and by 1980 nearly doubled again. The two-bedroom unit shown in Figure 7.3 by then had a price of $380,000. Total return for the 1976 buyer was stratospheric with equity after-tax *doubling* every year!

Could the 1980 buyer also profit? The Level 0, 1, and 2 yardsticks at the already inflated prices and interest rates look even worse. Certainly, *without* inflation, it would be at best a profitless venture and perhaps a big loser. But, with inflation of just 10 percent annually, attractive total returns still remain. (Nonetheless, we chose to invest in the similar-sized Florida unit analyzed in Chapter 5—at *one seventh* the cost.)

The cost of housing—for occupancy, rental, or resort use—has gotten scary. But will it drop significantly? Will replacement costs decline? Will people stop needing physical shelter and stop wanting more quality? In 1976, *U.S. News & World Report* headlined Chris Mader's advice to "Buy now." The authors haven't changed that advice. In our opinion, 1983 may perhaps offer some of the best values in housing for those that can muster the down payment and meet lender's requirements at today's interest rates. Huge, pent-up demand for housing should propel prices at rates significantly better than inflation once mortgage rates decline to the 10–13 percent area.

## Summary

Buying your home is one of the best possible investments if you plan to stay in a particular location two years or longer. In inflationary times, its fast-rising equity is a source of satisfaction and emergency funds. Perhaps most important, the rent you save by ownership is *after-tax* money. By contrast, the two major costs of ownership—mortgage interest and property taxes—are deductible and reduce income taxes otherwise due. (This presumes you itemize expenses rather than claim the standard deduction, or zero bracket, amount.) And while you cannot take depreciation deductions (except for strict business office use), homeowners who sell for a profit benefit from favorable capital gains rates and/or outright tax exemption.

Historically, waiting to purchase a home has been a poor policy. If ever there was cause to borrow, home ownership is it, especially for younger families with rising incomes. The startling rate of return, especially when leveraged and during inflation, ought to convince any prospective home or condominium buyer.

# 8 Residential Income Property

After home ownership, residential income property is perhaps your best, moderate-risk, possibly small-scale, next step. We have already introduced the selection, financing, buying, renting, operation, appreciation, and selling aspects of such property. And home ownership, presuming you have by now taken this step, has provided some firsthand experience with these issues. Therefore, we will focus on analyzing the *investment merits* of real estate. In this chapter we discuss some typical residential income properties, followed by Chapter 9's look at Commerical and Industrial Property and Chapter 10's Land Investing and Development.

## Analysis approach

Our analysis approach here and for the next chapters' examples is to provide a base case to determine *expected* rates of return and then to discuss *risk*. We will also illustrate the use of Part III's reference tables. This unique feature—actually a handbook— allows you to estimate, both quickly and accurately, the profitability and risk of most real estate opportunities.

As always, you must use skilled judgment, experience, and knowledge of local market data, current mortgage terms, taxation guidelines, and the like. This blend allows you to estimate the 13 key factors that determine a property's investment merit. Then a specific REAL analysis, or the tables of Part III, can be used to translate these assumptions into measures of investment performance. At that point, your judgment is again required to assess whether the projected results suit your investment objectives.

Stated simply, real estate investing becomes a four-step process:
1. Define your investment objectives.
2. Estimate the 13 key factors for each opportunity.
3. Project the investment outcome of each property.
4. Choose by comparing outcomes to objectives.

The weak link—and unnecessarily so—has been the analytical third step of projecting investment outcomes, including both *return* and *risk*. Historically these forecasts have been incomplete, no-inflation, first-year-only, before-sale, no-transaction-costs, seat-of-the-pants guesses. The results have often been inaccurate and misleading. Worse yet, this destroys the value of solid work done on the other three investing steps and leads to misguided investment decisions. Isn't there a better way?

## Sample multi-unit apartment building

This first example features the type of property you can reasonably aspire to own after experience with pyramiding smaller buildings and/or individual homes. Let's assume a 20-unit low-rise design commonly available in metropolitan areas. It need not be an elevator building, might feature a mix of studios, have one and two bedrooms, and offer off-street parking. The property could be about 10 to 20 years old with a remaining depreciable life, for tax purposes, of 15 years.

Having defined your investment objectives (Chapter 2), the second step is developing the 13 key factor values. This example's values are shown in Table 8.1. This form indicates that our 20-unit

TABLE 8.1
Key factors for sample multi-unit apartment building

|  | Real Estate Investment Analysis Form—Thirteen Key Factors | |
|---|---|---|
| Client _____ | Phone # _____ | |
| Address_____ | Project title _____ | |
| _____ | Years of analysis_____ | |

| 1. | Total project cost | $400,000 | |
|---|---|---|---|

**Mortgage Terms**

| 2. | Mortgage amount (show either $ or %) | $200,000 | or _____% of total project cost |
|---|---|---|---|
| 3. | Interest rate | 15% annually | |
| 4. | Mortgage life | 25 years | |

**Operating & Inflation Assumptions**

| 5. | Net resale price (today, before inflation, net of transaction costs) | $376,000 | or _____% of total project cost |
|---|---|---|---|
| 6. | Gross income (annually, before inflation, net of vacancy) | $60,000 | or _____% of total project cost |
| 7. | Operating expense (annually, before inflation) | $24,000 | or _____% of gross income |
| 8. | Annual inflation (resale price, income, expense) | 5% resale    10% income    15% expense | |

**Depreciation**

| 9. | Total depreciable base (not annual amount) | $320,000 | or _____% of total project cost |
|---|---|---|---|
| 10. | Depreciable life | 15 years | 200% for low-income housing 175% for most real estate* |
| 11. | Depreciable rate (percent of straight line) | 175% | 150% for tangible personal property 100% for all other† |

**Tax Rates**

| 12. | Ordinary income | 50% |
|---|---|---|
| 13. | Capital gains | 20% |

SOURCE: The Mader Group, Inc.
*Usually preferable for nonresidential property.
†Usually preferable for commercial property only because of ERTA recapture provisions.

apartment building requires $400,000 of total project cost, of which only 50 percent can be financed by a 25-year mortgage bearing 15 percent annual interest. This reduced amount of obtainable financing is based on a typical lender requiring a minimum "coverage" ratio of 1.15—that is, the cash flow before financing (our net operating income of $36,000) must be at least 1.15 times the debt service. In our example, with debt service of $30,740, our net operating income is 1.17 times the debt service. Any greater amount of debt and resulting debt service would not provide our lender with adequate coverage or security against potential default. Such mortgage rates are high by historical standards but have become typical during recent periods of tight money. Should such rates scare us away from investing? Could they go even higher?

The next key factor in Table 8.1 assumes that the property could be readily liquidated to net $376,000, based on a 6 percent allowance for transaction costs. The next factor shows that gross income of $60,000 can be expected in the first year. This averages $3,000 per unit, or a typical rent of $250 per month. From this, a vacancy allowance of 5 percent (or $3,000) is deducted. Then annual expenses are initially expected to be:

| | |
|---|---:|
| Vacancy[1] allowance at 5 percent ......... | $3,000 |
| Property taxes ....................... | 8,000 |
| Maintenance[2] ....................... | 6,000 |
| Utilities[3] ............................ | 2,000 |
| Supplies ............................. | 2,800 |
| Insurance ........................... | 1,200 |
| Administration ...................... | 1,000 |
| | $24,000 |

*The next factor is vital to a financial analysis, yet often over-simplified.* Average annual inflation assumed in this example is 10 percent annually for resale value, rental income, and operating expenses. This rate of increase is automatically factored into the year-by-year projections. After all, we bought the property seeking capital gains in addition to income. We ought to include such hoped-for—and probable—inflation/appreciation in our analysis. If you are unhappy with the inflation rates assumed, use risk or sensitivity analysis to project the results of lower rates or the benefits of higher ones.

The depreciation factors can usually be determined precisely. Based on tax laws and IRS guidelines, 175 percent of straight-line depreciation is allowed for residential property whether new or used, if acquired after 1980. This property's depreciation factors, assuming the land cost is 20 percent of the total project cost, are:

Depreciation amount . . . . $320,000 ($80,000 is land)

Depreciation life . . . . . . . . 15 years

Depreciation type . . . . . . . 175 percent (of straight line)

Finally, the investor's applicable tax rates are needed. In this example, they are assumed to be 50 percent on ordinary income and 20 percent on capital gains.

Table 8.2 presents the results of analyzing our sample multi-unit apartment building. Glancing swiftly to the rightmost column, you can see that the overall, after-tax total rate of return is over 12 percent per year for holding periods of a few years or longer. This result is satisfactory at best, although it probably meets or exceeds that routinely achievable from *most common types of investment,* despite our assumption of a mortgage bearing 15 percent interest.

Naturally, this investment does involve risks. What if the vacancy factor turns out to be not 5 percent, but 15 percent? What if an adverse or premature sale must be made? How about faster inflation of expenses but not of rents? What if your tax brackets, or the tax laws, change? What happens if catastrophic maintenance or personal liability expenses strike? These dire cases can be probed by risk analysis.

## Risk analysis

Tables 8.3 and 8.4 show a pessimistic turn in particular key factors as compared with their base-case values. For example, suppose our $400,000 budget for total project cost is overrun by 10 percent, such as from major unexpected repairs. *If all else remains the same,* we would then need another $40,000 in equity.

**TABLE 8.2**
Sample multi-unit apartment building—5/10/15% inflation

**KEY OPERATING FACTORS ARE ---**

| TOTAL PROJECT COST | ---MORTGAGE TERMS---<br>AMOUNT | % INTR | LIFE | ----OPERATING & INFLATION ASSUMPTIONS----<br>NET RESALE PRICE | % INFL | GROSS INCOME | % INFL | OPERATING EXPENSE | % INFL | ----DEPRECIATION---<br>AMOUNT | LIFE | RATE | ----TAX RATES---<br>INCOME | CAP GAIN |
|---|---|---|---|---|---|---|---|---|---|---|---|---|---|---|
| 400000 | 200000 | 15.00 | 25 | 376000 | 5 | 60000 | 10 | 24000 | 15 | 320000 | 15 | 175% | 50% | 20% |

| % NOI TO COST | % DEPREC TO COST |
|---|---|
| 9.0 | 80.0 |

**PRE-OPERATING SUMMARY ---**

| EQUITY AMOUNT | ---MORTGAGE TERMS---<br>% DEBT | MONTHLY | YEARLY | % NET RESALE TO COST | % INCOME TO COST | GROSS RENT MULT | % EXPENSE TO INCOME |
|---|---|---|---|---|---|---|---|
| 200000 | 50.00 | 2562 | 30740 | 94.0 | 15.0 | 6.7 | 40.0 |

**OPERATING RESULTS ---**

| YR | ---HOLDING RESULTS BEFORE INCOME TAXES---<br>GROSS INCOME | OPERATE EXPENSE | --MORTGAGE--<br>INTR | AMORT | CASH FLOW | % RE TURN | ---HOLDING RESULTS AFTER TAXES--<br>DEPREC IATION | TAXABLE INCOME | TAXES DUE | CASH FLOW | % RE TURN | ---OVERALL RESULTS IF SOLD AT YEAR END----<br>SALE PRICE | DEBT REPAY | TAXES DUE | CASH FLOW | TOTAL PROFIT | % IRR |
|---|---|---|---|---|---|---|---|---|---|---|---|---|---|---|---|---|---|
| 1 | 60000 | 24000 | 29947 | 793 | 5260 | 2.6 | 37333 | -31280 | -15640 | 20900 | 10.5 | 394800 | 199207 | 11227 | 184366 | 5267 | 2.6 |
| 2 | 66000 | 27600 | 29819 | 920 | 7660 | 3.8 | 32978 | -24397 | -12199 | 19859 | 9.9 | 414540 | 198287 | 25264 | 190990 | 31749 | 8.0 |
| 3 | 72600 | 31740 | 29672 | 1068 | 10120 | 5.1 | 29130 | -17942 | -8971 | 19091 | 9.5 | 435267 | 197218 | 37574 | 200475 | 60325 | 10.1 |
| 4 | 79860 | 36501 | 29500 | 1240 | 12619 | 6.3 | 25732 | -11873 | -5936 | 18555 | 9.3 | 457030 | 195978 | 48393 | 212660 | 91065 | 11.2 |
| 5 | 87846 | 41976 | 29300 | 1440 | 15130 | 7.6 | 22730 | -6160 | -3080 | 18210 | 9.1 | 479882 | 194538 | 57928 | 227416 | 124031 | 11.9 |
| 6 | 96631 | 48273 | 29069 | 1671 | 17618 | 8.8 | 20078 | -789 | -394 | 18013 | 9.0 | 503876 | 192867 | 66366 | 244643 | 159271 | 12.4 |
| 7 | 106294 | 55513 | 28800 | 1940 | 20040 | 10.0 | 17736 | 4244 | 2122 | 17918 | 9.0 | 529070 | 190928 | 73872 | 264270 | 196816 | 12.7 |
| 8 | 116923 | 63840 | 28489 | 2251 | 22343 | 11.2 | 16785 | 7809 | 3904 | 18438 | 9.2 | 555523 | 188676 | 81156 | 285691 | 236675 | 12.9 |
| 9 | 128615 | 73417 | 28127 | 2613 | 24459 | 12.2 | 16785 | 10287 | 5143 | 19315 | 9.7 | 583299 | 186063 | 88704 | 308533 | 278832 | 13.1 |
| 10 | 141477 | 84429 | 27707 | 3033 | 26308 | 13.2 | 16785 | 12556 | 6278 | 20030 | 10.0 | 612464 | 183030 | 96529 | 332905 | 323235 | 13.2 |

Reprinted with the permission of The Mader Group, Inc., Narberth, PA.

**TABLE 8.3**
Sample multi-unit apartment building—5/10/15% inflation
Sensitivity analysis results—revised key factor value at end of year and resulting IRR due to change of

| | TOTAL PROJECT COST | MORTGAGE TERMS | | | OPERATING ASSUMPTIONS | | | DEPRECIATION | | | TAX RATES | |
| | | AMOUNT | % INTR | LIFE | NET RESALE PRICE | GROSS INCOME | OPERATING EXPENSE | AMOUNT | LIFE | TYPE | INCOME | CAP GAIN |
| | 10% | -10% | 10% | -10% | -10% | -10% | 10% | -10% | 10% | -10% | -10% | 10% |
|---|---|---|---|---|---|---|---|---|---|---|---|---|
| | 440000. | 180000. | 16.50 | 22.5 | 355320. | 54000. | 26400. | 288000. | 16.5 | 157.50 | 45.0 | 22.0 |
| 1 | -9.1 | 3.1 | 1.9 | 2.6 | -10.7 | 1.1 | 2.0 | 2.3 | 2.3 | 2.6 | 2.2 | 2.5 |
| 2 | -0.1 | 8.0 | 7.3 | 8.0 | -0.4 | 6.4 | 7.4 | 7.7 | 7.7 | 8.0 | 7.7 | 7.7 |
| 3 | 4.1 | 9.8 | 9.3 | 10.1 | 4.5 | 8.4 | 9.4 | 9.7 | 9.7 | 10.0 | 9.7 | 9.8 |
| 4 | 6.4 | 10.9 | 10.5 | 11.2 | 7.1 | 9.5 | 10.5 | 10.8 | 10.8 | 11.1 | 10.9 | 10.9 |
| 5 | 7.8 | 11.5 | 11.2 | 11.9 | 8.8 | 10.2 | 11.1 | 11.5 | 11.5 | 11.7 | 11.6 | 11.6 |
| 6 | 8.7 | 12.0 | 11.7 | 12.4 | 9.9 | 10.6 | 11.6 | 12.0 | 12.0 | 12.2 | 12.1 | 12.1 |
| 7 | 9.4 | 12.3 | 12.0 | 12.7 | 10.7 | 10.9 | 11.9 | 12.3 | 12.3 | 12.5 | 12.4 | 12.5 |
| 8 | 9.9 | 12.5 | 12.3 | 12.9 | 11.3 | 11.1 | 12.1 | 12.5 | 12.6 | 12.7 | 12.7 | 12.7 |
| 9 | 10.3 | 12.6 | 12.4 | 13.0 | 11.7 | 11.2 | 12.2 | 12.6 | 12.7 | 12.9 | 12.9 | 12.9 |
| 10 | 10.5 | 12.7 | 12.6 | 13.1 | 12.0 | 11.3 | 12.3 | 12.7 | 12.8 | 13.0 | 13.0 | 13.0 |

Reprinted with the permission of The Mader Group, Inc., Narberth, PA.

TABLE 8.4
Sample multi-unit apartment building—5/10/15% inflation
Sensitivity analysis results—change in key factor value and resulting change in IRR (sensitivity minus original)

SENSITIVITY ANALYSIS RESULTS --- CHANGE IN KEY FACTOR VALUE AND RESULTING CHANGE IN IRR  (SENSITIVITY MINUS ORIGINAL)

| | TOTAL PROJECT COST | ---MORTGAGE TERMS--- | | | NET RESALE PRICE | ---------OPERATING ASSUMPTIONS--------- | | ----DEPRECIATION---- | | | ---TAX RATES--- | |
| | | AMOUNT | % INTR | LIFE | | GROSS INCOME | OPERATING EXPENSE | AMOUNT | LIFE | TYPE | INCOME | CAP GAIN |
| | 40000. | -20000. | 1.50 | -2.5 | -39480. | -6000. | 2400. | -32000. | 1.5 | -17.50 | -5.0 | 2.0 |
| 1 | -11.8 | 0.4 | -0.8 | 0.0 | -13.4 | -1.5 | -0.6 | -0.3 | -0.3 | -0.0 | -0.4 | -0.2 |
| 2 | -8.1 | -0.1 | -0.8 | 0.0 | -8.4 | -1.6 | -0.7 | -0.3 | -0.3 | -0.0 | -0.4 | -0.3 |
| 3 | -6.0 | -0.2 | -0.8 | 0.0 | -5.6 | -1.7 | -0.7 | -0.4 | -0.3 | -0.1 | -0.4 | -0.3 |
| 4 | -4.8 | -0.3 | -0.7 | -0.0 | -4.0 | -1.7 | -0.7 | -0.4 | -0.4 | -0.1 | -0.3 | -0.3 |
| 5 | -4.1 | -0.4 | -0.7 | -0.0 | -3.1 | -1.7 | -0.8 | -0.4 | -0.4 | -0.2 | -0.3 | -0.3 |
| 6 | -3.7 | -0.4 | -0.7 | -0.0 | -2.5 | -1.8 | -0.8 | -0.4 | -0.4 | -0.2 | -0.3 | -0.3 |
| 7 | -3.3 | -0.4 | -0.7 | -0.0 | -2.0 | -1.8 | -0.8 | -0.4 | -0.4 | -0.2 | -0.3 | -0.2 |
| 8 | -3.0 | -0.4 | -0.7 | -0.0 | -1.7 | -1.8 | -0.9 | -0.4 | -0.4 | -0.2 | -0.2 | -0.2 |
| 9 | -2.8 | -0.4 | -0.6 | -0.0 | -1.4 | -1.8 | -0.9 | -0.4 | -0.3 | -0.2 | -0.2 | -0.2 |
| 10 | -2.6 | -0.4 | -0.6 | -0.0 | -1.2 | -1.9 | -0.9 | -0.4 | -0.3 | -0.2 | -0.2 | -0.2 |

Reprinted with the permission of The Mader Group, Inc., Narberth, PA.

Under such circumstances, the rate of return declines—especially for shorter holding periods. This particular decline has two causes. First, profits are spread over a larger equity requirement. Second, the profits are lowered because the initial overrun lessens the ultimate capital gain, since the net resale price is assumed to be unchanged. The larger equity requirement and lower profits from resale are both factors that knock down total return.

To answer our query about the risk from high vacancy, look at the column in Table 8.3 reflecting shrunken gross income. The base case includes a 5 percent vacancy allowance. If vacancy is at the feared 15 percent level, then another 10 percent or $6,000 gets lopped off our $60,000 base-case gross income. Table 8.3 shows the lowered rate of return due to this vacancy problem. For example, the Year 5 rate of return in Table 8.2, the base cases, is 11.9 percent. Table 8.3 shows that the high vacancy alone lowers this to 10.2 percent, a decrease of 1.7 percent (found in Table 8.4), which might be judged a moderate risk and worth taking.

Other risks in this property can be similarly investigated. Premature sale is perhaps the biggest worry. As the base case (Table 8.2) shows, sale at the end of Year 1 results in a slightly positive rate of return. If sale must be rushed or the property unexpectedly drops in price, a loss might result, as shown in Table 8.3. If sold at the end of Year 1, the overall rate of return drops from an unexciting 2.6 percent to a terrible −9.1 percent. But, for perspective, look also at the loss possibilities in other types of investing. For instance, the Dow Jones Industrial Average first reached 800 in February 1964. *Eighteen years later,* in March 1982, it was still below 800—while the CPI had gone from 100 to 280. Even counting dividends, one would have been barely ahead for that "bearly" period.

## Using tables in Part III

For a quick approximation of key results, you can use the reference tables of Part III. Each chapter's tables feature the applicable depreciation and tax rules for a different category of real estate. The tables in Chapter 13 cover home (or condo) ownership. Chapters 14 and 15 cover residential and commercial property respectively. Chapter 16 illustrates the analysis of raw and developed land investing.

Part III's tables show the REAL analysis on a *per $1,000 basis*. That is, the total project cost factor is $1,000 in each case. This makes the tables easy to use, and since rates of return are percentages, these results apply to *any size investment*. Dollar values—such as total profit—can be easily scaled up to reflect the actual investment amount. Within each chapter, the different tables reflect variations in:

1. The percent mortgaged.
2. The mortgage interest rate.
3. The percent net income (NOI) to total project cost.[4]

For instance, our sample $400,000 apartment has a $300,000 (or 75 percent) mortgage at 15 percent interest. The net operating income is $60,000 gross, less $24,000 of expenses, or $36,000. This amount is 9 percent of the $400,000 total project cost (as Table 8.2 shows). These three values—the percent mortgaged, the mortgage interest rate, and the percent NOI to total project cost—dictate which table to consult within the appropriate chapter. In this case, the nearest table is Table 14.3 found in Chapter 14. It displays a REAL analysis for 60 percent mortgage at 15 percent interest and 9 percent net (NOI) to total. (All tables in that chapter use 175 percent of straight-line depreciation, the same as our sample multi-unit apartment building.) The remaining key factor values are common to all reference tables, except those found in Chapter 16:

1. A 25-year mortgage.
2. Transaction costs of 6 percent upon sale.
3. Operating expenses of 40 percent of gross income.
4. Zero percent and 10 percent inflation and 5–10–15 percent inflation for resale, gross income, and operating expenses, respectively (all combined on the same page for five years of analysis).
5. Eighty percent of the total project cost is the depreciation amount (hence 20 percent is land).

6. A depreciable life of 15 years.

7. Tax rate of 50 percent on ordinary income.

8. Tax rate of 20 percent on capital gains.

The chosen reference table closely approximates our sample multi-unit apartment building. In fact, it has identically proportioned data, except that our leverage is only 50 percent, not 60 percent as portrayed in the reference table. The dollar figures in this table reflect each $1,000 of project cost, of course. But all percentage figures—including the rate of return results—are closely applicable to our example.

Each reference table shows the no-inflation, the 5–10–15 percent case, and the 10 percent inflation results to help you judge the results of various inflation assumptions. But all reference tables are per $1,000, whereas our case is really 400 times that large. So to determine any dollar amount for our multi-unit apartment building, simply multiply by the scale factor: 400 times in this case. For example, after 5 percent annual resale increases, the Year 5 net sale price—shown as $1,200 in the table—multiplies into $480,000 for the actual property.

With only 50 percent leverage our investment will differ slightly from Table 14.3. So the rates of return calculated in other tables will help with this adjustment. Table 14.7 shows the effects of greater leverage. Interpolation of results between tables can yield quite accurate results for most cases.

## Impact of inflation

The sample 20-unit apartment building seems a marginal investment, especially when considering the sacrifice of near-term liquidity necessitated by the three- to five-year holding period. The 15 percent mortgage rate, which appears prohibitive on a historical basis, proves detrimental but not too burdensome because interest is tax deductible. A 10 percent rate (as from an assumable existing mortgage) would be much better, of course, boosting the Year 5 total return by approximately 6 points of annual return. *But neither of these mortgages would be acceptable if it were not for inflation.*

Our analysis assumed 10 percent annual inflation in resale, gross income, and operating expense. What happens if there is no inflation? Today, that seems an unlikely prospect. Nonetheless, the traditional analysis of real estate does assume constant selling prices, rents, and expenses—or, said another way, ignores inflation. Figure 8.1 graphs (from Table 14.3) the results of three different inflation assumptions, as used in the reference tables. All other factors are unchanged, including the 15 percent mortgage. A glance shows that our good investment sours in the absence of inflation. In fact, high mortgage rates *assume* inflation will continue and *impel* it to do so. A valid analysis certainly must include inflation in projecting profitability and risk.

FIGURE 8.1
Impact of inflation (from Table 14.3)

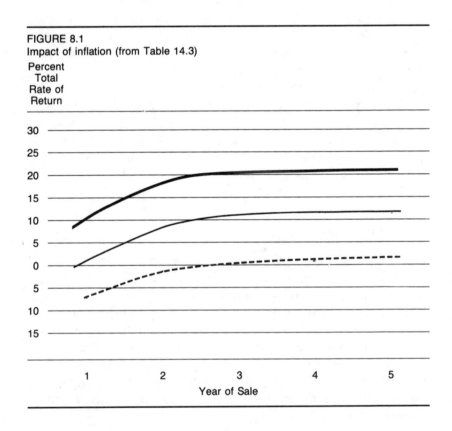

## New, large apartment complex

Next we will analyze a new, larger residential income property. This case will show why conventionally financed, nonsubsidized, multifamily housing construction has declined so severely. As builders reluctantly confess, "It's hard to make the numbers work," and the risks are numbing.

This case involves a 200-unit urban midrise (with development costing approximately $50,000 for each apartment). As residential housing, it is eligible for depreciation of 175 percent of straight-line. However, recent tax law changes have greatly reduced the tax deductions during the 18- to 24-month development period.

### Feasibility study

For new construction, a feasibility study is essential. And remember, every project ever done supposedly looked good on paper, so one should do a risk analysis as well! Economic feasibility means determining the most likely value for each key factor and its probable range. Then we can analyze the deal for return and risk.

For example, total project cost is uncertain (unless you contract for a reliable fixed cost). For our new residential midrise, the construction costs, which include hard costs; landscaping; architecture and engineering, legal development, and administration fees; financing fees; marketing fees; and miscellaneous costs totaling 10 million. The gross income estimate should reflect the regional market, the target tenant segment, and lease terms (e.g., central heat and air conditioning included; electricity separately metered and billed directly to tenant). It should be realistic in view of comparables and should be time adjusted to the normal occupancy date (two years hence, in our example).

Operating expenses are also more difficult to estimate for new properties. The property tax figure often awaits an official appraisal. The quality of insulation and future fuel bills are guesstimates. Lease-up rates, and the requisite marketing budget and preoperating loss, are hard to judge. The issues are discussed below for our proposed 200-unit apartment.

The key factors in this case require estimates of the timing and cost of development. With a development period of more than one year, phase-in of project financing is required. Then, with acceptable occupancy, an $8,000,000 mortgage amount at 13 percent "kicks in" for a 25-year maturity. This assumes probably unrealistically that a lender would make a loan where NOI does not cover debt service. But otherwise, the developer would have to put up an additional $2 million for a total of $4 million. And what developer has that kind of equity? Furthermore, the projected returns don't justify developing this property. But let's continue the example anyway.

An initial 20 percent developer's profit or 20 percent increase in value over construction costs is first assumed. Anticipated transaction costs on resale are expected to be 4 percent. (Multi-million-dollar properties generally encounter lower brokerage commissions and other closing costs, when figured as a percentage of market value.) Annual gross income of $1,360,000 is expected. This corresponds to $600 per month for the average unit and 5 to 6 percent vacancy. Annual expenses, including some utilities and the land lease, may be expected to approximate 50 percent of net rents, or $680,000.

Inflation of gross income at 8 percent, of operating expenses at 12 percent, and of resale at 4 percent are projected. Depreciation of 175 percent of the straight-line rate over 15 years is applicable. All construction costs are depreciable, since we assume the land is leased. The investor's tax rates are shown as 50 percent for income and 20 percent for capital gains.

Table 8.5 is a REAL analysis showing the two-year development/marketing period before the permanent mortgage and "normal" income and expense levels are attained. We can see that $2,000,000 of equity is required, resulting in 80 percent leverage. Also, the percent NOI to total project cost, or cap rate, is 6.8 percent. With 80 percent leverage and double-digit mortgage rates, no cash flow remains after debt service. Conventional lending practices would allow a mortgage of only about $4,000,000 based on the projected net operating income of this property. And if you could get the higher loan, conventional analysis says *don't build.* With moderate appreciation (and assuming you can obtain this leverage), the property's total return improves—but you have to risk more than $2,000,000 (possibly up to $6,000,000) for more than two years to find out!

## Risk analysis

Again it is appropriate to ask, "What can go wrong?" But even Solomon couldn't answer that. For example, during the 1970s there was a doubling and redoubling of fuel costs (who foresaw that one?). Taxes and insurance also added mightily to operating expenses. Rent controls or rent stabilization programs—a disconcerting surprise to some property owners—were legislated. And while inflation propelled resale values, it also penalized the purchasing power of cash flow received by those who didn't sell. To be sure, a rising cash flow was better than receiving a static number of dollars (like interest on a bond), but don't count on retiring comfortably on today's income levels. You need ongoing inflation protection.

To analyze risk, you can compute a revised total return based on a change in the key factor values. Tables 8.6 and 8.7 list the risks of adverse changes of 10 percent in selected factors. Fear a fuel cost rise? Suppose it would add 10 percent to operating expenses. Looking at the Year 5 return as a benchmark, we see in Tables 8.6 and 8.7 that each 10 percent rise in operating expense decreases the overall return by 0.9 percent. Thus we might expect spiraling property taxes to diminish returns by this amount if rents and other factors remain unchanged. If this cost rise is passed through, the risk is lowered or eliminated.

The most dramatic risk is a construction cost overrun, coupled with a short holding period. (Often the short holding period is not of the owner's choosing—*foreclosure* results if you cannot meet debt service requirements.) Worse still, under these conditions, the net resale price might also be depressed 10 percent, assuming distress-sale circumstances or a crisis economic climate.

## TABLE 8.5
### New construction—multi-unit apartment building

KEY CONSTRUCTION FACTORS ARE --

| YR | CUMULATIVE PROJECT COST | ----CONSTRUCTION LOAN----- YEAR END AVERAGE | % INTEREST | DEPRECIATION EXPENSE | GROSS INCOME | OPERATING EXPENSE | TAX RATE |
|---|---|---|---|---|---|---|---|
| 82 | 6000 | 4800 | 2400 | 15.00 | 0 | 0 | 0 | 50% |
| 83 | 10000 | 8000 | 7200 | 15.00 | 330 | 400 | 250 | 50% |

KEY OPERATING FACTORS ARE ---

| TOTAL PROJECT COST | ---MORTGAGE TERMS--- AMOUNT % INTR LIFE | | | NET RESALE PRICE | ------OPERATING & INFLATION ASSUMPTIONS------ % NET RESALE % INFL | GROSS INCOME | % INFL | OPERATING EXPENSE | % INFL | ---DEPRECIATION--- AMOUNT LIFE | | RATE | ----TAX RATES---- INCOME | CAP GAIN |
|---|---|---|---|---|---|---|---|---|---|---|---|---|---|---|
| 10000 | 8000 | 13.00 | 25 | 11520 | 115.2 | 4 | 1360 | 8 | 680 | 12 | 9670 | 15 | 175% | 50% | 20% |

PRE-OPERATING SUMMARY ---

| EQUITY AMOUNT | ---MORTGAGE TERMS---- % DEBT MONTHLY YEARLY | | | % NET RESALE TO COST | % INCOME TO COST | GROSS RENT MULT | % EXPENSE TO INCOME | % NOI TO COST | % DEPREC TO COST |
|---|---|---|---|---|---|---|---|---|---|
| 2000 | 80.00 | 90 | 1083 | 115.2 | 13.6 | 7.4 | 50.0 | 6.8 | 96.7 |

CONSTRUCTION RESULTS ---

------HOLDING RESULTS BEFORE INCOME TAXES------

| YR | GROSS INCOME | OPERATE EXPENSE | -LOAN INTR-- PAID DEDUCT | | CASH FLOW | EQTY FLOW | CASH & EQTY FLOW | ------HOLDING RESULTS AFTER TAXES------ DEPREC TAXABLE TAXES IATION INCOME DUE | | | CASH FLOW | EQTY FLOW | CASH AND NET DEBT EQTY FLOW INFLOW | | TOTAL NET CASH FLOW | CUM NET CASH FLOW |
|---|---|---|---|---|---|---|---|---|---|---|---|---|---|---|---|---|
| 82 | 0 | 0 | 360 | 45 | -360 | -1200 | -1560 | 0 | -45 | -23 | -338 | -1538 | 0 | 0 | -1538 | -1538 |
| 83 | 400 | 250 | 1080 | 120 | -930 | -800 | -1730 | 330 | -300 | -150 | -780 | -1580 | 0 | 0 | -1580 | -3118 |

Reprinted with the permission of The Mader Group, Inc., Narberth, PA.

TABLE 8.5 (concluded)

OPERATING RESULTS ---

| | ---HOLDING RESULTS BEFORE INCOME TAXES--- | | --MORTGAGE-- | | | | ---HOLDING RESULTS AFTER TAXES-- | | | | | ----OVERALL RESULTS IF SOLD AT YEAR END---- | | | | | |
|---|---|---|---|---|---|---|---|---|---|---|---|---|---|---|---|---|---|
| YR | GROSS INCOME | OPERATE EXPENSE | INTR | AMORT | CASH FLOW | % RE TURN | DEPREC IATION | TAXABLE INCOME | TAXES DUE | CASH FLOW | % RE TURN | SALE PRICE | DEBT REPAY | TAXES DUE | CASH FLOW | TOTAL PROFIT | % IRR |
| 1 | 1360 | 680 | 1037 | 45 | -403 | -12.9 | 1128 | -1651 | -825 | 423 | 13.6 | 11981 | 7955 | 545 | 3481 | 786 | 10.9 |
| 2 | 1469 | 762 | 1031 | 52 | -376 | -12.0 | 997 | -1485 | -743 | 367 | 11.8 | 12460 | 7903 | 979 | 3578 | 1251 | 11.6 |
| 3 | 1586 | 853 | 1024 | 59 | -349 | -11.2 | 880 | -1336 | -668 | 319 | 10.2 | 12958 | 7844 | 1358 | 3756 | 1747 | 12.1 |
| 4 | 1713 | 955 | 1016 | 67 | -325 | -10.4 | 778 | -1201 | -600 | 275 | 8.8 | 13477 | 7777 | 1690 | 4009 | 2276 | 12.4 |
| 5 | 1850 | 1070 | 1007 | 76 | -302 | -9.7 | 687 | -1078 | -539 | 237 | 7.6 | 14016 | 7701 | 1981 | 4334 | 2837 | 12.6 |
| 6 | 1998 | 1198 | 996 | 87 | -283 | -9.1 | 607 | -968 | -484 | 201 | 6.5 | 14576 | 7615 | 2236 | 4726 | 3430 | 12.7 |
| 7 | 2158 | 1342 | 984 | 99 | -267 | -8.6 | 536 | -869 | -435 | 168 | 5.4 | 15160 | 7516 | 2460 | 5183 | 4055 | 12.8 |
| 8 | 2331 | 1503 | 971 | 112 | -255 | -8.2 | 507 | -770 | -385 | 130 | 4.2 | 15766 | 7404 | 2666 | 5696 | 4698 | 12.7 |
| 9 | 2517 | 1684 | 955 | 128 | -249 | -8.0 | 507 | -629 | -314 | 65 | 2.1 | 16397 | 7276 | 2852 | 6268 | 5335 | 12.6 |
| 10 | 2719 | 1886 | 937 | 145 | -250 | -8.0 | 507 | -612 | -306 | 56 | 1.8 | 17052 | 7131 | 3043 | 6878 | 6001 | 12.5 |

Reprinted with the permission of The Mader Group, Inc., Narberth, PA.

TABLE 8.6
New construction—multi-unit apartment building
Sensitivity analysis results—revised key factor value at end of year and resulting IRR due to change of

| | 10% | -10% | 10% | -10% | -10% | -10% | 10% | -10% | 10% | -10% | -10% | 10% |
|---|---|---|---|---|---|---|---|---|---|---|---|---|
| | TOTAL PROJECT COST | ---MORTGAGE TERMS--- | | | ----------OPERATING ASSUMPTIONS---------- | | | ----DEPRECIATION---- | | | ---TAX RATES--- | |
| | | AMOUNT | % INTR | LIFE | NET RESALE PRICE | GROSS INCOME | OPERATING EXPENSE | AMOUNT | LIFE | TYPE | INCOME | CAP GAIN |
| | 11000. | 7200. | 14.30 | 22.5 | 10783. | 1224. | 748. | 8703. | 16.5 | 157.50 | 45.0 | 22.0 |
| 1 | -0.2 | 10.5 | 10.3 | 10.9 | -2.6 | 10.1 | 10.5 | 10.7 | 10.7 | 10.9 | 10.2 | 10.5 |
| 2 | 3.5 | 11.0 | 10.7 | 11.6 | 2.6 | 10.4 | 11.0 | 11.3 | 11.3 | 11.6 | 10.6 | 11.2 |
| 3 | 5.5 | 11.3 | 11.1 | 12.1 | 5.5 | 10.7 | 11.4 | 11.6 | 11.7 | 12.0 | 10.9 | 11.6 |
| 4 | 6.8 | 11.6 | 11.4 | 12.4 | 7.4 | 10.9 | 11.6 | 11.9 | 12.0 | 12.2 | 11.2 | 11.9 |
| 5 | 7.6 | 11.7 | 11.5 | 12.6 | 8.6 | 11.0 | 11.7 | 12.1 | 12.1 | 12.4 | 11.4 | 12.2 |
| 6 | 8.3 | 11.8 | 11.7 | 12.7 | 9.5 | 11.0 | 11.8 | 12.2 | 12.2 | 12.5 | 11.5 | 12.3 |
| 7 | 8.7 | 11.9 | 11.7 | 12.7 | 10.1 | 11.0 | 11.8 | 12.2 | 12.3 | 12.5 | 11.5 | 12.4 |
| 8 | 9.0 | 11.9 | 11.7 | 12.7 | 10.5 | 10.9 | 11.7 | 12.1 | 12.3 | 12.5 | 11.5 | 12.4 |
| 9 | 9.1 | 11.8 | 11.6 | 12.5 | 10.7 | 10.8 | 11.6 | 12.0 | 12.1 | 12.3 | 11.4 | 12.3 |
| 10 | 9.2 | 11.7 | 11.5 | 12.4 | 10.8 | 10.6 | 11.4 | 11.9 | 12.0 | 12.2 | 11.3 | 12.2 |

Reprinted with the permission of The Mader Group, Inc., Narberth, PA.

TABLE 8.7
New construction—multi-unit apartment building
Sensitivity analysis results—change in key factor value and resulting change in IRR (sensitivity minus original)

| TOTAL PROJECT COST | --MORTGAGE TERMS-- | | | --------OPERATING ASSUMPTIONS-------- | | | ---DEPRECIATION--- | | | ----TAX RATES--- | |
|---|---|---|---|---|---|---|---|---|---|---|---|
| | AMOUNT | % INTR | LIFE | NET RESALE PRICE | GROSS INCOME | OPERATING EXPENSE | AMOUNT | LIFE | TYPE | INCOME | CAP GAIN |
| 1000. | -800. | 1.30 | -2.5 | -1198. | -136. | 68. | -967. | 1.5 | -17.50 | -5.0 | 2.0 |
| 1 -11.1 | -0.4 | -0.7 | 0.0 | -13.6 | -0.9 | -0.4 | -0.2 | -0.2 | 0.0 | -0.8 | -0.4 |
| 2 -8.1 | -0.6 | -0.9 | 0.0 | -9.0 | -1.2 | -0.6 | -0.4 | -0.3 | -0.1 | -1.0 | -0.5 |
| 3 -6.6 | -0.7 | -1.0 | -0.0 | -6.6 | -1.4 | -0.7 | -0.4 | -0.4 | -0.1 | -1.1 | -0.5 |
| 4 -5.6 | -0.8 | -1.0 | -0.0 | -5.0 | -1.6 | -0.8 | -0.5 | -0.4 | -0.2 | -1.2 | -0.5 |
| 5 -5.0 | -0.9 | -1.1 | -0.0 | -4.0 | -1.6 | -0.9 | -0.5 | -0.5 | -0.2 | -1.2 | -0.4 |
| 6 -4.5 | -0.9 | -1.1 | -0.0 | -3.3 | -1.7 | -0.9 | -0.6 | -0.5 | -0.2 | -1.2 | -0.4 |
| 7 -4.1 | -0.9 | -1.1 | -0.1 | -2.7 | -1.8 | -1.0 | -0.6 | -0.5 | -0.3 | -1.2 | -0.4 |
| 8 -3.8 | -0.9 | -1.0 | -0.1 | -2.3 | -1.8 | -1.0 | -0.6 | -0.5 | -0.3 | -1.2 | -0.4 |
| 9 -3.5 | -0.9 | -1.0 | -0.1 | -2.0 | -1.9 | -1.1 | -0.6 | -0.5 | -0.3 | -1.2 | -0.3 |
| 10 -3.3 | -0.8 | -1.0 | -0.1 | -1.7 | -1.9 | -1.1 | -0.6 | -0.5 | -0.3 | -1.2 | -0.3 |

1/ 8 OF CONSTRUCTION LOAN INTEREST PAID IN 1982 IS TAX DEDUCTIBLE IN 1982
THE BALANCE IS DEDUCTIBLE OVER THE FIRST 7 YEARS OF OPERATION

1/ 9 OF CONSTRUCTION LOAN INTEREST PAID IN 1983 IS TAX DEDUCTIBLE IN 1983
THE BALANCE IS DEDUCTIBLE OVER THE FIRST 8 YEARS OF OPERATION

Reprinted with the permission of The Mader Group, Inc., Narberth, PA.

Then you *compound* the worst risks. A virtually complete wipeout could occur in the two years—most developers would see (and have seen) this risk/reward ratio in conventional multi-family housing as too adverse.

## Condo conversion

Given the costs and uncertainties of new residential construction, most new housing demand is being met by condo conversion. (Some would say much of this demand is being forced, as well.) Increasingly, as renters realize the benefits of ownership and accept apartment-style living as appropriate for them, they buy the unit they used to rent. Whole buildings are generally converted (in a year or two) to individual ownership in this manner. Over 10 percent of new ownership demand is now met by conversion, although the technique has often stirred political sanctions and tenants'-rights issues. Table 8.8 shows local market trends toward conversion.

TABLE 8.8
Number of apartments converted to condominiums (figures estimated)

| City | 1977 | 1978 | 1979 (est.) |
|---|---|---|---|
| Atlanta | — | 200 | 2,000 |
| Boston | — | 3,000 | 2,000 |
| Chicago | 16,000 | 24,000 | 30,000 |
| Dallas | 1,000 | 1,000 | 1,000 |
| Denver | 1,000 | 4,000 | 8,000 |
| Detroit | — | 1,000 | 2,500 |
| Houston | 13,000 | 5,000 | 1,500 |
| Los Angeles-Orange County | 1,000 | 3,000 | 7,000 |
| Miami-Ft. Lauderdale | — | 2,000 | 2,000 |
| Minneapolis-St. Paul | 1,500 | 2,000 | 3,000 |
| New York* | 10,500 | 20,500 | 34,000 |
| Philadelphia | — | 500 | 2,000 |
| Phoenix | — | 1,000 | 2,000 |
| San Diego | 1,000 | 2,000 | 3,000 |
| San Francisco-Oakland | 1,500 | 2,000 | 2,000 |
| Seattle | 1,000 | 4,000 | 2,000 |
| Tampa-St. Petersburg | — | 2,500 | 2,500 |
| Washington, D.C., area | 4,000 | 7,500 | 12,000 |

*Includes conversions to cooperatives.
Basic data: Advance Mortgage Corporation; Community Associations Institute.

SOURCE: *U.S. News & World Report*, Dec. 24, 1979.

## Summary

Should you invest in residential income property? It seems a reasonable place to begin, possibly on a small scale and after the experience of home ownership. Our examples show good total returns are available, despite current market conditions, when you include the prospect of inflation in resale values. *New* residential property has the advantage of creating value through development (if you are the developer). On the other hand, *used* residential property has an already established market and financial history; it has less construction risk and provides relatively predictable lease income and operating expenses. Current high mortgage rates are acceptable *only if* overcome by rising rents and an inflation-swollen resale price. But doesn't this seem likely? Again, you must judge the returns and risks.

## Notes

1. A vacancy allowance of 5 percent implies, for example, a 19-month occupancy followed by a one-month vacancy, for a one-twentieth or 5 percent vacancy average. This factor may be accounted for as a reduction in gross income or as an operating expense; either way the analysis results are the same.

2. The maintenance cost might include a rent subsidy to a resident part-time supervisor.

3. Utilities expenses are only those paid by the owner and exclude tenant services, which are assumed to be separately metered and billed.

4. The percent net (NOI) to total is used because it combines two factors into one. It is the surplus of income over expense, taxable as ordinary income. Thus your proposed investment's gross income and operating expense figures need not match those in the reference table. It is enough that the percent NOI to total be close to that in the reference table.

# 9 Commercial and Industrial Property

The commercial and industrial property marketplace is surprisingly large. Business and industry currently spend $100 billion annually on new construction. By contrast, the residential housing marketplace is no larger and in 1980 and 1981 proved more cyclical, as well. But just as the majority of housing is owner-occupied, so, too, is a large portion of commercial and industrial property, especially manufacturing facilities. Still, there are many opportunities for investors, including the four examples discussed here: an office building, shopping center, warehouse, and resort facility.

## Office building

Demand for urban and suburban office space has grown for decades as workplaces have shifted from manufacturing to service facilities and jobs from blue collar to white collar. General-purpose facilities find a large market of prospective tenants, because many organizations prefer to rent rather than own space. This gives them location and expansion flexibility and keeps depreciation "expenses" from reducing a publicly held corporation's reported accounting profits.

This large demand for office space has, naturally enough, stimulated a large supply. But periodic localized overbuilding resulting from the long lead time (normally two to four years) necessary to plan and build an office project, accentuated by the national business cycle, can make office building ownership more risky than investing in residential income property. Rental rates and occupancy fluctuate more and are particularly affected by location, transportation, parking, architecture, floor size, lease length, and features such as an attractive lobby, the tenant improvement package; adequate elevator service; reliable heating, ventilation, and air conditioning (HVAC); cleaning services; and so forth. Fortunately, these risks are balanced by potential gross rents of $18 to $60 (in New York) per square foot annually for class-A urban space and of $10 to $20 per square foot for prime suburban space.

Before we study our example, a final qualitative observation is in order. Location has been emphasized before, but for office space it is *crucial.* Think about it. Demand for offices is derived from business needs, including proximity to other offices, hotels, and restaurants and to transportation hubs that allow easy commuting. Good locations tend to get even better.

By contrast, industrial facilities often need large land areas and can *create* jobs rather than relying on local space demand, often precipitated by too many people working in too small a space. Also a business spends a lower percentage of its revenues on rent than does a homeowner or apartment renter. It can afford to buy the best. You should be choosy, too. "Bargain" office space in a wrong or declining area may prove too troublesome to rent profitably.

## Sample high-rise office building

Today's office buildings are literally small cities, occupied by day when demands for services and utilities are highest. New York's twin 110-story World Trade Center towers can accommodate nearly 50,000 people, for example, in their seven million square feet of space. Chicago's John Hancock Center contains almost 50 stories of office space, topped by 20 stories of condominiums with retail facilities such as a grocery store at the top.

Residents could conceivably live, work, and shop in the same structure. Highly automated elevator and security systems reduce operating personnel, but cleaning services remain excruciatingly labor intensive. Care to apply as window washer?

We will analyze a more typical 35-story office building having 20,000 square feet of gross space per floor. Since lease length on such commercial property is usually quite long—typically between five and ten years and occasionally longer—rents do not keep pace smoothly with inflation as they might with residential properties. However, office leases in many major urban and suburban areas often contain Consumer Price Index escalators that raise rents by a portion of the annual increases in inflation—currently between 25 and 50 percent. Furthermore, rentals can swing widely when leases renew due to local capacity and economic factors. Based on today's land and building costs, current financing costs, and rental rates, many high-rise office buildings must reach occupancy levels of between 75 and 90 percent just to break even, measured in before-tax cash flow.

The New York City office market provides a yo-yo example. Wall Street structures commanded up to $12 per square foot in 1969 but dropped to $8 in 1975. With resurgence of the Big Apple, particularly uptown, due mainly to demand far exceeding the available supply, rents by 1980 had more than doubled their previous high. By late 1981 and early 1982, premium space was demanding as high as $55 per square foot, with rental rates averaging $38.

The key factor values used in Table 9.1 reflect these special considerations of office buildings. Since the initial outlays for a highrise are so huge, the dollar figures are shown in thousands. And while it may take two years or more from ground breaking to rent-check cashing, we have illustrated an operating property. The developer joint-ventured for financing since, for a building of 600,000 rentable square feet, $60 million is required. This represents a total cost including land, construction costs (hard costs), soft costs (commissions, development and financing fees, architectural and space planning fees, legal expenses, insurance, taxes, title, and other expenses of $100 per rentable square foot. Mort-

**TABLE 9.1**
Office building—joint venture

Real Estate Investment Analysis Form—Thirteen Key Factors

Client_____   Phone # _____

Address_____   Project title _____

_____   Years of analysis _____

| | | | |
|---|---|---|---|
| 1. Total project cost | $33,000 | | |

**Mortgage Terms**

| | | | |
|---|---|---|---|
| 2. Mortgage amount (show either $ or %) | $30,000 | or _____ | % of total project cost |
| 3. Interest rate | 12% annually | | |
| 4. Mortgage life | 30 years | | |

**Operating & Inflation Assumptions**

| | | | |
|---|---|---|---|
| 5. Net resale price (today, before inflation, net of transaction costs) | | or 98% | of total project cost |
| 6. Gross income (annually, before inflation, net of vacancy) | $ 5,700 | or _____ | % of total project cost |
| 7. Operating expense (annually, before inflation) | $ 1,800 | or _____ | % of gross income |
| 8. Annual inflation (resale price, income, expense) | 3% resale  2% income  0% expense | | |

**Depreciation**

| | | | |
|---|---|---|---|
| 9. Total depreciable base (not annual amount) | $27,000 | or _____ | % of total project cost |
| 10. Depreciable life | 15 years | 200% for low-income housing | |
| 11. Depreciable rate (percent of straight line) | 100% | 175% for most real estate* 150% for tangible personal property 100% for all other† | |

**Tax Rates**

| | |
|---|---|
| 12. Ordinary income | 50% |
| 13. Capital gains | 20% |

SOURCE: The Mader Group, Inc.
*Usually preferable for nonresidential property.
†Usually preferable for commercial property only because of ERTA recapture provisions.

gages of fairly long duration can be arranged, usually with an insurance company or pension fund. Financing may be contingent on construction completion or certain occupancy goals. For instance, the first 80 percent of the financing may be funded once the construction, except for tenant improvements, is complete. Then the remainder of the loan may become available as the building leases, or once the building reaches 95 percent occupancy. The first portion is called the "floor" loan and the remainder is called the "ceiling." Typically, if certain occupancy achievements are not met within a predetermined time period, the ceiling portion of the loan may never be funded. This adds to the risk of any delay or vacancy problems. In our example, the lender provides all capital, structured as a first mortgage, and also gets a 50 percent ownership. The developer puts up land rights and leaves builder's profit worth $3 million in the deal as his equity.

To determine the key operating factors as seen by the developer, we show only his *half* of the total project cost, including $3 million of equity in foregone opportunity. The mortgage allocation is also half of cash costs, or $30 million. It bears a below-market interest rate, in view of the lender's equity participation.

High gross rents meet operating expenses that run at approximately 30 percent of gross rentals before vacancy, as shown in Table 9.1. Both leasing agents and property managers are typically retained, for instance, and between-tenant remodeling costs are usually necessary. About 15 percent of the gross area goes for unrentable space such as elevators, ventilating shafts, stairways, and main lobbies. Net leasable area rentals of $20 per square foot would then produce about $5,700,000 as the initial rent roll, allowing 5 percent vacancy, and reflecting just the developer's half.

Inflation of 3 percent per year in resale is illustrated, with an allowance of 2 percent for transaction costs to sell. The income stream increases at 2 percent per year representing ten-year leases with a 25 percent CPI escalation clause, with 8 percent assumed inflation and full-expense escalators, meaning all operating expenses and property taxes are paid by the tenants. So the landlord's responsibility for operating expenses and taxes is fixed, except for a possible lag in collecting year-to-year increases from the tenants. A risk, however, would be having to re-lease during a weak market period. Then a decline in income could dry up the developer's cash flow, especially if the available tax shelter could not be applied to offset other taxable income, as assumed by our analysis.

In this example, depreciation is taken on a straight-line basis over 15 years as currently allowed for new commercial construction. Three million dollars for the developer's share of the land cost is assumed. Some mechanical equipment, fixtures, and leasehold improvements would qualify for a shorter life. And certain personal property such as elevators, security and fire control equipment, and certain tenant improvements would normally qualify for investment tax credits—direct offsets against taxes owed. For a joint-ownership vehicle (just a type of partnership), as assumed, the applicable tax rates are the individual partners' brackets, say 50 percent on income and 20 percent on capital gains. Table 9.1 shows all our key factor inputs.

Now take a look at the results of our computerized analysis in Table 9.2 and the risk analysis found in Tables 9.3 and 9.4. How do you interpret this analysis? As always, it's nice to have high income with low expenses, leverage, tax shelter, and appreciation. But commercial property has long leases that limit net operating income increases, and less tax shelter than residential income property. Although 175 percent declining-balance depreciation is allowed for both commercial and residential property, recapture rules favor accelerated over straight line for residential but straight line over accelerated for commercial property.

Total project cost and operating expenses are huge and typically run higher per square foot of space than for a residential building, but so does the rental income. Unless marred by bad location or design, weak local market, or persistent vacancies, an office building should return more than residential property. The risk is that, since breakeven requires high occupancy levels, vacancy problems or lowered income might not cover mortgage payments and operating expenses or that a developer can't use all the tax shelter. Also, changing demand for a location or the building's

TABLE 9.2
Office building—joint venture

KEY OPERATING FACTORS ARE ---

| TOTAL PROJECT COST | ---MORTGAGE TERMS--- | | | ------OPERATING & INFLATION ASSUMPTIONS------ | | | | | | ----DEPRECIATION--- | | | ----TAX RATES--- | |
|---|---|---|---|---|---|---|---|---|---|---|---|---|---|---|
| | AMOUNT | % INTR | LIFE | NET RESALE PRICE | % RESALE INFL | GROSS INCOME INFL | % INCOME INFL | OPERATING EXPENSE | % EXPENSE INFL | AMOUNT | LIFE | RATE | INCOME | CAP GAIN |
| 33000 | 30000 | 12.00 | 30 | 32340 | 3 | 5700 | 2 | 1800 | 0 | 27000 | 15 | 100% | 50% | 20% |

PRE-OPERATING SUMMARY ---

| EQUITY AMOUNT | ----MORTGAGE TERMS---- | | | % NET RESALE TO COST | % INCOME TO COST | GROSS RENT MULT | % EXPENSE TO INCOME | % NOI TO COST | % DEPREC TO COST |
|---|---|---|---|---|---|---|---|---|---|
| | % DEBT | MONTHLY | YEARLY | | | | | | |
| 3000 | 90.91 | 309 | 3703 | 98.0 | 17.3 | 5.8 | 31.6 | 11.8 | 81.8 |

OPERATING RESULTS ---

| YR | ---HOLDING RESULTS BEFORE INCOME TAXES--- | | | | | | ---HOLDING RESULTS AFTER TAXES--- | | | | | ---OVERALL RESULTS IF SOLD AT YEAR END--- | | | | | |
|---|---|---|---|---|---|---|---|---|---|---|---|---|---|---|---|---|---|
| | GROSS INCOME | OPERATE EXPENSE | ---MORTGAGE--- INTR | AMORT | CASH FLOW | % RE TURN | DEPREC IATION | TAXABLE INCOME | TAXES DUE | CASH FLOW | % RE TURN | SALE PRICE | DEBT REPAY | TAXES DUE | CASH FLOW | TOTAL PROFIT | % IRR |
| 1 | 5700 | 1800 | 3594 | 109 | 197 | 6.6 | 1800 | -1494 | -747 | 944 | 31.5 | 33310 | 29891 | 422 | 2997 | 941 | 31.4 |
| 2 | 5814 | 1800 | 3580 | 123 | 311 | 10.4 | 1800 | -1366 | -683 | 994 | 33.1 | 34310 | 29768 | 982 | 3559 | 2497 | 39.9 |
| 3 | 5930 | 1800 | 3565 | 138 | 427 | 14.2 | 1800 | -1234 | -617 | 1045 | 34.8 | 35339 | 29630 | 1548 | 4161 | 4144 | 41.5 |
| 4 | 6049 | 1800 | 3547 | 156 | 546 | 18.2 | 1800 | -1098 | -549 | 1095 | 36.5 | 36399 | 29474 | 2120 | 4805 | 5882 | 41.6 |
| 5 | 6170 | 1800 | 3527 | 176 | 667 | 22.2 | 1800 | -958 | -479 | 1146 | 38.2 | 37491 | 29299 | 2698 | 5494 | 7717 | 41.2 |
| 6 | 6293 | 1800 | 3505 | 198 | 790 | 26.3 | 1800 | -812 | -406 | 1196 | 39.9 | 38616 | 29101 | 3283 | 6231 | 9651 | 40.6 |
| 7 | 6419 | 1800 | 3480 | 223 | 916 | 30.5 | 1800 | -661 | -331 | 1247 | 41.6 | 39774 | 28878 | 3875 | 7021 | 11687 | 40.0 |
| 8 | 6548 | 1800 | 3452 | 251 | 1045 | 34.8 | 1800 | -504 | -252 | 1297 | 43.2 | 40967 | 28627 | 4473 | 7867 | 13830 | 39.5 |
| 9 | 6678 | 1800 | 3420 | 283 | 1175 | 39.2 | 1800 | -342 | -171 | 1346 | 44.9 | 42196 | 28344 | 5079 | 8773 | 16082 | 39.0 |
| 10 | 6812 | 1800 | 3384 | 319 | 1309 | 43.6 | 1800 | -172 | -86 | 1395 | 46.5 | 43462 | 28025 | 5692 | 9744 | 18449 | 38.6 |

Reprinted with the permission of The Mader Group, Inc., Narberth, PA.

TABLE 9.3
Office building—joint venture
Sensitivity analysis results—revised key factor value at end of year and resulting IRR due to change of

| | 10% | -10% | 10% | -10% | -10% | -10% | 10% | -10% | 10% | -10% | -10% | 10% |
|---|---|---|---|---|---|---|---|---|---|---|---|---|
| | TOTAL PROJECT COST | ---MORTGAGE TERMS--- | | | --------OPERATING ASSUMPTIONS-------- | | | ---DEPRECIATION--- | | | ---TAX RATES--- | |
| | | AMOUNT | % INTR | LIFE | NET RESALE PRICE | GROSS INCOME | OPERATING EXPENSE | AMOUNT | LIFE | TYPE | INCOME | CAP GAIN |
| | 36300. | 27000. | 13.20 | 27.0 | 29979. | 5130. | 1980. | 24300. | 16.5 | 90.00 | 45.0 | 22.0 |
| 1 | -27.0 | 18.7 | 25.3 | 31.4 | -57.5 | 21.9 | 28.4 | 29.5 | 29.7 | 31.4 | 28.9 | 29.9 |
| 2 | -1.2 | 23.3 | 34.2 | 39.7 | -5.0 | 30.7 | 37.0 | 38.0 | 38.2 | 39.9 | 37.6 | 38.6 |
| 3 | 8.5 | 24.6 | 36.2 | 41.1 | 17.3 | 32.6 | 38.8 | 39.5 | 39.7 | 41.5 | 39.4 | 40.4 |
| 4 | 13.3 | 25.0 | 36.5 | 41.0 | 27.3 | 33.0 | 38.9 | 39.5 | 39.7 | 41.6 | 39.6 | 40.7 |
| 5 | 16.0 | 25.1 | 36.3 | 40.5 | 32.1 | 32.8 | 38.6 | 39.1 | 39.2 | 41.2 | 39.3 | 40.5 |
| 6 | 17.6 | 25.1 | 36.0 | 39.8 | 34.6 | 32.5 | 38.1 | 38.5 | 38.7 | 40.6 | 38.8 | 40.0 |
| 7 | 18.6 | 25.1 | 35.6 | 39.1 | 35.9 | 32.0 | 37.6 | 37.9 | 38.1 | 40.0 | 38.3 | 39.6 |
| 8 | 19.3 | 24.9 | 35.1 | 38.5 | 36.6 | 31.6 | 37.1 | 37.3 | 37.5 | 39.5 | 37.8 | 39.1 |
| 9 | 19.7 | 24.8 | 34.7 | 38.0 | 36.9 | 31.2 | 36.6 | 36.8 | 37.0 | 39.0 | 37.4 | 38.7 |
| 10 | 20.0 | 24.7 | 34.4 | 37.5 | 37.0 | 30.8 | 36.2 | 36.4 | 36.6 | 38.6 | 37.0 | 38.4 |

Reprinted with the permission of The Mader Group, Inc., Narberth, PA.

TABLE 9.4
Office building—joint venture
Sensitivity analysis results—change in key factor value and resulting change in IRR (sensitivity minus original)

| | TOTAL PROJECT COST | ---MORTGAGE TERMS--- | | | NET RESALE PRICE | ---------OPERATING ASSUMPTIONS--------- | | ----DEPRECIATION---- | | | ---TAX RATES--- | |
|---|---|---|---|---|---|---|---|---|---|---|---|---|
| | | AMOUNT | % INTR | LIFE | | GROSS INCOME | OPERATING EXPENSE | AMOUNT | LIFE | TYPE | INCOME | CAP GAIN |
| | 3300. | -3000. | 1.20 | -3.0 | -3331. | -570. | 180. | -2700. | 1.5 | -10.00 | -5.0 | 2.0 |
| 1 | -58.3 | -12.7 | -6.0 | 0.0 | -88.8 | -9.5 | -3.0 | -1.8 | -1.7 | 0.0 | -2.5 | -1.4 |
| 2 | -41.2 | -16.6 | -5.7 | -0.2 | -45.0 | -9.2 | -2.9 | -1.9 | -1.7 | -0.0 | -2.3 | -1.3 |
| 3 | -33.0 | -17.0 | -5.3 | -0.4 | -24.2 | -8.9 | -2.8 | -2.0 | -1.8 | -0.0 | -2.1 | -1.1 |
| 4 | -28.2 | -16.5 | -5.0 | -0.5 | -14.3 | -8.6 | -2.7 | -2.1 | -1.9 | 0.0 | -2.0 | -0.9 |
| 5 | -25.1 | -16.0 | -4.8 | -0.7 | -9.0 | -8.3 | -2.6 | -2.1 | -1.9 | -0.0 | -1.9 | -0.7 |
| 6 | -23.0 | -15.5 | -4.6 | -0.8 | -6.0 | -8.1 | -2.5 | -2.1 | -1.9 | -0.0 | -1.8 | -0.6 |
| 7 | -21.4 | -15.0 | -4.5 | -0.9 | -4.1 | -8.0 | -2.5 | -2.2 | -2.0 | 0.0 | -1.7 | -0.5 |
| 8 | -20.2 | -14.6 | -4.4 | -1.0 | -2.9 | -7.9 | -2.4 | -2.2 | -2.0 | -0.0 | -1.7 | -0.4 |
| 9 | -19.3 | -14.2 | -4.3 | -1.1 | -2.1 | -7.9 | -2.4 | -2.2 | -2.0 | 0.0 | -1.6 | -0.3 |
| 10 | -18.6 | -13.9 | -4.2 | -1.1 | -1.5 | -7.8 | -2.4 | -2.2 | -2.0 | -0.0 | -1.6 | -0.2 |

Reprinted with the permission of The Mader Group, Inc., Narberth, PA.

functional obsolescence can retard its resale price. Without additional cash, you could be forced to sell disadvantageously. On the other hand, high rents driving up initial lease-up or at lease renewal time can result in huge increases in the value of an office building.

It takes big bucks and professional management to play the office building game—something to try with your *second* million. And structures of the size illustrated above are the province of large developers, corporations, and major financial institutions. Only a very few individuals have the assets and expertise to consider high-rise office investments. However, syndication can bring these opportunities within the ownership scope of investors participating as a group.

## Shopping center

Stores and shopping centers, be they community *strip malls* or giant regional *enclosed malls*, also attract sophisticated owners. The risks are moderate when dealing with triple-A credit-rated tenants on long-term leases. Financing, however, is often relatively short (20 years) because of the specialized structures and potential for new, nearby competition. Tax shelter is limited. Much of the investment is attributable to nondepreciable land. So why invest?

Store leases frequently include *overage*, or a percentage of the occupant's sales if that exceeds the fixed minimum rent. So the task is to be the first and timed with development (not ahead of it). Then pick the right location, get a good participation, and ride it with inflation. To produce steadily rising rents, most centers prelease to reliable "anchor" stores, such as a department store, giant discounter, or a food and drugstore pair. They are important traffic builders and consequently will pay low rents—roughly breakeven. Your profits stem from the overage on growing sales and from the many smaller specialty shops that gather to serve the attracted traffic—and pay higher rents.

Shopping center owners have done well in the past two decades. Such property is almost synonymous with shopping-by-auto and suburban sprawl. Rezoning and rising land values have contributed to their hefty gains. Inflation has driven up their overage rent receipts with pleasing regularity. But hindsight can be like looking in a mirror. It shows what is going on behind you as if it were in front, while obscuring what truly lies ahead. Will we see a shift to the cities, mass transit, shopping-by-computer, and below-zero population growth? Place your bets.

## Distribution warehouse

A distribution warehouse, situated in a zoned industrial park with good transportation access, is usually leasable and appreciates nicely. Trammell Crow, the respected Dallas entrepreneur, initially specialized in this type of development.

A warehouse facility is typically dedicated to one or a few tenants who can control its use, so a "triple net" lease is often written so that the user pays the taxes, operating expenses including maintenance, and insurance. This keeps down the owner's management time as well as his operating risk. The goal is a stream of leveraged, tax-sheltered cash flow with inflation/appreciation in the property's collateral value and sale price. The big risk lies in the fact that these types of properties are usually leased by one (single purpose) or just a few tenants. Thus, failure to find "the tenant" or the risk of your single user going "belly up" (bankrupt) can leave you with an entire building unleased, with some operating costs, taxes, and financing costs continually payable. A long lease-up period can easily cause a great strain on an investor's liquidity, with potential foreclosure right around the corner.

Other significant differences exist in the economies of a typical warehouse versus an office building or shopping center. Warehouses are inexpensive and quickly built. With a quality, financially strong long-term tenant, mortgage credit is more easily obtainable. A general-purpose building, usually with standard 20-foot ceiling heights, sprinklers, 5 percent office space, and rail access might be built on "spec," without a tenant. Even if subdivided, these buildings yield a much lower gross income per square foot than office space but also have lower operating expenses. In view of the low project cost, however, this produces an acceptable "% NOI to total," or Level 1 rate of return.

Leverage, tax shelter, and inflation add the remainder of return. Straight-line depreciation is allowed with a 15-year life. Recapture rules are the same as for office buildings. Also, if cheap outlying land is used, the depreciation amount can be as high as 95 percent of the total project cost. This positive effect is augmented by inflation in lease rates, given a strong market. To maintain high leverage, a somewhat earlier sale or refinancing of the distribution warehouse may be in order.

A recent nationwide phenomenon—though over ten years old in California—is the public "mini-warehouse." Spaces roughly the size of a garage are offered to consumers on a month-to-month basis. Rentals prove to be very high on a per-square-foot basis for storage space which is typically used for boats, furniture, equipment, and the like. Office and retail tenants can store inventory and less often used supplies at substantially lower rates than what they pay at their main location. One tenant just used it for peace and quiet on weekends as a hobby shop and for reading. The low-cost structure allows high returns, but a visible location and large-scale operation are needed to cover marketing. Security can also pose a problem.

## Resort property

This final example of commercial and industrial property represents highly specialized facilities. Thus risks and potential rewards are highest here. Whether it be indoor tennis courts, beach club, motel, restuarant, bowling alley, or parking garage, you are marketing a *service* first and investing in real estate second. Success depends primarily on the business rather than on construction, financing, or property-management expertise. Our illustration consists of an actual situation, including the limited partnership syndicate formed to do the deal. But first let's explain what a syndication is and what purpose it serves.

## Syndication

This form of ownership organizes many investors and pools their funds. Small groups (often five or fewer) may buy a single property in this manner. Often the organizer acts as the general partner, and other investors have a limited control and liability status. More visible, however, are the large syndications, such as those publicized and offered by large brokerage houses.

For example, JMB Realty of Chicago has pooled the funds of more than 35,000 investors into several "public" limited partnerships and a few dozen "private" ones. The distinction is that publicly offered interests are deemed to be securities and must be registered with the federal Securities and Exchange Commission, and with state agencies. Also, suitability for the investor must be assured—usually by his or her affirmation of sufficient income and net worth to absorb the tax shelter provided.

The raised funds, net of selling commissions and the organizer's fee, are invested in real estate. JMB chooses a mix of office, shopping center, warehouse, and apartment buildings and favors Sun Belt locations. Its subsidiaries arrange the property purchase, financing, and management, plus eventual resale when thought timely. Standard industry fees are charged. This provides close control of the syndicate's diverse property portfolio and of the individual investor's account with the partnership. A syndicate's sizable pool of capital and economies of scale allow it to consider larger, specialized deals. In evaluating a syndication, the most important factor to consider is the general partner and his track record. Focus on the fees or percentage ownership being paid to him or his affiliates and then the investment itself. Read on for a discussion of a particular example of a syndication deal of a resort property that we looked at years ago.

In the early 1970s, an innovative proposal was presented to the partners of a prestigious investment banking firm. A city-owned, unused, riverside pier structure would be leased and renovated for indoor tennis. Land so near the city center was prohibited for this use, so why not locate over water? The investment proposal was accepted.

The development firm became the general partner, and the investment banker and its clients put up the major equity and became limited partners. Work was initiated on the eight-court facility, but ran nearly 7 percent over budget by completion. To their chagrin, a schedule slippage crimped three weeks from the first 30-week prime season and disgruntled the newly enrolled members. Worse still, the city slowed completion of the adjacent highway while designing out the two exit ramps nearest the subject site. Attempting to avoid the highway construction or crossing the highway from the nearby residential developments was like rushing the net while facing a slam.

The developer's projected profitability and risk were based on 70, 80, and 90 percent occupancy levels for the eight courts, using a 15-hour day and a seven-day week. Other courts in the region, which were neither numerous nor close by, were packed from 8:00 A.M. until midnight. Suffice it to say that for the first two years court utilization averaged only 50 percent. This was below breakeven, after operating expenses and payments on the pier lease and ten-year leasehold improvement loan. The third year was nicely profitable, however, due to revamped marketing and creation of a pier-front parking alcove. And today, ten years later, the adjacent highway has just been completed.

What is the lesson? As verified in psychological research, people tend to underestimate risk. Optimism kept the organizers and investors from projecting the results of such low occupancy. A 70, 80, or 90 percent occupancy seemed more likely. But uncontrollable business risks often occur—the stock market's gyrations prove that. These amplify, and for specialized property, often outweigh the real estate risks, such as the construction cost and time overruns. With tennis booming nationwide, and indoor play gaining devotees during both winter and summer, it was difficult *not* to make money on indoor courts. Instead, this case documents the risk of a specialized facility and underscores the need for a thorough analysis.

Based on this hard-won experience, the tennis-court operator decided in the mid-1970s to try it again. A four-court facility in

TABLE 9.5
Example: limited partnership investment proposal
(For instructional use only. Not an offering or solicitation)

Sundance Tennis Courts
A four-court tennis facility located in Rutland, Vermont.
Cash Flow Analysis (assumed 70% capacity)

| Operations | | |
|---|---|---|
| Revenues: | | |
| Membership fees | $ 10,500 | |
| Court time | 124,110 | |
| Pro shop | 20,050 | |
| Refreshments and miscellaneous | 6,020 | |
| Total revenues | | 160,680 |
| Expenses: | | |
| Insurance | 2,000 | |
| Management | 10,000 | |
| Staff | 6,580 | |
| Benefits (15%) | 2,490 | |
| Maintenance | 4,350 | |
| Materials | 1,800 | |
| Light and heat | 25,020 | |
| Advertising and printing | 3,000 | |
| Legal and accounting | 1,500 | |
| Real estate taxes | 12,000 | |
| Office and miscellaneous | 6,500 | |
| Total expenses | | 75,240 |
| Operational net income | | 85,440 |
| Mortgage constant @ 10%, 20 years | | 57,900 |
| Cash flow in excess of expenses and debt service | | $ 27,540 |

SOURCE: Landtect Corporation, 1616 Walnut Street, Philadelphia, PA

a medium-sized New England town was available. The following case shows the projections and financial analysis provided to prospective syndicate investors.

Table 9.5 shows a "typical" year analysis. Note that to affirm these estimates, one would have to *know this service business*. For a $10,000 or so participation, could you economically investigate these particulars? In this business? Out of your town? Most investors, therefore, rely on the experience, integrity, and incentives of the general partner when reviewing such proposals.

Table 9.6 is a risk analysis, of sorts, around the key variable of occupancy. Notice the range it assumes—from 55 to 100 per-

TABLE 9.6
Sundance Tennis Courts, Rutland, Vermont
Sensitivity analysis

|  | OCCUPANCY RATE | | | | | |
|---|---|---|---|---|---|---|
| REVENUES: | 100% | 90% | 80% | 70% | 60% | 55% |
| Court Time – Winter | $134,100 | $120,690 | $107,280 | $ 93,870 | $ 80,460 | $ 73,755 |
| Court Time – Summer | 43,200 | 38,900 | 34,560 | 30,240 | 25,920 | 23,760 |
| Memberships | 15,000 | 13,500 | 12,000 | 10,500 | 9,000 | 8,250 |
| Pro Shop | 28,640 | 25,780 | 22,910 | 20,050 | 17,180 | 15,750 |
| Refreshments and Miscellaneous | 8,600 | 7,740 | 6,880 | 6,020 | 5,160 | 4,730 |
| Total Revenue | $229,540 | $206,610 | $183,630 | $160,680 | $137,720 | $126,245 |
| EXPENSES: | | | | | | |
| Manager | $ 10,000 | $ 10,000 | $ 10,000 | $ 10,000 | $ 10,000 | $ 10,000 |
| Assistants | 6,580 | 6,580 | 6,580 | 6,580 | 6,580 | 6,580 |
| Benefits | 2,490 | 2,490 | 2,490 | 2,490 | 2,490 | 2,490 |
| Maintenance | 4,750 | 4,750 | 4,350 | 4,350 | 4,350 | 4,250 |
| Materials | 2,000 | 2,000 | 1,800 | 1,800 | 1,800 | 1,800 |
| Light and Heat | 32,340 | 29,900 | 27,460 | 25,020 | 22,580 | 21,360 |
| Insurance | 2,000 | 2,000 | 2,000 | 2,000 | 2,000 | 2,000 |
| Advertising and Printing | 3,000 | 3,000 | 3,000 | 3,000 | 2,000 | 2,000 |
| Legal and Accounting | 1,500 | 1,500 | 1,500 | 1,500 | 1,500 | 1,500 |
| Real Estate Taxes | 12,000 | 12,000 | 12,000 | 12,000 | 12,000 | 12,000 |
| Office and Miscellaneous | 6,500 | 6,500 | 6,500 | 6,500 | 6,500 | 6,500 |
| Total Expenses (excl. depr. & int.) | $ 83,160 | $ 80,720 | $ 77,680 | $ 75,240 | $ 72,300 | $ 70,980 |
| Cash Flow Before Debt Service | 146,380 | 125,890 | 105,950 | 85,440 | 65,420 | 55,265 |
| Debt Service | 57,900 | 57,900 | 57,900 | 57,900 | 57,900 | 57,900 |
| Cash Flow | $ 88,480 | $ 67,990 | $ 48,050 | $ 27,540 | $ 7,520 | $( 2,635) |

percent. Results for revenue, operating income, and cash flow after debt service indicate that 70 percent occupancy is expected. However, in these syndicator-provided figures, are you skeptical of any budgeted items and the fixed/variable costs? Is staff compensation sufficient? Can pro shop sales be that high and where is the cost of goods sold? Would *you* cut advertising at low occupancy? *Can* you cut the heat bill significantly on unused courts?

Table 9.7 shows a total return calculation, wherein the syndicator footnoted certain inflation assumptions. For example, income and expense were expected to rise sharply until 70 percent occupancy, then climb further thereafter. Footnote 9 implies a resale value after ten years of over $1 million, or ten times the net operating income for that year. The cash flow from holding, plus the equity recouped from resale, are shown.

We've asked seminar participants about this case during 50-plus meetings of the Real Estate Investment Analysis seminar sponsored by The Wharton School. Invariably, there is skepticism about the financial assumptions reflected in Tables 9.5 through 9.7. (Arizona residents even wonder why anyone would go *indoors* to play tennis!)

Yet this partnership was sold, and in the last year it was possible to do so—1975. Since then, the revised tax law has required that partnership losses, prepaid interest, and upfront fees be calculated on the *accrual* method of accounting. That is, deductions must be prorated over the owner's holding period. Also, construction interest is no longer tax deductible during the development period but must be capitalized for later write-off. So when we ask seminar participants, "Who would buy this offering because they have the money, like tax shelters, and believe the analysis?" they answer, in chorus, "Doctors!"

## Summary

Commercial and industrial property can provide higher returns and risks than residential income property. Its more specialized nature and typically larger scale make it the province of sophisiticated, experienced investors. Financing may be subject

## TABLE 9.7
### Sundance Tennis Courts, Rutland, Vermont
Projected cash flow—70% usage

| YEAR (SEPT–AUG) | REVENUES (1) | OPERATING EXPENSES (1) | AVAILABLE FOR DEBT SERVICE | INTEREST (2) | PRINCIPAL (2) | CASH FLOW | DEPRECIATION (3) | TAXABLE INCOME | INCOME TAXES (4) | CASH FLOW LESS TAXES (5) |
|---|---|---|---|---|---|---|---|---|---|---|
| 1976 (Mar–Aug) | (Const. Period) | $20,000 (6) | – | $25,000 (7) | – | | | $(45,000) | $(22,500) | $ 22,500 (8) |
| 1976-77 | $126,245 | 70,980 | $ 55,265 | 50,000 | $ 7,900 | $(2,635) | $26,250 | (20,985) | (10,493) | 7,858 |
| 1977-78 | 149,195 | 73,770 | 75,425 | 49,210 | 8,690 | 17,525 | 24,938 | 1,277 | 639 | 16,886 |
| 1978-79 | 160,680 | 75,240 | 85,440 | 48,341 | 9,559 | 27,540 | 23,690 | 13,409 | 6,705 | 20,835 |
| 1979-80 | 168,714 | 79,002 | 89,712 | 47,385 | 10,515 | 31,812 | 22,506 | 19,821 | 9,911 | 21,901 |
| 1980-81 | 168,714 | 79,002 | 89,712 | 46,334 | 11,566 | 31,812 | 21,381 | 21,997 | 10,999 | 20,813 |
| 1981-82 | 177,150 | 82,952 | 94,198 | 45,177 | 12,723 | 36,298 | 20,312 | 28,709 | 14,355 | 21,943 |
| 1982-83 | 177,150 | 82,952 | 94,198 | 43,905 | 13,995 | 36,298 | 19,296 | 30,997 | 15,499 | 20,799 |
| 1983-84 | 186,007 | 87,100 | 98,907 | 42,505 | 15,395 | 41,007 | 18,331 | 38,071 | 19,036 | 21,971 |
| 1984-85 | 186,007 | 87,100 | 98,907 | 40,966 | 16,934 | 41,007 | 17,415 | 40,526 | 20,263 | 20,744 |
| 1985-86 | 195,308 | 91,455 | 103,853 | 39,272 | 18,628 | 45,953 | 16,544 | 48,037 | 24,019 | 21,934 |
| 1986 | (Sale of Project for 10 X Cash Flow Before Debt Service) | | | | | | | | | 378,263 (9) |

1) Assumes 55% usage 1st year, 65% 2nd year, 70% 3rd year, and increases in revenues and expenses of 5% every other year.

2) Assumes $500,000., 10%, 20 year mortgage ($57,900/year).

3) Assumes $525,000 depreciable value, 150% declining balance method, 30 year life.

4) Assumes 50% Tax Rate.

5) Total Return; negative taxes counted as positive return.

6) Developer's Fees

7) $525,000 x 12% x 6 months x 1/2 average, plus financing fees

8) Total construction period tax savings

9) Net Proceeds Calculation:

| | | |
|---|---|---|
| Sale Price | | $1,040,000 |
| Less: 6% Commission | | 62,400 |
| Net Price | | 977,600 |
| Less Mtge. Pymt. | $374,095 (10) | |
| Taxes | 225,242 (11) | 599,337 |
| Net Proceeds | | $ 378,263 |

10) Mortgage Payment:
| | |
|---|---|
| Original Mortgage | $500,000 |
| Principal Repayments | 125,905 |
| Balance Due | $374,095 |

11) Tax Calculations:
| | |
|---|---|
| Total Depreciation Taken | $210,663 |
| S/L Depreciation, 10 yrs. | 175,000 |
| | $ 35,663 x .50 = $17,832 (Ordinary) |

Book Values
| | | |
|---|---|---|
| Original | $525,000 | |
| S/L Depreciation | 175,000 | |
| Book Value – Improvements | 350,000 | |
| Land | 35,000 | |
| Book Value | 385,000 | |

| | | |
|---|---|---|
| Net Sales Price | 977,600 | |
| Book Value | 385,000 | |
| Capital Gain | 592,600 | |
| Capital Gain Rate | x .35 | |
| Capital Gains Tax | $207,410 | $207,410 |
| | | $225,242  Total Tax |

to occupancy goals and minimum standards on lease quality and may involve joint ventures. The construction cycle can be lengthy with interior finishing and renovation surprisingly costly. And single-purpose properties, such as manufacturing facilities or resorts, are particularly illiquid.

An attractive, well-located building leased during good economic times can do very well. But overbuilding, especially in mature urban markets, can drop rental rates sharply or produce sustained high vacancies. Demand for commercial and industrial space simply is *not* as responsive to price cutting as is residential property. A business operation has too many other considerations that dominate minor changes in rental expenses.

If you can ensure occupancy, as in a small office building occupied by your own firm, then owning may be especially favorable. Longer-term leases and a longer holding period should be a part of your plan. If you want to operate a service, such as a motel, restaurant, or resort facility, then business success or lack of it dominates the real estate aspects of your investment. The investor profiles best met by commercial and industrial property seem to be those of the wealthy or the occupant-owner. Syndication is a good vehicle for passive, smaller-scale participation in this marketplace, but study the record of the organizers as well as their property portfolio.

# 10 Land Investing and Development

Will Rogers once said, "Buy land. They aren't making any more of it." Not a particularly funny line for Will and not particularly true, either. For example, *Forbes* magazine once noted that "at least 25 percent of Manhattan Island has been created by landfill"—a "New Amsterdam" even the Dutch would be proud of. Malcolm Forbes himself has been selling off land sites for development at his 250,000-acre Trinchera Ranch in southern Colorado. It is such new-land *use* that creates investment values, and this goes on all the time.

## Why own land?

To this point, we have focused on analyzing income property. Usually, rental income offsets both the operating expenses and debt service, providing a residual cash flow. Then depreciation acts to shield this return from taxation. Even if 1980s-style interest rates cause debt service to consume all the net operating income, income property should still provide a positive after-tax cash flow.

Some land generates income from crops, timber, grazing, a driving range, sod farm, or whatever. But these are essentially specialized businesses, like the indoor tennis courts discussed in Chapter 9. They require operating skills and the marketing of a product or service to get the income. The landowner may lease his or her acreage to remain a passive investor, but its rentable value then depends on its usefulness to others. So land derives income only from operations using it, or none at all.

Land is also held for appreciation. Your yard or neighboring wooded lot yields personal satisfaction, perhaps, but we will focus on economic objectives. Upgrading the usefulness of land, plus inflation, is the source of its capital gain. But in the absence of current income, this appreciation must generate *all* of the return as well as cover carrying costs during the holding period. When leveraging land with little equity, delays in upgrading have a magnified impact on return. Leveraged land investment, analyzed in Table 10.1, is the most volatile way to invest in real estate.

TABLE 10.1
Total returns from land doubling in market value

Assume land doubles in value during the time periods shown. Then, the after-tax, annualized, total rate of return is as listed for the various leverage levels. (A land loan of 12$\frac{1}{2}$ percent interest only is assumed. No income, annual expense of 2 percent of purchase cost, 10 percent selling costs, and capital gains taxes at 20 percent are assumed except for a one-year holding period where ordinary taxation at 50 percent is assumed.)

| Years to Double | Leverage Level (Percent Financed) | | | | |
|---|---|---|---|---|---|
| | 0% | 50% | 70% | 80% | 90% |
| 1 | 39.0 | 71.7 | 115.4 | 170.0 | 333.7 |
| 2 | 27.1 | 44.1 | 63.0 | 82.9 | 128.4 |
| 3 | 17.0 | 25.1 | 33.6 | 41.8 | 58.5 |
| 5 | 9.4 | 11.6 | 9.3 | 15.8 | 19.2 |
| 7 | 6.2 | 6.2 | 6.2 | 6.2 | 6.2 |
| 10 | 3.8 | 2.2 | 0.8 | −0.4 | −2.1 |

## Land and inflation

"You can't go wrong buying land." It's a common euphemism but untrue. People *expect* land to rise in price and it almost always does. But with only moderate appreciation (10 percent per year) or even with good growth (15 percent per year), the carrying costs can prove damaging, if not devastating. Add to this the typically higher transaction costs, such as sales commissions, and the investment can prove mediocre, even if held several years. Figure 10.1 shows the total return (all from capital gain, not income) from various rates of land appreciaition/inflation. It reveals that return is very sensitive to both the holding period and the inflation factor. Note, however, that these returns are achieved with 12½ percent fixed-rate, interest-only financing—a far cry from land loan rates that have floated typically two to three points over the prime rate, which has stayed between 12 percent and 22 percent for the most part of the early 80s. Since most land produces little or no income, a great deal of cash is normally required to carry leveraged land until capital gains can be realized. This is where the major risk lies. Nevertheless, many fortunes have been made in land throughout history.

FIGURE 10.1
Land investing and inflation/appreciation

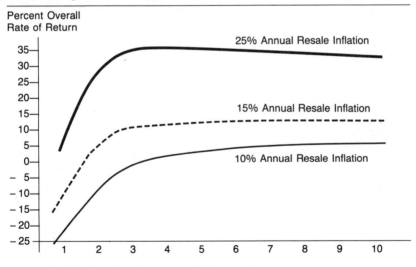

Percent Overall
Rate of Return

25% Annual Resale Inflation

15% Annual Resale Inflation

10% Annual Resale Inflation

- 75% interest-only mortgage at 12.5%.
- 10% selling costs
- 2% per year expenses

Despite the success stories of some speculators, unless you are in the path of immediate development (perhaps undertaken by yourself), land values rise *gradually*. Land that appreciates due only to inflation, say at 10 percent, is not profitable when it must carry a mortgage. The 15 percent appreciation curve shows that economic upgrading of the land's actual or potential use can produce modest profitability. But even faster appreciation rates verify the speculators' war stories. When financed with very high leverage and correctly timed, spurting land prices can indeed make millionaires of modest investors. This is the happy side of land investing and development, as you can see in Figure 10.1.

## Five fortunes made in land

Five strategies for investing in land will be discussed, with each illustrated by an actual case example. They are:
1. Farmland purchase, for operation or lease.
2. Land speculation, with quick resale.
3. Land accumulation and packaging.
4. Long-term land investment.
5. Land development and resale.

### Farmland

The largest single land-use category is agricultural. Of two billion acres of land in the United States (excluding Alaska), one billion acres are used in farming. During 1980, the average price per acre was $550 to $600. For perspective, this aggregate farmland value—two thirds of a *trillion* dollars—roughly equals the value of all common stocks listed on the New York Stock Exchange.

Appreciation in farmland reflects inflation and specific grain and livestock prices. Thus, prices rose gently in the 25-year post–World War II period through 1970. Then inflation took off in the 1970s, coupled with a worldwide grain-price explosion. These twin effects dramatically multiplied the value of farmland, as shown in Figure 10.2. Owners in the Midwest's corn and soybean belt enjoyed both the sharpest percentage increase and the highest land values—exceeding $3,000 per acre for prime parcels. With the flattening out of grain prices in 1981 and 1982, farmland prices have also flattened, and even fallen in some cases.

---

FIGURE 10.2
Average value per acre: farmland

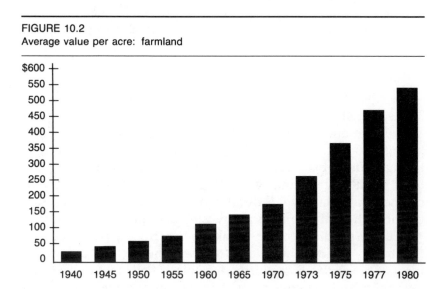

---

Nearly all farmland is bought by individuals. Partnerships and corporations recently accounted for only one-seventh of farm buyers. And the much-discussed foreign buying sums to only 1 or 2 percent of farmland owned by noncitizens. Farmland financing is also an individual affair, with half of farmland being seller financed. One fourth of needed buyer credit—about a half million loans altogether—comes from the Federal Land Bank, an association supervised by the Farm Credit Adminstration, an independent federal agency. The remaining fourth of land loans are from conventional sources such as banks and insurance companies.

As with real estate, investment returns consist of net operating income (NOI) and capital gains or losses. Taxation effects, transaction costs, and inflation must be included, of course. Farmland, when rented for cash, yields only 4 percent or so of the land's current value. If leased under a 50-50 crop sharing arrangement (with greater risk to the owner), a 5 percent yield might result. Clearly, the rest of the return is expected from appreciation. At today's required rates of return, in view of bond and mortgage yields, for example, appreciation of 10 percent annually or more is already factored into investors' thinking and into farmland prices.

## Land speculation

The speculator, in land or other commodities, pits his or her knowledge and judgment against that of the seller and other potential buyers in the marketplace. He or she hopes that risk taking, differential knowledge or analysis, unpublicized negotiations, creative financing, or similar factors will produce an extraordinary rate of return. Naturally, timing is crucial. It is said that the definition of a long-term investor is a speculator who lost.

In the first edition of this book we described a parcel of land that nearly doubled in a year because of nearby rapid development of the Dallas-Fort Worth Metroplex—then a new airport/industrial complex. Similar opportunities also existed in the late 1970s.

Another example, cited by a seminar participant, involved the changing land use in Southern California's Orange County area following the sale of the Irvine Ranch and its subsequent rapid development. Raw land suitable for light industrial property doubled from one dollar to two dollars per square foot. Remaining raw land in the area now goes for as much as $7 per square foot. Developed land, with proper zoning, onsite utilities, and transportation access jumped from $2 to $4 per square foot in little over a year. Fully improved land in the original Irvine Ranch has recently sold for as much as $19 per square foot.

This appreciation far exceeded the inflation in development costs because the rate of fresh demand outpaced the regulation- and leadtime-constrained rate of new supply. (On the country's other coastline, land speculation also surged in Atlantic City's new beachfront gambling center when regulations changed and timing became key.)

## Land packaging

If it succeeds, land packaging is another route to riches. This is the concept of buying at wholesale and selling at retail, usually to a new class of user. Land is purchased or optioned—possibly in secret and over a few years—until a suitable contiguous *package* is controlled, sometimes called land assemblage. Then plans are announced for upgrading, redevelopment, or new construction. The pieces or the entire property are then resold at values reflecting the now-possible high usefulness of the land. Alternately, as at Disney World in Florida, the land can be held for income from business operations rather than resold.

Zeckendorf is a name that, among real estate aficionados, sparks images of daring, creativity, and ultimately, bankruptcy. In perhaps his most famous deal, William Zeckendorf used land packaging for profit and publicity. He noticed that midtown land on Manhattan's East River, while close to the city center, was used for a slaughterhouse district that lowered neighboring land values. But take away the smell and that area *and its neighborhood* would suddenly be more valuable.

Zeckendorf's plan was to upgrade this land by development consistent with a higher use. But control of the whole district was necessary and adjacent purchases were also desirable. Working covertly, he acquired properties at $17 and up per square foot. A few blocks west, Grand Central and Fifth Avenue locations then commanded up to $300 per square foot. Prime locations in mid-town have recently sold for as much as $2,000 per square foot (that's almost $100 million per acre—incredible!). The surprising, dramatic conclusion was that the United Nations, which had just abandoned efforts to find a suitable urban site, was offered the package for a mere $2 million profit. The Rockefellers, donors of the land under the U.N., jumped at the chance and the resale was negotiated within a week.

## Long-term land investment

This fourth strategy has the least risk but requires the most patience and staying power. A long-term land investor usually sustains a negative cash flow until the property is developed to generate income or is resold. Yet fabulous capital gains can be produced over decades of inflation/appreciation. And our tax structure encourages exactly this type of holding, since expenses are immediately deductible against ordinary income while capital gains taxes are at lower rates and deferred until realized.

One extremely successful holding, producing a 200-fold capital gain, was made by Philadelphia's Seltzer family. In addition to their industrial land holdings in northern New Jersey's metropolitan suburbs, the Seltzers had owned some acreage adjacent to Philadelphia's city line. The parcel, situated between the city and its Main Line residential suburb, lay on a plateau overlooking the river—and the subsequently developed expressway—as it flowed into town. Originally bought for $1,000 an acre in 1934, the last acre was sold in 1972 for $200,000.

The magnitude of a 200-fold multiple seems staggering until we compute the compound annual rate of return involved. The 38-year holding period is one that aggressive youths or habitual speculators will find hard to comprehend. It literally spans a working lifetime, say from age 24 to 62. Yet reduced to a compound annual rate of return, the result is 14.9 percent per year.[1] This is hardly staggering, though very good indeed. Furthermore, property taxes and other holding costs would lower this rate of return. On the other hand, any leverage used would have improved the return on equity. And such long-term gains enjoy favored tax treatment.

We can put long-term investing into further perspective by recalling the case of Manhattan Island itself. Purchased in 1624 for $24, it has appreciated at only 6 percent compounded annually during the intervening 356 years. But this produces a land value of perhaps $25 billion today! (If the Indians had bought $24 worth of certificates of deposit at 8 percent, they would now be way ahead—before taxes and other forms of expropriation, of course.)

The conclusion? Land almost certainly appreciates over time. Whether bought for farmland operations or short-term speculative gain, repackaged for a higher economic use, or held for the long pull, profit opportunities exist. But the question is: Will the land appreciate *fast enough* to produce worthwhile profits? And staying power is required to pay ongoing taxes and expenses—and high interest costs if leveraged.

Most of all, patience provides impressive rewards. Ask the thankful third-generation descendants of property-owning Californians, or second-generation Floridians, or first-generation Hawaiians about the wealth produced by land and time. While the rates of appreciation may vary, and some will get high, quicker returns, long-term land investing usually provides only moderate profitability. Still, even fourth-generation Bostonians can be grateful for property-owning ancestors who bequeathed land holdings.

## Land development

Land speculation, packaging, and long-term investment each seek appreciation based on improved land-use *potential*. This can stem from mere inflation—the same potential use for which more dollars must be paid. Or it can result from true appreciation, such as from population growth exceeding new land availability or from greater per capita expenditures directed toward land. Farming partly closes this gap between the land's potential for income and its *developed* usage. The land developer, therefore, takes the major risk—much like the leap from theory to practice. And to the land developer, the marketplace accords the highest returns when the deal works.

Development, from the investor's perspective, incurs substantial upfront costs to enhance market value. Few development costs are tax deductible: construction interest and financing points must now be capitalized, as must closing costs, architect's fees, roads, utilities, landscaping, and the like. These costs are deducted through depreciation charges over each improvement's useful life.

Construction or development interest costs incurred in 1983 or later must be capitalized and written off over ten years. If the developer then chooses to sell the land, his income or profits may be taxed as ordinary income. Alternatively, if the developer chooses to build, several years may pass before operating profits are realized. Gross income and operating expenses both depend on the type of development undertaken. As we have seen, a net lease on industrial property has a low-rent/low-expense pattern. A motel/restaurant, by contrast, usually generates high gross income, but 60 percent or more goes for operating expenses.

The leverage employed is also a key determinant of the rate of return. Here the developer has a major advantage. He might buy raw land at its existing price, then package it, get it rezoned for a higher and more valuable usage, arrange "in the ground" improvements such as roads, utilities, sewers, and water and upgrade the quality of its use through further development. By keeping the land and profits from development invested, it may be possible for the developer to borrow or joint-venture for the full amount of development costs. This happy situation is called *mortgaging out*. That is, the loan amount equals total costs so the developer is not out any cash, is also untaxed, and therefore has a "free" equity ride on the finished project. With no equity (except foregone opportunity), no rate of return on equity can be calculated—it is infinite, since there is no out-of-pocket equity. Of course, leverage is a two-edged sword, with an unprofitable project resulting in an infinitely *negative* return.

Many developers have bootstrapped themselves in exactly this way. During tight money, with inflation-swollen interest rates, with escalating materials and labor costs, and with shortages causing construction delays, the developer may be called on for additional capital beyond that provided by a mortgage or development loan. This whipsaw effect can easily wipe out the developer's working capital. The stalled project then defaults on completion or interest payment. Standing unfinished, it deteriorates in value, threatening the loan principal, as well. Foreclosed and sold at auction, the property may be a bargain for another developer but represents the failure of the first one. In the mid-1970s REIT debacle, as many as two-thirds of the construction loans made were in such troubled abeyance. Again, recall that development *risk* is commensurate with the potential for *reward*.

## New rules for developers

Along with other businesses, developers must increasingly deal with consumer concern, government regulation, environmental impact statements, no-growth referenda, securities regulations, recalcitrant zoning boards, tenant associations, rent controls, home warranties, and so on. These make the developer's job more complex, and thus construction more costly. Tight monetary policy, and the resultant high interest rates, especially hit development and construction when the government attempts to choke off inflation.

Government programs *aiding* development also exist, although they have a checkered record. Urban homestake programs offer hope for generating homeowner equity from abandoned buildings. Rapid depreciation (straight line over only five years) has spurred rehabilitation of some substandard or historical housing. The U.S. Department of Housing and Urban Development program for funding new towns tried to diffuse jobs and living patterns based on sensible land-use planning. Mortgage insurance and rent supplements fund some housing but compete with other housing and business needs for loan capital.

Finally, there is a trend toward consolidation in what has always been a fragmented industry. The 100 largest home builders, for example, have improved their market share in the past decade, partly by acquisition. U.S. Homes, Kaufman and Broad, Ryan Homes, and Centex are among the largest, but no single firm has more than 1 percent of the market. Counterbalancing this trend, many large corporations who ventured into development, such as Boise Cascade, Chrysler, Gulf, U.S. Steel, and Westinghouse, have since exited. It seems that entrepreneurial skill and risk taking are still vital elements of the business.

## Phased development example

Development projects may easily take a few to several years to complete. Usually, a phased plan of equity plus debt precedes the eventual sale or rental income stream from the developed land sites or buildings. To illustrate this complex situation, the REAL analysis in Table 10.2 shows a phased development example.

Equity of $20,000 in Year 1 is augmented by a $40,000 raw-land acquisition loan at 3 percent over prime. With $60,000 in total, a three-acre site suitably zoned for industrial development can be bought (or it might be optioned). Let us assume that design, premarketing, arranging financing, and development all take a year following acquisition, so that the equity and debt are not needed until Year 2.

The required development doubles the initial purchase cost. Development includes streets designed in width and for the weight of heavy trucks; water flow and pressure ample for tenant and fire-control usage; storm and sanitary sewer capacity; gas, electric, and phone utilities; and zoning covenants specifying a maximum land-coverage ratio, architectural and sign standards, setbacks, landscaping, light and air access, and objectionable uses. (Zoning covenants are more common with larger developments.)

In Year 2, a speculative general-purpose warehouse, possibly 60,000 square feet (or a smaller low-rise office building), could be built and partially leased by year end. Here a conventional mortgage, possibly with a second, would nearly cover construction costs. (Alternately, a joint venture or investor and syndication could be arranged to finance the building.)

We have presented over ten intensive two-and-a-half day seminars covering exactly this situation to members and guests of the Society of Industrial Realtors (SIR). We use a specifically prepared computerized simulator such as that mandated for airline-pilot training and recertification. Participants compress time 1,000 to 1, making a year's development decisions in a few hours. Five years' evolution of one or more developments unfolds under their direction – in competition with the other seminar participants. And the simulator allows us to vary the economic and market conditions to provide participants with the ability to test different development strategies and see the results of their decisions almost immediately, while their reasoning is still fresh.

# TABLE 10.2
## Phased-in development example

### KEY CONSTRUCTION FACTORS ARE --

| YR | CUMULATIVE PROJECT COST | ----CONSTRUCTION LOAN---- YEAR END | AVERAGE | % INTEREST | DEPRECIATION EXPENSE | GROSS INCOME | OPERATING EXPENSE | TAX RATE |
|---|---|---|---|---|---|---|---|---|
| 82 | 120000 | 80000 | 60000 | 15.00 | 0 | 0 | 0 | 50% |
| 83 | 1320000 | 1000000 | 800000 | 15.00 | 0 | 18750 | 18750 | 50% |
| 84 | 1320000 | 1000000 | 1000000 | 15.00 | 80000 | 112500 | 25000 | 50% |

### KEY OPERATING FACTORS ARE ---

| | TOTAL PROJECT COST | --MORTGAGE TERMS--- AMOUNT | % INTR | LIFE | ----OPERATING & INFLATION ASSUMPTIONS----- NET RESALE PRICE | % INFL | GROSS INCOME | % INFL | OPERATING EXPENSE | % INFL | ----DEPRECIATION--- AMOUNT | LIFE | RATE | ---TAX RATES--- INCOME | CAP GAIN |
|---|---|---|---|---|---|---|---|---|---|---|---|---|---|---|---|
| | 1320000 | 1000000 | 13.00 | 25 | 1400000 | 5 | 150000 | 0* | 7500 | 0* | 1120000 | 14 | 100% | 50% | 20% |
| 1 | 1320000 | | | | 1470000 | 5 | 150000 | 0 | 7500 | 0 | | | | 50% | 20% |
| 2 | 1320000 | | | | 1543500 | 5 | 150000 | 0 | 7500 | 0 | | | | 50% | 20% |
| 3 | 1320000 | | | | 1620675 | 5 | 150000 | 0 | 7500 | 0 | | | | 50% | 20% |
| 4 | 1320000 | | | | 1701709 | 5 | 150000 | 0 | 7500 | 0 | | | | 50% | 20% |
| 5 | 1320000 | | | | 1786794 | 5 | 187500 | 25 | 9375 | 25 | | | | 50% | 20% |
| 6 | 1320000 | | | | 1876134 | 5 | 187500 | 0 | 9375 | 0 | | | | 50% | 20% |
| 7 | 1320000 | | | | 1969941 | 5 | 187500 | 0 | 9375 | 0 | | | | 50% | 20% |
| 8 | 1320000 | | | | 2068438 | 5 | 187500 | 0 | 9375 | 0 | | | | 50% | 20% |
| 9 | 1320000 | | | | 2171859 | 5 | 187500 | 0 | 9375 | 0 | | | | 50% | 20% |
| 10 | 1320000 | | | | 2280452 | 5 | 234375 | 25 | 11719 | 25 | | | | 50% | 20% |

### PRE-OPERATING SUMMARY ---

| EQUITY AMOUNT | ---MORTGAGE TERMS--- % DEBT | MONTHLY | YEARLY | % NET RESALE TO COST | % INCOME TO COST | GROSS RENT MULT | % EXPENSE TO INCOME | % NOI TO COST | % DEPREC TO COST |
|---|---|---|---|---|---|---|---|---|---|
| 320000 | 75.76 | 11278 | 135340 | 106.1 | 11.4 | 8.8 | 5.0 | 10.8 | 84.8 |

Reprinted with the permission of The Mader Group, Inc., Narberth, PA.

TABLE 10.2 (concluded)

|  | HOLDING RESULTS BEFORE INCOME TAXES | | | | | | | HOLDING RESULTS AFTER TAXES | | | | | | | |
|---|---|---|---|---|---|---|---|---|---|---|---|---|---|---|---|
| YR | GROSS INCOME | OPERATE EXPENSE | –LOAN INTR– PAID | –LOAN INTR– DEDUCT | CASH FLOW | EQTY FLOW | CASH & EQTY FLOW | DEPREC IATION | TAXABLE INCOME | TAXES DUE | CASH FLOW | CASH AND EQTY FLOW | NET DEBT INFLOW | TOTAL NET CASH FLOW | CUM NET CASH FLOW |
| 82 | 0 | 0 | 9000 | 900 | -9000 | -40000 | -49000 | 0 | -900 | -450 | -8550 | -48550 | 0 | -48550 | -48550 |
| 83 | 18750 | 18750 | 120000 | 12000 | -120000 | -280000 | -400000 | 0 | -12000 | -6000 | -114000 | -394000 | 0 | -394000 | -442550 |
| 84 | 112500 | 25000 | 150000 | 15000 | -62500 | 0 | -62500 | 80000 | -7500 | -3750 | -58750 | -58750 | 0 | -58750 | -501300 |

OPERATING RESULTS ---

|  | HOLDING RESULTS BEFORE INCOME TAXES | | | | | | HOLDING RESULTS AFTER TAXES | | | | | OVERALL RESULTS IF SOLD AT YEAR END | | | | | |
|---|---|---|---|---|---|---|---|---|---|---|---|---|---|---|---|---|---|---|
| YR | GROSS INCOME | OPERATE EXPENSE | –MORTGAGE– INTR | –MORTGAGE– AMORT | CASH FLOW | % RE TURN | DEPREC IATION | TAXABLE INCOME | TAXES DUE | CASH FLOW | % RE TURN | SALE PRICE | DEBT REPAY | TAXES DUE | TOTAL CASH FLOW | TOTAL PROFIT | % IRR |
| 1 | 150000 | 7500 | 129670 | 5670 | 7160 | 1.4 | 80000 | -95070 | -47535 | 54695 | 10.9 | 1470000 | 994330 | 3400 | 472270 | 25665 | 1.9 |
| 2 | 150000 | 7500 | 128887 | 6453 | 7160 | 1.4 | 80000 | -94287 | -47144 | 54303 | 10.8 | 1543500 | 987877 | 85640 | 469983 | 77681 | 4.2 |
| 3 | 150000 | 7500 | 127997 | 7344 | 7160 | 1.4 | 80000 | -93397 | -46698 | 53858 | 10.7 | 1620675 | 980533 | 146655 | 493487 | 155043 | 6.4 |
| 4 | 150000 | 7500 | 126983 | 8357 | 7160 | 1.4 | 80000 | -92383 | -46191 | 53351 | 10.6 | 1701709 | 972176 | 208442 | 521091 | 235998 | 7.8 |
| 5 | 187500 | 9375 | 125829 | 9511 | 42785 | 8.5 | 80000 | -55604 | -27802 | 70587 | 14.1 | 1786794 | 962665 | 271039 | 553090 | 338585 | 9.1 |
| 6 | 187500 | 9375 | 124517 | 10824 | 42785 | 8.5 | 80000 | -54292 | -27146 | 69931 | 13.9 | 1876134 | 951841 | 334487 | 589806 | 445231 | 10.0 |
| 7 | 187500 | 9375 | 123023 | 12318 | 42785 | 8.5 | 80000 | -52798 | -26399 | 69184 | 13.8 | 1969941 | 939524 | 398828 | 631589 | 556197 | 10.7 |
| 8 | 187500 | 9375 | 121322 | 14018 | 42785 | 8.5 | 80000 | -51097 | -25549 | 68333 | 13.6 | 2068438 | 925506 | 464108 | 678824 | 671766 | 11.2 |
| 9 | 187500 | 9375 | 119387 | 15953 | 42785 | 8.5 | 80000 | -49162 | -24581 | 67366 | 13.4 | 2171859 | 909553 | 530372 | 731935 | 792242 | 11.6 |
| 10 | 234375 | 11719 | 117185 | 18155 | 87316 | 17.4 | 80000 | 25471 | 12735 | 74581 | 14.9 | 2280452 | 891398 | 592090 | 796984 | 931852 | 12.0 |

Reprinted with the permission of The Mader Group, Inc., Narberth, PA.

The types of decisions discussed *and actually practiced* in this seminar are illustrated in Table 10.3.

TABLE 10.3
Real estate simulation decision sheet

```
FIRM___    YEAR 19___   TEAM NAME _____      DECISION SHEET

:::: L A N D   O P T I O N E D   O R   P U R C H A S E D ::::

A                                     PROJ #     .....    .....    .....    .....

1 OPTION COST (IF ANY)                DOLLARS    .....    .....    .....    .....
2 PURCHASE PRICE / ACRE               DOLLARS    .....    .....    .....    .....
3 LAND ACQUISITION LOAN               % COST     .....    .....    .....    .....

:::: L A N D   T O   B E   S O L D ::::

B                                     PROJ #     .....    .....    .....    .....

1 # OF ACRES OFFERED FOR SALE         ACRES      .....    .....    .....    .....
2 SALE PRICE / ACRE (0="AT MARKET")   DOLLARS    .....    .....    .....    .....

:::: L A N D   T O   B E   D E V E L O P E D ::::

C                                     PROJ #     .....    .....    .....    .....

1 # OF ACRES TO BE DEVELOPED          ACRES      .....    .....    .....    .....
2 MAXIMUM BUILDING / AREA RATIO       PERCENT    .....    .....    .....    .....
3 MARKETING EXPENDITURES              DOLLARS    .....    .....    .....    .....
4 AMENITIES                           DOLLARS    .....    .....    .....    .....
5 LAND DEVELOPMENT LOAN               % COST     .....    .....    .....    .....

:::: B U I L D I N G S   T O   B E   C O N S T R U C T E D ::::

D                                     PROJ #     .....    .....    .....    .....

1 # OF ACRES USED BY BUILDING         ACRES      .....    .....    .....    .....
2 PURCHASE (1) OR LEASE (2) LAND      1 OR 2     .....    .....    .....    .....
3 GEN PURP (1) OR OFFICE (2) BLDG     1 OR 2     .....    .....    .....    .....
4 SIZE OF BUILDING                    SQ FT      .....    .....    .....    .....
5 AMENITIES                           DOLLARS    .....    .....    .....    .....
6 ANNUAL LEASE RATE                   CENTS/SF   .....    .....    .....    .....

7 CONSTRUCTION LOAN                   % COST     .....    .....    .....    .....
8 PERMANENT MTG -- 1ST                % VALUE    .....    .....    .....    .....
9 PERMANENT MTG -- 2ND                % VALUE    .....    .....    .....    .....
10 INVESTOR PARTICIPATION (0 OR 80%)  % EQUITY   .....    .....    .....    .....
11 JOINT VENTURE (0 OR 100%)          % COST     .....    .....    .....    .....

:::: S P A C E   T O   B E   L E A S E D ::::

E                                     PROJ #     .....    .....    .....    .....

1 NEW LEASE RATE (IF CHANGED)         CENTS/SF   .....    .....    .....    .....

:::: B U I L D I N G S   T O   B E   S O L D ::::

F                                     PROJ #     .....    .....    .....    .....

1 SALE PRICE (0="AT MARKET")          DOLLARS    .....    .....    .....    .....

:::: C A S H   M A N A G E M E N T ::::

G
1 INVEST IN CERTIFICATES OF DEPOSIT   $1000      .....
2 ONE YEAR LOAN REQUESTED             $1000      .....

        ADDITIONAL INPUT FORMS MAY BE FILED IF NECESSARY.
```

## Summary

Half of U.S. land (excluding Alaska) is used for agriculture. Land can also be held with a view toward short-term resale (upgrading its usage), for long-term holding, or for early development—the highest-risk, highest-reward route. Unless farmed or operated in some enterprise, land produces negligible income. Yet ongoing tax, insurance, and upkeep costs must be met. Leveraged holdings also face the drain of interest payments. Transaction costs often include 10 percent commissions for raw-land brokerage.

All this means that land must appreciate rapidly to provide suitable profitablilty. And the investor must have working capital to "feed" the land, if leveraged, while waiting for it to appreciate. Yet holders do receive some tax benefits: Operating and financing costs are deductible, and sale profits are taxed as capital gains, assuming investor (not dealer) status and more than one year of holding. Impressive capital multiplication can occur over long holding periods.

Development requires managerial skill and experience beyond that of mere ownership. In this labor-intensive, highly leveraged, delays-are-costly environment, the potential rewards and risks are highest. Successful developers can sometimes mortgage out on a project with no residual investment on their part. The returns are then incalculable—even for a computer! Today, it is more likely that substantial equity or a joint-venture partner is needed to carry the investor through the entire development process.

## Notes

1. A convenient way to estimate compound annual rates of return relies on the "rule of 72." Based on logarithms, this rule says that a doubling is achieved by any combination of years and rates multiplying to 72. For example, 7.2 years of 10 percent compound annual growth doubles your money (before tax considerations). Also, 10 years at 7.2 percent growth provides a double. So does 5 years at 14.4 percent, or 72 years at 1 percent (a terrible thought). Our 200-fold gain represents nearly eight consecutive doubles. This is about one doubling every 5 years during the 38-year holding period. Applying the rule of 72, a double in 5 years indicates a 14.4 percent compound annual rate of return, close to the actual 14.9 percent figure.

# 11 Advanced Analysis

In addition to probing the investment merits of the different types of real estate—houses, condos, apartments, commercial/industrial property, and land—we can use the REAL analysis to aid in deciding operating and management policies. That is: What mortgage terms and leverage level are best? How long should leases be? How vital is it to control operating costs and pass on escalating expenses? How do your tax circumstances affect returns? Should you sell, trade, or refinance your property? When? Can a particular investment be syndicated on favorable terms? And so on. These and other crucial issues are explored in this chapter.

## Mortgage terms in the 1980s

The method by which you finance your investment has a major impact on profitability and risk. The type and level of your leverage also influences your other investing objectives: liquidity, expenses, tax shelter, and inflation protection. We have already discussed today's variety of mortgages (see Chapter 3) and have analyzed self-amortizing mortgages of fairly long duration.

But for 1980, 1981, and the first half of 1982, the fixed-interest rate on these instruments fell victim to inflation. New- and used-home sales volumes plummeted and prices softened for only the third time in 14 years (as in the 1970 and 1974–75 tight-money periods). Variable-rate, flexible, and graduated mortgages increasingly prevail.

Financing by the seller is also frequently provided to lubricate sales. Options and extended-time agreements of sale are other techniques to control property in a cash-tight era. How does traditional analysis change? How are measures of profitability and risk influenced by use of nonconventional mortgages?

The only complication in evaluating such financing is that it introduces another significant factor for risk analysis. That is, if the average mortgage rate should prove to be higher or lower than a constant interest rate, what would that do to the investment's rate of return? Figure 11.1 reflects a likely outcome. Suppose a variable-rate mortgage (VRM) was issued in 1979 with 10

FIGURE 11.1
Conventional versus variable-rate mortgage

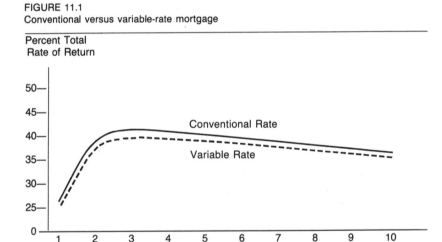

Percent Total
Rate of Return

- 80% debt
- 12% net operating income
- 10% inflation

percent initial interest. Then interest on it rose 1 percent per year and leveled off at 12.5 percent, its upper limit. The reduced return *does* pose a risk but *does not* eliminate real estate's strong returns.

## Leverage level

Our reference tables represent conventional mortgages of either 60 or 80 percent of value, but greater leverage is sometimes achievable if it suits your objectives. The incremental loan funds may be costly, but a good project will nonetheless show a higher rate of return. In Figure 11.2, we have graphed the Year 5 total return (a convenient, representative benchmark) for various leverage levels. The effects of 0 percent and 10 percent inflation show how return and risk are amplified by high leverage.

FIGURE 11.2
Year 5 rate of return for various leverage levels

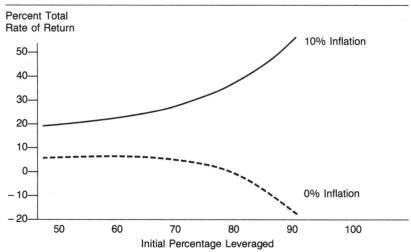

Percent Total
Rate of Return

10% Inflation

0% Inflation

Initial Percentage Leveraged

• 15% mortgage rate
• 12% net operating income

Figure 11.2 also shows the main incentive for high leverage—the inflation/appreciation factor. Despite transaction costs and high mortgage rates, and after a reasonably long holding period (five years), price increases account for most of the profits. No inflation, no gains. But with inflation, the greater leverage lets your money control proportionately more property, so you benefit more from swollen prices.

The catch, or course, is risk. The highly leveraged policy is correct, despite high rates, with inflation and no operating problems. Your experience, reserve capital, personal goals, and other factors should be considered in arriving at your own policy on leverage. But leverage becomes a nightmare with high vacancy, deterioration, maintenance cost overruns, rent controls that retard resale prices as well as rents, a downgrading of the neighborhood, *or any other cause of constant or declining resale value.*

## Lease length

Historically, real estate investors tried to contract for relatively long leases to lock in income. Businesses in particular sought such long-term location and price stability. But with inflation, it may not be in the owner's best interest to lease long term. Furthermore, for residential property, the usual remedy for lease breaking by the renter is merely forfeiture of the security deposit. Thus the long lease binds the landlord more than it does the tenant. The inability to raise rents periodically may mean a missed opportunity, or worse, a shrinking profit due to rising expenses.

On the other hand, tenant turnover is expensive, and good renter relationships are valuable. Advertising, showing the space, agent commissions, renovation, and redecorating are all typical but expensive ingredients in remarketing vacancies. What is a proper policy on lease length? And which cost increases can and should be passed on automatically by lease-escalator clauses? (With today's inflation, one colleague now calls these *elevator* clauses!)

For residential property, a one-year initial lease plus optional one-year renewals seems best. An escalator clause might be included but not used until renewal time. For longer leases, with today's utility, fuel, supplies, labor, and tax cost increases, it is an increasingly acceptable and necessary practice to include a rent-escalator clause. Recovering expense increases is the minimum goal—increasing NOI is better.

With commercial and industrial property, lease length is typically three to ten years. Many leases have annual increases in rates based on a percentage of increase in the Consumer Price Index or some other measure of inflation. Often leases then allow current tenant renewal, perhaps with rental levels readjusted to the then-current market values based on appraisal, expense recovery, or CPI adjustment. Since marketing commercial space can be costly, these longer leases are in the owner's best interest, as well as the occupant's. But some form of rent escalation is necessary to bring about protection and profit from inflation.

With shopping centers, rents are often keyed to a percentage of sales (called "overage" because rents then increase proportionately with sales), which hopefully increase as prices increase. By contrast, a long-term net-net-net (meaning the lease rate is net of property taxes, maintenance, and insurance) lease has the tenant pay all operating costs and hence all increases. But only at lease-expiration time (sometimes after 20 years) can the owner then increase income due to inflation. The long-term, fixed-income lease inhibits any potential rise in resale price. The important factor is to have NOI catch up with inflation relatively often. Annually is great, every three to five years is acceptable for commercial property, but five to ten years of constant net operating income restrains the owner's rate of return significantly. And having constant gross income, without the ability to pass on expense increases, is a formula for disaster.

## Escalating expenses

What if the marketplace won't accept rental boosts as fast as expenses go up? Any building, whether new or used, gets older and might go out of style with the passage of time, despite good maintenance and administrative policies. The REAL analysis helps develop understanding of this likely event.

Suppose that, instead of sale price, gross income, and operating expenses all rising uniformly at 10 percent per year, we assume to following:

1. 5 percent inflation of the resale price, recognizing aging.
2. 10 percent increases in annual gross rents, recognizing inflation.
3. 15 percent annual jumps in operating expenses, given utility and other cost pressures.

Many experts feel that this is an accurate, perhaps conservative, estimate of inflation's likely impact on investment property during the 1980s. The reference tables of Part III illustrate such cases. What does this pattern of operating results do to the overall rate of return?

Figure 11.3 graphs total return for a typical property financed with an initial leverage level of 75 percent with a 12.5 percent mortgage. For various holding periods, it shows the effect of 0 percent inflation, a uniform 10 percent annually, and our 5-10-15 percent inflation pattern defined above. As you can see, inflation makes a big impact on total return—an impact too large and too attractive to ignore.

## Inflation adjustment

By now, an underlying worry might be, "But how much *food* or *energy* will I be able to buy with my real estate profits?" In other words, if real estate profits now depend on inflation, what does that same inflation do to *purchasing power*? To adjust the REAL report for inflation, either a simple or a more detailed procedure can be followed.

First, the rightmost column of the REAL analysis reporting total return (IRR) *is* an annual percentage rate. Thus, to correct for inflation's erosion of the dollar, simply slice off the inflation rate from the total return. (Except for annual compounding effects, this simple modification would be correct—see Table 11.1(A)). Then, remember to adjust your other investments for inflation.

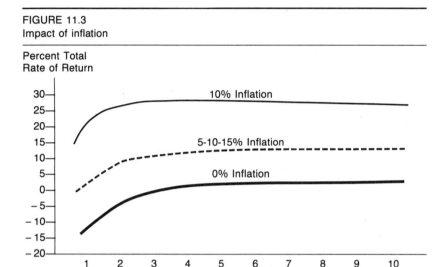

FIGURE 11.3
Impact of inflation

Percent Total
Rate of Return

- 75% debt
- 12.5% interest rate

also—*savings, bonds, mortgages,* and probably *stocks* would all show *negative after-tax real returns!*

Second, to be more precise with your inflation adjustment, take each year's after-tax cash flow and reduce (discount) the dollar amount for purchasing-power erosion. Thus a sale cash flow received two years hence, with 10 percent inflation, is worth only 82 cents on the present dollar. With both holding and sale cash flows adjusted to their inflation-sapped buying power, a new total return (a "real" IRR) can be calculated. This is demonstrated in Table 11.1 (B).

## Declining property values

We have asserted that appreciation/inflation is the major driving force behind high real estate returns. But what if resale prices

TABLE 11.1
Adjusting the IRR for the effects of 10% annual inflation

(A) Adjust the internal rate of return as shown for Year 5 of our REAL analysis by the 10 percent inflation rate.

Inflation-adjusted IRR = 20.5% − 10.0% = 10.5%

OR

(B) Adjust each year's cash flow by the appropriate discount factor for 10 percent inflation.

| Year | Cash Flows | Present Value Factor (10%) | Adjusted Cash Flow |
|------|-----------|----------------------------|--------------------|
| 0 | − $200,000 | 1.000 | − $200,000 |
| 1 | + $ 24,000 | 0.909 | + $ 21,816 |
| 2 | + $ 26,000 | 0.826 | + $ 21,476 |
| 3 | + $ 28,000 | 0.751 | + $ 21,028 |
| 4 | + $ 30,000 | 0.683 | + $ 20,490 |
| 5 | + $ 32,000 | 0.621 | + $ 19,872 |
| 5 | + $305,000 | 0.621 | + $189,405 |

Inflation-adjusted IRR = 9.6% (using a Hewlett-Packard calculator)

do not go up, or worse, if they decline, as has happened on a short-term basis recently to many properties? The answer is: You are in trouble, more than traditional analysis approaches indicate if they ignore sale price and transaction-cost effects.

Suppose our typical property has a net income before leverage that is 10 percent of the total project cost. A price decline of 5 percent per year would sharply cut the total return (remember, it's defined as income plus capital gain or *loss*). Before considering resale, results are undamaged. Leverage and tax shelter would seem to be working for you. But the price decline comes all from the owner's hide. The total returns to equity are negative and, if leveraged, might lead to a total loss.

Suppose you choose to hold the property to postpone realizing your accumulating loss. Fine. But to overlook it is to deceive yourself. Although the property still provides a cash flow from holding, this amounts to a return *of* investment, not a return *on* investment. When you sell, you won't recoup your full equity. You are consuming principal to pay income. That may suit some investors' objectives, but they should realize what they are doing. Inflation and true appreciation provide high returns, not milking declining properties.

## Refinancing

Refinancing increases your leverage level, boosting overall return. Suppose you decide, as a matter of systematic policy, to reset your leverage back to 75 percent of value whenever leverage gets below 60 percent. The leverage level, unless reset, naturally drops due to property appreciation and mortgage amortization.

For example, a $400,000 property with a $300,000 mortgage might appreciate/inflate in resale price at 5 percent per year. In five years we could expect a 25 percent higher market value, equalling $500,000 (or more, counting compounded growth). Meanwhile, some mortgage amortization has also been paid. The less than $300,000 of remaining debt is below the owner's 60 percent leverage standard on the current $500,000 value; so it's time to refinance.

Figure 11.4 illustrates this scenario. It shows the sale price, debt level, and cash inflow from holding, including refinancing proceeds every five years. And this is *after-tax* cash because the increased loan funds are not taxable, since they are not income. Yet refinancing has brought liquidity to the owner and a way to realize inflation gains without selling.

FIGURE 11.4
Market value, debt balance, and cash inflow of a refinanced property (in $1,000)

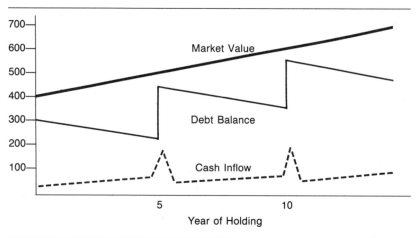

However, this is not the complete bonanza it seems. More of the property's net operating income must go to service the higher debt balance. That is why the "cash inflow" line of Figure 11.4 drops lower after each refinancing. Also, with the passage of time, depreciation (especially if accelerated) will have lost most of its zip. This lowers the property's tax-shelter capability. Most significant, an ever-larger tax liability and higher transaction costs build up for when you *do* sell, when your sale price net of transaction costs might only cover the repayment of the mortgage balance to the lender.

Since leverage boosts the total return of good projects, maintaining high leverage through refinancing helps even further.

FIGURE 11.5
Total returns with and without refinancing

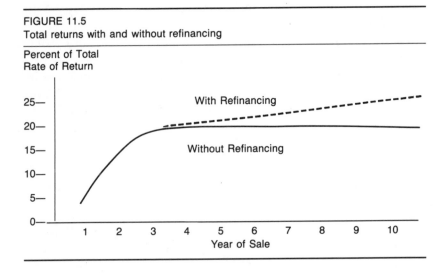

Figure 11.5 shows the effect of refinancing, assuming the new debt carries the same mortgage terms as the original financing. This profitability difference is significant. Furthermore, a later refinancing again jacks up the total return. And liquidity is improved due to the periodic inflow of fresh loan proceeds. If you choose never to sell the property, the accruing capital gain tax liability is not your problem (nor, under the current suspension of the "carry over" basis for taxes, is it your heirs' problem. Their tax basis is the property's market value upon their acquiring it

as a part of your estate.). Thus refinancing is a sound policy for long-term investors who desire liquidity and are able to withstand the heightened risk of periodically resetting a high leverage level.

## Property trading

Property trading is another useful, sophisticated technique for maintaining leverage and parlaying the principal untaxed. A "tax-free exchange of assets of like kind" is allowed by the tax code. Thus real estate can be swapped without either side being required to recognize gains as from a sale. As a practical matter, the properties will not have identical market values or equity portions. And one party may really want liquidity, not another property. So trades must be engineered to meet various needs.

Many advertised properties note that the owner is willing to trade. In many other instances, the would-be seller can be persuaded to trade instead. Or a third party can be found to immediately buy from the reluctant trader, giving the trader (taxable) liquidity. Being interested in capital growth, you will probably want a larger property in swap for your existing equity. The terms of the trade may include assuming or obtaining a first mortgage on the property being acquired, plus a second mortgage taken back by the seller who is trading down, plus perhaps some additional cash, called *boot*. All boot, including mortgages assumed by the seller, is taxable under the present tax laws. Trades are complex, and it is best to use a specialist when considering property trading.

Both refinancing and trading let you postpone paying your accruing capital gain tax liability. More important, you can own a larger property on which inflation can boost profits. But arranging the trade generally costs more in brokerage commissions and title, appraisal, and closing expenses than would a refinancing. The main consideration, therefore, is your operating forecast for your present property. If it no longer suits your appreciation, tax shelter, or other goals, trade it or, failing that, sell it. Otherwise, refinancing and holding can be the easiest as well as the most profitable policy.

## Partnership syndicates

When a property is too large for one owner, or when some investors desire a passive status, a syndicate is often formed. In its simplest form, it can be two partners sharing responsibility and liability. It may be a joint venture of two operating entities, or it may be organized as a corporation. Usually organized by a developer or professional syndicator acting as general partner, it offers qualified investors a passive, limited-liability entrée to real estate deals.

How should you analyze a piece of such a syndicate if offered to you? The most knowledgeable source is the general partner. Unfortunately, he (and any commissioned salesperson) may be the least objective. In public offerings, all material data and risks are required to be disclosed in a prospectus registered with the SEC. A private offering memorandum should provide equal disclosure. The general partner's obligations and compensation must be spelled out. The limited partner's expectations should be presented. The track record of the developer/manager is crucial. Finally, you must judge whether the degree of expected return, risk, liquidity, tax shelter, and so forth suit your needs. But, if you are willing to be an active investor, you can avoid the sales and management overhead of syndicates, illustrated in Figure 11.6

## Summary

Each property is unique. So, the analysis must include the timing and key factor values specific to the situation. Several common situations and operating tactics are reviewed here to show such analysis.

If the property is a good investment, leverage should make it better. However, high leverage, especially at high interest rates, also raises risk. During inflation, the contractual right and ability to recover rising costs is vital, causing owners to shorten the lease length and include rent-escalator clauses. To gain liquidity from owned properties, investigate refinancing. To postpone capital

FIGURE 11.6
Syndication terms—a representative 1981 offering

Acquisition Stage*

| | Dollar Amount | Percent |
|---|---|---|
| Gross proceeds | 10,000,000 | 100.0 |
| Less public offering expenses | | |
| Selling commissions | 800,000 | 8.0 |
| Organizational expenses | 500,000 | 5.0 |
| Available for investment, net of public offering expenses | 8,700,000 | 87.0 |
| Less legal and other property acquisition fees (nonaffiliates) | 400,000 | 4.0 |
| Acquisition fees (real estate commissions) (payable to affiliates) | 900,000 | 9.0 |
| Working capital reserve | 200,000 | 2.0 |
| Net proceeds available for investment | 7,200,000 | 72.0 |

*These are only estimates; actual proceeds will vary within prescribed limits as set out in the offering documents.

Operational Stage

General partners receive:

1) 10 percent of all yearly disbursable cash after limited partners receive 6 percent of their adjusted capital contributions.
2) Approximately 1 percent annually for administration and operation of the partnership.
3) Commissions on the sale of insurance coverage—approximately 1/2 percent annually.
4) Property-management fees—approximately 5 percent of gross receipts.
5) 4 percent of profits or losses for tax purposes (not on sale or refinancing).

Liquidation or Refinancing Stage

General partners receive:

1) 3 percent of the selling price of the property.
2) 15 percent of remaining sale or refinancing proceeds after limited partners have received adjusted capital contributions.

gains taxes on appreciated properties you don't want to hold, consider trading. Such tactics can improve total returns, partly by keeping leverage high. For passive investors, syndications offer opportunities.

# 12 Conclusions and Strategy

Many books discuss real estate. And many provide insight on how to select, develop, appraise, finance, improve, operate, and sell real property. But few adequately discuss property's investment merits. No other book that we know of has quantified inflation's impact as have the two editions of this book. We have addressed this gap because the answers are too important and too attractive to oversimplify. Both theory and fact verify that, with inflation, investors can reasonably hope to achieve *after-tax rates of return of 15 percent to 30 percent compounded annually.*

Favorable results have been achieved by most, but not all, real estate investors. Take homeowners, for example. One friend, a stockbroker, made more money on the sale of his house than he had in several years from his stock-market trading. No doubt your acquaintances could tell similar stories. And in every town large enough to spread a rumor, certain somebodies are always "Making a fortune in real estate."

While such intuitive and unsubstantiated evidence abounds, we have sought more comprehensive, consistent, and accurate measures of real estate investment performance. The respectable literature is sparse. But what does exist, coupled with both professional and personal experience, leads us to conclude that real estate suits the objectives of many investors. Its after-tax return surpasses savings, bonds, stocks, or tangibles as investment alternatives. The kicker is inflation. Rising rents and resale prices, coupled with leverage even at historically high mortgage rates, provide not only inflation protection but also inflated profits.

We developed and applied the REAL analysis to deal with these issues. The analysis serves three broad purposes:

1. To illuminate the general characteristics of real estate investing.
2. To discover the specific merits of particular opportunities.
3. To analyze management and operating policies.

Part I discussed investing during inflation and offered a guide for determing your own objectives. We described the real estate marketplace and presented sample investments and risk analysis. Part II reviewed the types of properties you can select from and suggested operating policies. You are invited to use the reference tables of Part III for specific applications of the real analysis, or you may contact the Mader Group, Inc., for that purpose.

## Leverage, tax shelter, and inflation

We have seen that real estate's traditional advantages are a good rate of return, augmented by *leverage* and *tax shelter*. But *inflation,* which generally causes rising net incomes and resale prices, can double the investor's total rate of return.

Other key factors also influence returns and risks. The major ones are the total project cost relative to its immediate liquidation value, the percentage leveraged, and net operating income. Of important but lesser influence is the mortgage interest rate. Perhaps surprisingly, changes in the mortgage life; in the amount, life, and type of depreciation; and in the investor's tax rates cause only minor changes in total returns.

Figure 12.1 graphs the cap rate and the before-tax, after-tax, and after-sale rates of return provided by a typical leveraged income property. We have called these Levels 1, 2, 3, and 4, respectively.

FIGURE 12.1
Cap rate and before-tax, after-tax, and after-sale rates of return

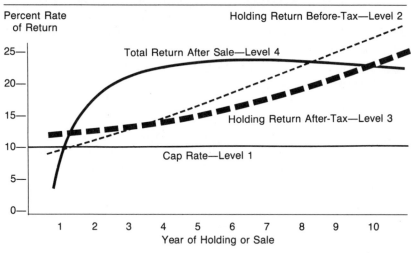

Clearly it is not sufficient to compute just the Year 1 results when making an investment analysis. Nor can transaction costs be ignored because they provide a strong incentive for holding a few years (or until about 25 percent appreciation). Tax shelter has a perverse effect—at first improving the holding returns when viewed after tax, before succumbing partially to the tax collector's grasp and declining from the before-tax return.

Strongest in impact is inflation—or the risk of decline—in the property's resale price. We'll cite one final example to remind you that property values *can decline* and that, in any case, analysis is helpful.

## How REAL began—a final caution

In the late 1960s, the principal author's doctoral training and investment research indicated that stock-and-bond investing offered limited opportunities compared to real estate. To enter real estate, we first focused on the familiar—housing for university students. Since *systems* was the fashionable term of the era, and factory-built mobile units offered economy, we formed University Housing Systems, Inc., to rent furnished mobile homes to students.

To guarantee a rental market and gain sponsorship, we surveyed 2,000 colleges and universities and identified about 50 willing prospects. Growing enrollments created their housing need, and constrained finances meant outside suppliers would be welcome. Using university land would ensure a prime location with limited competition. Besides, land is not depreciable. We wanted our investment in depreciable assets to capture the tax shelter presently unusable by our untaxed university clientele. In addition to a ready market, prime land access, and tax benefits, the big feature was the mobile unit: quick to install, furnished, and having a desirable home-style layout unlike the traditional dormitory.

Recall that we have labeled a gross rent multiplier *level zero.* Unfortunately, our initial thinking was only to this depth. We reasoned that inexpensive housing (then seven dollars per square foot furnished) with guaranteed occupancy at acceptable rent would mean our total project cost was a low multiplier of gross rent, and payback would be quick.

To teach ourselves more about real estate economics—including the intricacies of *leverage, tax shelter,* and *inflation*—we then wrote the original version of the REAL computer program. Soon it became apparent that our university housing idea was *not* a good one. Imagine how much operating expenses would run for student-occupied mobile homes! (We envisioned Saturday nights and beer bottles crashing through quarter-inch panel walls.) By the time we figured the net operating income as a percent of total cost (Level 1), the concept had lost some luster but was still good.

Next, the financing then available was horrible—for mobiles, lenders said, "See our car loan department." Their mortgage interest rate was 3 percent higher and the amortization three times quicker than for conventional housing financing. Clearly Level 2, our return on equity, suffered with such lousy leverage.

Level 3 was an improvement, at least. Rapid write-off, short life, and no cost in land would provide plenty of tax shelter. The REAL revelation, however, was Level 4. What appreciation/inflation rate should we use for our student-occupied mobile homes? Experience at that time had shown that rental mobile homes had *declined* in resale value—falling by half in about five to seven years. When this *negative* appreciation was plugged into our key factors, projected total returns were poor, indeed. We terminated our venture. We've since met five other investors who *did* rent mobile homes to students, and each had lost money. At least we learned that *analytically* and were able to cut our losses to the cost of the feasibility study.

## Key features of the REAL analysis

Real estate investing has become more sophisticated. Curbside analysis no longer suffices. In this book we have described and applied an analysis method to quickly, accurately, and economically enhance your experienced and knowledgeable judgments about particular properties. The REAL analysis succinctly develops and displays a property's investment merits— including rates of return before and after tax, before and after sale, and with or without inflation. Multiple runs or a sensitivity analysis allow the quantification of risk, liquidity, and leverage effects. These key features are summarized below.

1. The 13 KEY FACTORS must be *estimated* (or guessed).
2. The results are a *projection* (not final accounting statements).
3. Inflation rates (or real appreciation rates) may *differ* for the gross income, operating expense, and resale price.
4. Year-to-year *fluctuations* may occur in rent, expense, and resale price and in the investor's tax brackets.
5. Management *time* is an often-hidden operating expense or added investment.
6. Contingent liabilities and unbudgeted catastrophes are assumed to be insured.
7. Total return (internal rate of return) is an *overall,* compound annual result.
8. Total profit and total return should perhaps be *inflation-adjusted.*

9. The required computations are *tedious* without reference tables or computer access.
10. Results must/should be recomputed for *any changes* (different scenarios) in the KEY FACTORS (risk or sensitivity analysis).

## Investing in the 1980s

Investing, investments, and investors have each been affected by events of the 1980s. No longer can we assume a stable U.S. marketplace and money market. Changing demographics, tastes, and capital and energy costs will profoundly alter investing patterns. Table 12.1 expresses these shifts at three stages and over three decades.

*Investing* must now cope with "throbbing variables" that once were static or predictable. *Investments* include so many new alternatives—gold, options, futures, collectibles, money market funds, and syndications, among them. Plus, in real estate, a dynamic market has created problems of its own with costs, with tenants, and with financing. *Investors,* too, have changed their criteria. They once looked for income property and expected leverage to enhance returns due to seemingly added risk. Then inflation came and boosted returns, while shifting mortgage risk to the *lender.* Tax shelter elsewhere was restricted by law, so real estate boomed. Today's investor hopes to hedge inflation and taxes and analyze property accordingly, including not just Levels 1, 2, and 3, but also Level 4 and risk.

## Summary

If you decide to invest in real estate, following home ownership, we suggest existing residential income property as the best beginning point, especially for the '80s. High leverage—around 75 percent or more—is a must. Appreciation, which enhances mere inflation, is the most important selection criterion. Then management and operating policies should try to provide maximum and growing net income. Sale, or possibly refinancing or trading, should be used to pyramid to larger, similar properties and to

TABLE 12.1
How real estate investing has changed

| | 1950s–1960s | 1970s | 1980s |
|---|---|---|---|
| Investing Environment | U.S. population growth<br>High real income growth<br>Inflation minimal<br>Movement southwest<br>Suburban sprawl | U.S. population stabilizes<br>Low real income growth<br>Inflation surges<br>Movement southwest<br>Urban revitalization | U.S. population static<br>Medium real income growth<br>Inflation continues<br>Movement to Sun Belt<br>Transportation sensitive |
| Investment Concerns | Real estate stable<br>Low-interest, long-term financing<br>Utility costs stable<br>Tenants nonassertive | Real estate soars<br>High-interest, long-term financing<br>Utility costs soar<br>Land-use restrictions<br>Tenants increasingly militant | Real estate selective<br>Variable rate (but high), flexible length financing<br>Energy-efficiency sensitive<br>Land-use regulated<br>Tenants demand rent controls |
| Investing Criteria | "Income property"<br>Cap rates steady<br>Leverage<br>Tax shelter<br>Value stability | "Income and capital gain property"<br>Cap rates volatile<br>Debt = flight from paper money<br>Shelter + long-term capital gains<br>Value appreciation | "Try to hold and hedge property"<br>Total return analysis<br>After financing<br>After tax<br>After inflation |

multiple properties. Invest for yourself, guided by the counsel of professionals. Then hire someone to run your properties so that you can preserve your time for investing and supervision—and before you know it, leisure.

# PART III

# Real Estate Reference Tables

# 13 Home or Condominium Property

This chapter presents four reference tables detailing the *implied profitability* of *home or condominium ownership*. *No depreciation* is allowed, but capital gains tax exclusions are available. Below is an index to this chapter's specific tables, showing the key factors varied and summarized results.

| Table | Percent Mortgaged | Percent Mortgage Interest Rate | Percent Net Income to Total Project Cost | Percent Year 5 Rates of Return | | |
|-------|-------------------|--------------------------------|------------------------------------------|------------------|----------------------|-------------------|
| | | | | 0% Inflation | 5-10-15% Inflation | 10% Inflation |
| 13.1 | 60 | 10 | 8 | 8.5 | 20.8 | 28.7 |
| 13.2 | 60 | 15 | 8 | 3.1 | 16.5 | 25.0 |
| 13.3 | 80 | 10 | 8 | 10.0 | 30.8 | 42.0 |
| 13.4 | 80 | 15 | 8 | −4.9 | 20.9 | 33.7 |

## TABLE 13.1
## Home or condominium ownership with no depreciation (per $1,000)

KEY FACTORS ARE ----

| | ----MORTGAGE TERMS---- | | |
|---|---|---|---|
| TOTAL INVESTED | AMOUNT | % INTR | LIFE |
| 1000 | 600 | 10.00 | 25 |

----OPERATING & INFLATION ASSUMPTIONS----

| NET SALE PRICE | IMPLIED GROSS INCOME | PROP. TAX OPERATING EXPENSE | % ANNUAL INFLATION |
|---|---|---|---|
| 940 | 100 | 20 | 0.0 |

| ----DEPRECIATION---- | | | | ----TAX RATES---- | |
|---|---|---|---|---|---|
| AMOUNT | LIFE | TYPE | | INCOME | CAP GAIN |
| 0 | 0 | 0% | | 30% | 0% |

COMPUTED SUMMARY ----

| | ----MORTGAGE TERMS---- | | |
|---|---|---|---|
| EQUITY AMOUNT | % DEBT | MONTHLY | YEARLY |
| 400 | 60.0 | 5.45 | 65 |

| % NET SALE TO TOTAL | % INCOME TO TOTAL | % EXPENSE TO INCOME | % NET TO TOTAL |
|---|---|---|---|
| 94.0 | 10.0 | 20.0 | 8.0 |

| % DEPREC TO TOTAL |
|---|
| 0.0 |

COMPUTED RESULTS ----

| | ---HOLDING RESULTS BEFORE INCOME TAXES--- | | | | | | ---HOLDING RESULTS AFTER TAXES--- | | | | | ---OVERALL RESULTS WITH SALE AT YEAR END--- | | | | | |
|---|---|---|---|---|---|---|---|---|---|---|---|---|---|---|---|---|---|
| | GROSS | OPERATE | -MORTGAGE-- | | CASH | % RE | DEPREC | TAXABLE | TAXES | CASH | % RE | SALE | DEBT | TAXES | CASH | TOTAL | % |
| YR | INCOME | EXPENSE | INTR | AMORT | FLOW | TURN | IATION | INCOME | DUE | FLOW | TURN | PRICE | REPAY | DUE | FLOW | PROFIT | IRR |
| 1 | 100 | 20 | 60 | 6 | 15 | 3.6 | 0 | -80 | -24 | 38 | 9.6 | 940 | 594 | 0 | 346 | -16 | -4.0 |
| 2 | 100 | 20 | 59 | 6 | 15 | 3.6 | 0 | -79 | -24 | 38 | 9.6 | 940 | 588 | 0 | 352 | 29 | 3.7 |
| 3 | 100 | 20 | 58 | 7 | 15 | 3.6 | 0 | -78 | -24 | 38 | 9.5 | 940 | 581 | 0 | 359 | 74 | 6.4 |
| 4 | 100 | 20 | 56 | 8 | 15 | 3.6 | 0 | -78 | -23 | 38 | 9.5 | 940 | 573 | 0 | 367 | 119 | 7.7 |
| 5 | 100 | 20 | 57 | 8 | 15 | 3.6 | 0 | -77 | -23 | 38 | 9.4 | 940 | 565 | 0 | 375 | 166 | 8.5 |

TABLE 13.1 (concluded)

| YR | GROSS INCOME | OPERATE EXPENSE | INTR | AMORT | CASH FLOW | % RE TURN | DEPREC IATION | TAXABLE INCOME | TAXES DUE | CASH FLOW | % RE TURN | SALE PRICE | DEBT REPAY | TAXES DUE | CASH FLOW | TOTAL PROFIT | % IRR |
|---|---|---|---|---|---|---|---|---|---|---|---|---|---|---|---|---|---|
| | HOLDING RESULTS BEFORE INCOME TAXES | | MORTGAGE | | | | HOLDING RESULTS AFTER TAXES | | | | | OVERALL RESULTS WITH SALE AT YEAR END | | | | | |
| 1 | 100 | 20 | 60 | 6 | 15 | 3.6 | 0 | -80 | -24 | 38 | 9.6 | 987 | 594 | 0 | 393 | 31 | 7.8 |
| 2 | 110 | 23 | 59 | 6 | 22 | 5.4 | 0 | -82 | -25 | 46 | 11.6 | 1036 | 588 | 0 | 448 | 133 | 16.1 |
| 3 | 121 | 26 | 58 | 7 | 29 | 7.3 | 0 | -85 | -25 | 55 | 13.7 | 1088 | 581 | 0 | 507 | 246 | 18.8 |
| 4 | 133 | 30 | 58 | 8 | 37 | 9.3 | 0 | -88 | -26 | 64 | 15.9 | 1143 | 573 | 0 | 569 | 372 | 20.1 |
| 5 | 146 | 35 | 57 | 8 | 46 | 11.5 | 0 | -92 | -28 | 74 | 18.4 | 1200 | 565 | 0 | 635 | 511 | 20.8 |

INFLATION OF SALE PRICE, INCOME & EXPENSE AT 10% ANNUALLY

| YR | GROSS INCOME | OPERATE EXPENSE | INTR | AMORT | CASH FLOW | % RE TURN | DEPREC IATION | TAXABLE INCOME | TAXES DUE | CASH FLOW | % RE TURN | SALE PRICE | DEBT REPAY | TAXES DUE | CASH FLOW | TOTAL PROFIT | % IRR |
|---|---|---|---|---|---|---|---|---|---|---|---|---|---|---|---|---|---|
| | HOLDING RESULTS BEFORE INCOME TAXES | | MORTGAGE | | | | HOLDING RESULTS AFTER TAXES | | | | | OVERALL RESULTS WITH SALE AT YEAR END | | | | | |
| 1 | 100 | 20 | 60 | 6 | 15 | 3.6 | 0 | -80 | -24 | 38 | 9.6 | 1034 | 594 | 0 | 440 | 78 | 19.5 |
| 2 | 110 | 22 | 59 | 6 | 23 | 5.6 | 0 | -81 | -24 | 47 | 11.7 | 1137 | 588 | 0 | 549 | 235 | 27.0 |
| 3 | 121 | 24 | 58 | 7 | 31 | 7.8 | 0 | -83 | -25 | 56 | 14.0 | 1251 | 581 | 0 | 670 | 412 | 28.6 |
| 4 | 133 | 27 | 58 | 8 | 41 | 10.3 | 0 | -84 | -25 | 66 | 16.6 | 1376 | 573 | 0 | 803 | 611 | 28.3 |
| 5 | 146 | 29 | 57 | 8 | 52 | 12.9 | 0 | -86 | -26 | 78 | 19.4 | 1514 | 565 | 0 | 949 | 834 | 28.7 |

Reprinted with the permission of The Mader Group, Inc., Narberth, PA.

**TABLE 13.2**
Home or condominium ownership with no depreciation (per $1,000)

KEY FACTORS ARE ---

| TOTAL INVESTED | ----MORTGAGE TERMS---- | | | ----OPERATING & INFLATION ASSUMPTIONS---- | | | | ----DEPRECIATION---- | | | ----TAX RATES---- | |
|---|---|---|---|---|---|---|---|---|---|---|---|---|
| | AMOUNT | % INTR | LIFE | NET SALE PRICE | IMPLIED GROSS INCOME | PROP. TAX OPERATING EXPENSE | % ANNUAL INFLATION | AMOUNT | LIFE | TYPE | INCOME | CAP GAIN |
| 1000 | 600 | 15.00 | 25 | 940 | 100 | 20 | 0.0 | 0 | 0 | 0% | 30% | 0% |

COMPUTED SUMMARY ---

| EQUITY AMOUNT | ----MORTGAGE TERMS---- | | | % NET SALE TO TOTAL | % INCOME TO TOTAL | % EXPENSE TO INCOME | % NET TO INCOME | % DEPREC TO TOTAL |
|---|---|---|---|---|---|---|---|---|
| | % DEBT | MONTHLY | YEARLY | | | | | |
| 400 | 60.0 | 7.68 | 92 | 94.0 | 10.0 | 20.0 | 8.0 | 0.0 |

COMPUTED RESULTS ---

| YR | ----HOLDING RESULTS BEFORE INCOME TAXES---- | | | | | | ----HOLDING RESULTS AFTER TAXES---- | | | | | ----OVERALL RESULTS WITH SALE AT YEAR END---- | | | | | |
|---|---|---|---|---|---|---|---|---|---|---|---|---|---|---|---|---|---|
| | GROSS INCOME | OPERATE EXPENSE | --MORTGAGE-- INTR | AMORT | CASH FLOW | % RE TURN | DEPREC IATION | TAXABLE INCOME | TAXES DUE | CASH FLOW | % RE TURN | SALE PRICE | DEBT REPAY | TAXES DUE | CASH FLOW | TOTAL PROFIT | % IRR |
| 1 | 100 | 20 | 90 | 2 | -12 | -3.1 | 0 | -110 | -33 | 21 | 5.2 | 940 | 598 | 0 | 342 | -37 | -9.2 |
| 2 | 100 | 20 | 89 | 3 | -12 | -3.1 | 0 | -109 | -33 | 21 | 5.2 | 940 | 595 | 0 | 345 | -14 | -1.7 |
| 3 | 100 | 20 | 89 | 3 | -12 | -3.1 | 0 | -109 | -33 | 20 | 5.1 | 940 | 592 | 0 | 348 | 10 | 0.9 |
| 4 | 100 | 20 | 88 | 4 | -12 | -3.1 | 0 | -108 | -33 | 20 | 5.1 | 940 | 588 | 0 | 352 | 34 | 2.2 |
| 5 | 100 | 20 | 88 | 4 | -12 | -3.1 | 0 | -108 | -32 | 20 | 5.0 | 940 | 584 | 0 | 356 | 59 | 3.1 |

Reprinted with the permission of The Mader Group, Inc., Narberth, PA.

TABLE 13.2 *(concluded)*

INFLATION OF SALE PRICE, INCOME & EXPENSE AT 5-10-15% ANNUALLY

| | ----HOLDING RESULTS BEFORE INCOME TAXES---- | | | | | ----HOLDING RESULTS AFTER TAXES--- | | | | | ---OVERALL RESULTS WITH SALE AT YEAR END-- | | | | | |
| | GROSS INCOME | OPERATE EXPENSE | --MORTGAGE-- INTR | AMORT | CASH FLOW | % RE TURN | DEPRECIATION | TAXABLE INCOME | TAXES DUE | CASH FLOW | % RE TURN | SALE PRICE | DEBT REPAY | TAXES DUE | CASH FLOW | TOTAL PROFIT | % IRR |
| YR | | | | | | | | | | | | | | | | | |
| 1 | 100 | 20 | 90 | 2 | -12 | -3.1 | 0 | -110 | -33 | 21 | 5.2 | 987 | 598 | 0 | 389 | 10 | 2.5 |
| 2 | 110 | 23 | 89 | 3 | -5 | -1.3 | 0 | -112 | -34 | 29 | 7.1 | 1036 | 595 | 0 | 441 | 91 | 11.0 |
| 3 | 121 | 26 | 89 | 3 | 2 | 0.6 | 0 | -115 | -35 | 37 | 9.2 | 1088 | 592 | 0 | 497 | 183 | 14.0 |
| 4 | 133 | 30 | 88 | 4 | 10 | 2.6 | 0 | -119 | -36 | 46 | 11.5 | 1143 | 588 | 0 | 555 | 287 | 15.6 |
| 5 | 146 | 35 | 88 | 4 | 19 | 4.8 | 0 | -123 | -37 | 56 | 14.0 | 1200 | 584 | 0 | 616 | 405 | 16.5 |

INFLATION OF SALE PRICE, INCOME & EXPENSE AT 10% ANNUALLY

| | ----HOLDING RESULTS BEFORE INCOME TAXES---- | | | | | ----HOLDING RESULTS AFTER TAXES--- | | | | | ---OVERALL RESULTS WITH SALE AT YEAR END-- | | | | | |
| | GROSS INCOME | OPERATE EXPENSE | --MORTGAGE-- INTR | AMORT | CASH FLOW | % RE TURN | DEPRECIATION | TAXABLE INCOME | TAXES DUE | CASH FLOW | % RE TURN | SALE PRICE | DEBT REPAY | TAXES DUE | CASH FLOW | TOTAL PROFIT | % IRR |
| YR | | | | | | | | | | | | | | | | | |
| 1 | 100 | 20 | 90 | 2 | -12 | -3.1 | 0 | -110 | -33 | 21 | 5.2 | 1034 | 598 | 0 | 436 | 57 | 14.3 |
| 2 | 110 | 22 | 89 | 3 | -4 | -1.1 | 0 | -111 | -33 | 29 | 7.3 | 1137 | 595 | 0 | 543 | 192 | 22.2 |
| 3 | 121 | 24 | 89 | 3 | 5 | 1.1 | 0 | -113 | -34 | 39 | 9.6 | 1251 | 592 | 0 | 659 | 348 | 24.2 |
| 4 | 133 | 27 | 88 | 4 | 14 | 3.6 | 0 | -115 | -35 | 49 | 12.2 | 1376 | 588 | 0 | 788 | 526 | 24.8 |
| 5 | 146 | 29 | 88 | 4 | 25 | 6.2 | 0 | -117 | -35 | 60 | 15.0 | 1514 | 584 | 0 | 930 | 728 | 25.0 |

Reprinted with the permission of The Mader Group, Inc., Narberth, PA.

## TABLE 13.3
### Home or condominium ownership with no depreciation (per $1,000)

KEY FACTORS ARE ---

| TOTAL INVESTED | ----MORTGAGE TERMS---- | | | ----OPERATING & INFLATION ASSUMPTIONS---- | | | | ----DEPRECIATION---- | | | ---TAX RATES--- | |
|---|---|---|---|---|---|---|---|---|---|---|---|---|
| | AMOUNT | % INTR | LIFE | NET SALE PRICE | IMPLIED GROSS INCOME | PROP.TAX OPERATING EXPENSE | % ANNUAL INFLATION | AMOUNT | LIFE | TYPE | INCOME | CAP GAIN |
| 1000 | 800 | 10.00 | 25 | 940 | 100 | 20 | 0.0 | 0 | 0 | 0% | 30% | 0% |

COMPUTED SUMMARY ---

| EQUITY AMOUNT | ---MORTGAGE TERMS--- | | | % NET SALE TO TOTAL | % INCOME TO TOTAL | % EXPENSE TO INCOME | % NET TO TOTAL | % DEPREC TO TOTAL |
|---|---|---|---|---|---|---|---|---|
| | % DEBT | MONTHLY | YEARLY | | | | | |
| 200 | 80.0 | 7.27 | 87 | 94.0 | 10.0 | 20.0 | 8.0 | 0.0 |

COMPUTED RESULTS ---

| | ---HOLDING RESULTS BEFORE INCOME TAXES--- | | | | | | ---HOLDING RESULTS AFTER TAXES--- | | | | | ---OVERALL RESULTS WITH SALE AT YEAR END--- | | | | | |
|---|---|---|---|---|---|---|---|---|---|---|---|---|---|---|---|---|---|
| YR | GROSS INCOME | OPERATE EXPENSE | --MORTGAGE-- INTR | AMORT | CASH FLOW | % RE TURN | DEPREC IATION | TAXABLE INCOME | TAXES DUE | CASH FLOW | % RE TURN | SALE PRICE | DEBT REPAY | TAXES DUE | CASH FLOW | TOTAL PROFIT | % IRR |
| 1 | 100 | 20 | 80 | 8 | -7 | -3.6 | 0 | -100 | -30 | 23 | 11.3 | 940 | 792 | 0 | 148 | -30 | -14.9 |
| 2 | 100 | 20 | 79 | 8 | -7 | -3.6 | 0 | -99 | -30 | 22 | 11.2 | 940 | 784 | 0 | 156 | 1 | 0.3 |
| 3 | 100 | 20 | 78 | 9 | -7 | -3.6 | 0 | -98 | -29 | 22 | 11.1 | 940 | 775 | 0 | 165 | 32 | 5.7 |
| 4 | 100 | 20 | 77 | 10 | -7 | -3.6 | 0 | -97 | -29 | 22 | 10.9 | 940 | 765 | 0 | 175 | 65 | 8.4 |
| 5 | 100 | 20 | 76 | 11 | -7 | -3.6 | 0 | -96 | -29 | 22 | 10.8 | 940 | 753 | 0 | 187 | 97 | 10.0 |

Reprinted with the permission of The Mader Group, Inc., Narberth, PA.

# TABLE 13.3 (concluded)

## INFLATION OF SALE PRICE, INCOME & EXPENSE AT 5-10-15% ANNUALLY

| YR | HOLDING RESULTS BEFORE INCOME TAXES | | | | | | HOLDING RESULTS AFTER TAXES | | | | | OVERALL RESULTS WITH SALE AT YEAR END | | | | | |
|---|---|---|---|---|---|---|---|---|---|---|---|---|---|---|---|---|---|
| | GROSS INCOME | OPERATE EXPENSE | MORTGAGE INTR | AMORT | CASH FLOW | % RETURN | DEPREC IATION | TAXABLE INCOME | TAXES DUE | CASH FLOW | % RE TURN | SALE PRICE | DEBT REPAY | TAXES DUE | CASH FLOW | TOTAL PROFIT | % IRR |
| 1 | 100 | 20 | 80 | 8 | -7 | -3.6 | 0 | -100 | -30 | 23 | 11.3 | 987 | 792 | 0 | 195 | 17 | 8.6 |
| 2 | 110 | 23 | 79 | 8 | 0 | -0.1 | 0 | -102 | -31 | 30 | 15.2 | 1036 | 784 | 0 | 252 | 105 | 24.7 |
| 3 | 121 | 26 | 78 | 9 | 7 | 3.7 | 0 | -104 | -31 | 39 | 19.3 | 1088 | 775 | 0 | 313 | 205 | 28.9 |
| 4 | 133 | 30 | 77 | 10 | 15 | 7.7 | 0 | -107 | -32 | 48 | 23.8 | 1143 | 765 | 0 | 378 | 317 | 30.4 |
| 5 | 146 | 35 | 76 | 11 | 24 | 12.1 | 0 | -111 | -33 | 57 | 28.7 | 1200 | 753 | 0 | 446 | 443 | 30.8 |

## INFLATION OF SALE PRICE, INCOME & EXPENSE AT 10% ANNUALLY

| YR | HOLDING RESULTS BEFORE INCOME TAXES | | | | | | HOLDING RESULTS AFTER TAXES | | | | | OVERALL RESULTS WITH SALE AT YEAR END | | | | | |
|---|---|---|---|---|---|---|---|---|---|---|---|---|---|---|---|---|---|
| | GROSS INCOME | OPERATE EXPENSE | MORTGAGE INTR | AMORT | CASH FLOW | % RETURN | DEPREC IATION | TAXABLE INCOME | TAXES DUE | CASH FLOW | % RE TURN | SALE PRICE | DEBT REPAY | TAXES DUE | CASH FLOW | TOTAL PROFIT | % IRR |
| 1 | 100 | 20 | 80 | 8 | -7 | -3.6 | 0 | -100 | -30 | 23 | 11.3 | 1034 | 792 | 0 | 242 | 64 | 32.1 |
| 2 | 110 | 22 | 79 | 8 | 1 | 0.4 | 0 | -101 | -30 | 31 | 15.5 | 1137 | 784 | 0 | 353 | 207 | 44.4 |
| 3 | 121 | 24 | 78 | 9 | 10 | 4.8 | 0 | -102 | -31 | 40 | 20.1 | 1251 | 775 | 0 | 476 | 370 | 45.0 |
| 4 | 133 | 27 | 77 | 10 | 19 | 9.6 | 0 | -104 | -31 | 50 | 25.2 | 1376 | 765 | 0 | 612 | 556 | 43.6 |
| 5 | 146 | 29 | 76 | 11 | 30 | 14.9 | 0 | -105 | -32 | 61 | 30.7 | 1514 | 753 | 0 | 761 | 766 | 42.0 |

Reprinted with the permission of The Mader Group, Inc., Narberth, PA.

## TABLE 13.4
### Home or condominium ownership with no depreciation (per $1,000)

KEY FACTORS ARE ---

| TOTAL INVESTED | ---MORTGAGE TERMS--- | | |
|---|---|---|---|
| | AMOUNT | % INTR | LIFE |
| 1000 | 800 | 15.00 | 25 |

----OPERATING & INFLATION ASSUMPTIONS----

| NET SALE PRICE | IMPLIED GROSS INCOME | PROP.TAX OPERATING EXPENSE | % ANNUAL INFLATION |
|---|---|---|---|
| 940 | 100 | 20 | 0.0 |

----DEPRECIATION----

| AMOUNT | LIFE | TYPE |
|---|---|---|
| 0 | 0 | 0% |

----TAX RATES----

| INCOME | CAP GAIN |
|---|---|
| 30% | 0% |

COMPUTED SUMMARY ---

| EQUITY AMOUNT | ---MORTGAGE TERMS--- | | |
|---|---|---|---|
| | % DEBT | MONTHLY | YEARLY |
| 200 | 80.0 | 10.25 | 123 |

| % NET SALE TO TOTAL | % INCOME TO TOTAL | % EXPENSE TO INCOME | % NET TO TOTAL | % DEPREC TO TOTAL |
|---|---|---|---|---|
| 94.0 | 10.0 | 20.0 | 8.0 | 0.0 |

COMPUTED RESULTS ---

| YR | ---HOLDING RESULTS BEFORE INCOME TAXES--- | | | | | | ---HOLDING RESULTS AFTER TAXES--- | | | | | ---OVERALL RESULTS WITH SALE AT YEAR END--- | | | | | |
|---|---|---|---|---|---|---|---|---|---|---|---|---|---|---|---|---|---|
| | GROSS INCOME | OPERATE EXPENSE | ---MORTGAGE--- INTR | AMORT | CASH FLOW | % RE TURN | DEPREC IATION | TAXABLE INCOME | TAXES DUE | CASH FLOW | % RE TURN | SALE PRICE | DEBT REPAY | TAXES DUE | CASH FLOW | TOTAL PROFIT | % IRR |
| 1 | 100 | 20 | 120 | 3 | -43 | -21.5 | 0 | -140 | -42 | -1 | -0.5 | 940 | 797 | 0 | 143 | -58 | -28.9 |
| 2 | 100 | 20 | 119 | 4 | -43 | -21.5 | 0 | -139 | -42 | -1 | -0.6 | 940 | 793 | 0 | 147 | -55 | -14.9 |
| 3 | 100 | 20 | 119 | 4 | -43 | -21.5 | 0 | -139 | -42 | -1 | -0.7 | 940 | 789 | 0 | 151 | -52 | -9.6 |
| 4 | 100 | 20 | 118 | 5 | -43 | -21.5 | 0 | -138 | -41 | -2 | -0.8 | 940 | 784 | 0 | 156 | -49 | -6.7 |
| 5 | 100 | 20 | 117 | 6 | -43 | -21.5 | 0 | -137 | -41 | -2 | -0.9 | 940 | 778 | 0 | 162 | -45 | -4.9 |

Reprinted with the permission of The Mader Group, Inc., Narberth, PA.

# TABLE 13.4 (concluded)

## INFLATION OF SALE PRICE, INCOME & EXPENSE AT 5-10-15% ANNUALLY

| YR | ---HOLDING RESULTS BEFORE INCOME TAXES--- GROSS INCOME | OPERATE EXPENSE | --MORTGAGE-- INTR | AMORT | CASH FLOW | % RE TURN | ---HOLDING RESULTS AFTER TAXES--- DEPREC IATION | TAXABLE INCOME | TAXES DUE | CASH FLOW | % RE TURN | ---OVERALL RESULTS WITH SALE AT YEAR END--- SALE PRICE | DEBT REPAY | TAXES DUE | CASH FLOW | TOTAL PROFIT | % IRR |
|----|----|----|----|----|----|----|----|----|----|----|----|----|----|----|----|----|----|
| 1 | 100 | 20 | 120 | 3 | -43 | -21.5 | 0 | -140 | -42 | -1 | -0.5 | 987 | 797 | 0 | 190 | -11 | -5.4 |
| 2 | 110 | 23 | 119 | 4 | -36 | -18.0 | 0 | -142 | -43 | 7 | 3.4 | 1036 | 793 | 0 | 243 | 49 | 11.5 |
| 3 | 121 | 26 | 119 | 4 | -28 | -14.2 | 0 | -145 | -44 | 15 | 7.6 | 1088 | 789 | 0 | 299 | 120 | 17.1 |
| 4 | 133 | 30 | 118 | 5 | -20 | -10.1 | 0 | -148 | -45 | 24 | 12.1 | 1143 | 784 | 0 | 359 | 204 | 19.6 |
| 5 | 146 | 35 | 117 | 6 | -12 | -5.8 | 0 | -152 | -46 | 34 | 17.1 | 1200 | 778 | 0 | 422 | 301 | 20.9 |

## INFLATION OF SALE PRICE, INCOME & EXPENSE AT 10% ANNUALLY

| YR | ---HOLDING RESULTS BEFORE INCOME TAXES--- GROSS INCOME | OPERATE EXPENSE | --MORTGAGE-- INTR | AMORT | CASH FLOW | % RE TURN | ---HOLDING RESULTS AFTER TAXES--- DEPREC IATION | TAXABLE INCOME | TAXES DUE | CASH FLOW | % RE TURN | ---OVERALL RESULTS WITH SALE AT YEAR END--- SALE PRICE | DEBT REPAY | TAXES DUE | CASH FLOW | TOTAL PROFIT | % IRR |
|----|----|----|----|----|----|----|----|----|----|----|----|----|----|----|----|----|----|
| 1 | 100 | 20 | 120 | 3 | -43 | -21.5 | 0 | -140 | -42 | -1 | -0.5 | 1034 | 797 | 0 | 237 | 36 | 18.1 |
| 2 | 110 | 22 | 119 | 4 | -35 | -17.5 | 0 | -141 | -42 | 7 | 3.7 | 1137 | 793 | 0 | 344 | 151 | 32.3 |
| 3 | 121 | 24 | 119 | 4 | -26 | -13.1 | 0 | -143 | -43 | 17 | 8.4 | 1251 | 789 | 0 | 462 | 285 | 34.5 |
| 4 | 133 | 27 | 118 | 5 | -16 | -8.2 | 0 | -145 | -43 | 27 | 13.5 | 1376 | 784 | 0 | 592 | 442 | 34.4 |
| 5 | 146 | 29 | 117 | 6 | -6 | -2.9 | 0 | -146 | -44 | 38 | 19.1 | 1514 | 778 | 0 | 736 | 624 | 33.7 |

Reprinted with the permission of The Mader Group, Inc., Narberth, PA.

# 14 Residential Property

This chapter presents eight reference tables detailing the profitability of *residential property,* which qualifies for *175 percent of straight-line depreciation.* Below is an index to this chapter's specific tables, showing the key factors varied and summarized results.

| Table | Percent Mortgaged | Percent Mortgage Interest Rate | Percent Net Operating Income (NOI) to Total Project Cost | Percent Year 5 Rates of Return | | |
|---|---|---|---|---|---|---|
| | | | | 0% Inflation | 5-10-15% Inflation | 10% Inflation |
| 14.1 | 60 | 10 | 9 | 6.4 | 16.4 | 24.4 |
| 14.2 | 60 | 10 | 12 | 10.7 | 20.3 | 28.1 |
| 14.3 | 60 | 15 | 9 | 2.1 | 12.9 | 21.5 |
| 14.4 | 60 | 15 | 12 | 6.5 | 16.9 | 25.2 |
| 14.5 | 80 | 10 | 9 | 8.2 | 26.4 | 38.4 |
| 14.6 | 80 | 10 | 12 | 17.7 | 33.9 | 45.0 |
| 14.7 | 80 | 15 | 9 | −5.9 | 17.9 | 31.6 |
| 14.8 | 80 | 15 | 12 | 5.1 | 25.5 | 38.2 |

# TABLE 14.1
Residential—175 percent of straight line depreciation (per $1,000)

## KEY OPERATING FACTORS ARE ---

| TOTAL PROJECT COST | --MORTGAGE TERMS--- | | | ----OPERATING & INFLATION ASSUMPTIONS----- | | | | | | ----DEPRECIATION--- | | | ----TAX RATES--- | |
|---|---|---|---|---|---|---|---|---|---|---|---|---|---|---|
| | AMOUNT | % INTR | LIFE | NET RESALE PRICE | % INFL | GROSS INCOME | % INFL | OPERATING EXPENSE | % INFL | AMOUNT | LIFE | RATE | INCOME | CAP GAIN |
| 1000 | 600 | 10.00 | 25 | 940 | 0 | 150 | 0 | 60 | 0 | 800 | 15 | 175% | 50% | 20% |

## PRE-OPERATING SUMMARY ---

| EQUITY AMOUNT | ---MORTGAGE TERMS---- | | | % NET RESALE TO COST | % INCOME TO COST | GROSS RENT MULT | % EXPENSE TO INCOME | % NOI TO COST | % DEPREC TO COST |
|---|---|---|---|---|---|---|---|---|---|
| | % DEBT | MONTHLY | YEARLY | | | | | | |
| 400 | 60.00 | 5 | 65 | 94.0 | 15.0 | 6.7 | 40.0 | 9.0 | 80.0 |

## OPERATING RESULTS ---

| YR | ---HOLDING RESULTS BEFORE INCOME TAXES---- | | | | | | ----HOLDING RESULTS AFTER TAXES--- | | | | | ----OVERALL RESULTS IF SOLD AT YEAR END---- | | | | | |
|---|---|---|---|---|---|---|---|---|---|---|---|---|---|---|---|---|---|
| | GROSS INCOME | OPERATE EXPENSE | --MORTGAGE-- INTR | AMORT | CASH FLOW | % RE TURN | DEPREC IATION | TAXABLE INCOME | TAXES DUE | CASH FLOW | % RE TURN | SALE PRICE | DEBT REPAY | TAXES DUE | CASH FLOW | TOTAL PROFIT | % IRR |
| 1 | 150 | 60 | 60 | 6 | 25 | 6.1 | 93 | -63 | -32 | 56 | 14.0 | 940 | 594 | 17 | 329 | -15 | -3.7 |
| 2 | 150 | 60 | 59 | 6 | 25 | 6.1 | 82 | -52 | -26 | 50 | 12.6 | 940 | 588 | 44 | 308 | 15 | 1.9 |
| 3 | 150 | 60 | 58 | 7 | 25 | 6.1 | 73 | -41 | -21 | 45 | 11.3 | 940 | 581 | 64 | 295 | 46 | 4.3 |
| 4 | 150 | 60 | 58 | 8 | 25 | 6.1 | 64 | -32 | -16 | 41 | 10.2 | 940 | 573 | 80 | 286 | 78 | 5.6 |
| 5 | 150 | 60 | 57 | 8 | 25 | 6.1 | 57 | -24 | -12 | 36 | 9.1 | 940 | 565 | 93 | 282 | 111 | 6.4 |

Reprinted with the permission of The Mader Group, Inc., Narberth, PA.

## TABLE 14.1 (concluded)

### INFLATION OF SALE PRICE, INCOME, AND EXPENSE AT 5-10-15% ANNUALLY

| YR | GROSS INCOME | OPERATE EXPENSE | MORTGAGE INTR | AMORT | CASH FLOW | % RETURN | DEPREC IATION | TAXABLE INCOME | TAXES DUE | CASH FLOW | % RETURN | SALE PRICE | DEBT REPAY | TAXES DUE | CASH FLOW | TOTAL PROFIT | % IRR |
|---|---|---|---|---|---|---|---|---|---|---|---|---|---|---|---|---|---|
| | ---HOLDING RESULTS BEFORE INCOME TAXES--- | | | | | | ---HOLDING RESULTS AFTER TAXES--- | | | | | ---OVERALL RESULTS IF SOLD AT YEAR END--- | | | | | |
| 1 | 150 | 60 | 60 | 6 | 25 | 6.1 | 93 | -63 | -32 | 56 | 14.0 | 987 | 594 | 28 | 365 | 21 | 5.2 |
| 2 | 165 | 69 | 59 | 6 | 31 | 7.6 | 82 | -46 | -23 | 53 | 13.3 | 1036 | 588 | 63 | 385 | 95 | 11.9 |
| 3 | 181 | 79 | 58 | 7 | 37 | 9.2 | 73 | -29 | -15 | 51 | 12.8 | 1088 | 581 | 94 | 413 | 174 | 14.4 |
| 4 | 200 | 91 | 58 | 8 | 43 | 10.7 | 64 | -14 | -7 | 50 | 12.5 | 1143 | 573 | 121 | 448 | 259 | 15.6 |
| 5 | 220 | 105 | 57 | 8 | 49 | 12.3 | 57 | 1 | 0 | 49 | 12.2 | 1200 | 565 | 145 | 490 | 349 | 16.4 |

### INFLATION OF SALE PRICE, INCOME, AND EXPENSE AT 10% ANNUALLY

OPERATING RESULTS ---

| YR | GROSS INCOME | OPERATE EXPENSE | MORTGAGE INTR | AMORT | CASH FLOW | % RETURN | DEPREC IATION | TAXABLE INCOME | TAXES DUE | CASH FLOW | % RETURN | SALE PRICE | DEBT REPAY | TAXES DUE | CASH FLOW | TOTAL PROFIT | % IRR |
|---|---|---|---|---|---|---|---|---|---|---|---|---|---|---|---|---|---|
| | ---HOLDING RESULTS BEFORE INCOME TAXES--- | | | | | | ---HOLDING RESULTS AFTER TAXES--- | | | | | ---OVERALL RESULTS IF SOLD AT YEAR END--- | | | | | |
| 1 | 150 | 60 | 60 | 6 | 25 | 6.1 | 93 | -63 | -32 | 56 | 14.0 | 1034 | 594 | 37 | 402 | 58 | 14.6 |
| 2 | 165 | 66 | 59 | 6 | 34 | 8.4 | 82 | -43 | -21 | 55 | 13.7 | 1137 | 588 | 83 | 466 | 177 | 21.3 |
| 3 | 181 | 73 | 58 | 7 | 43 | 10.9 | 73 | -22 | -11 | 55 | 13.7 | 1251 | 581 | 127 | 544 | 309 | 23.4 |
| 4 | 200 | 80 | 58 | 8 | 54 | 13.6 | 64 | -2 | -1 | 56 | 13.9 | 1376 | 573 | 168 | 635 | 456 | 24.2 |
| 5 | 220 | 88 | 57 | 8 | 66 | 16.6 | 57 | 18 | 9 | 57 | 14.3 | 1514 | 565 | 208 | 741 | 620 | 24.4 |

Reprinted with the permission of The Mader Group, Inc., Narberth, PA.

# TABLE 14.2
## Residential—175 percent of straight line depreciation (per $1,000)

KEY OPERATING FACTORS ARE ---

| TOTAL PROJECT COST | ----MORTGAGE TERMS---- AMOUNT | % INTR | LIFE |
|---|---|---|---|
| 1000 | 600 | 10.00 | 25 |

| ----OPERATING & INFLATION ASSUMPTIONS------ NET RESALE PRICE | % INFL | GROSS INCOME | % INCOME INFL | OPERATING EXPENSE | % EXPENSE INFL |
|---|---|---|---|---|---|
| 940 | 0 | 200 | 0 | 80 | 0 |

| ----DEPRECIATION--- AMOUNT | LIFE | RATE |
|---|---|---|
| 800 | 15 | 175% |

| ----TAX RATES--- INCOME | CAP GAIN |
|---|---|
| 50% | 20% |

PRE-OPERATING SUMMARY ---

| EQUITY AMOUNT | ----MORTGAGE TERMS---- % DEBT | MONTHLY | YEARLY |
|---|---|---|---|
| 400 | 60.00 | 5 | 65 |

| % NET RESALE TO COST | % INCOME TO COST | GROSS RENT MULT | % EXPENSE TO INCOME |
|---|---|---|---|
| 94.0 | 20.0 | 5.0 | 40.0 |

| % NOI TO COST | % DEPREC TO COST |
|---|---|
| 12.0 | 80.0 |

OPERATING RESULTS ---

| | ----HOLDING RESULTS BEFORE INCOME TAXES---- | | --MORTGAGE-- | | | | ----HOLDING RESULTS AFTER TAXES-- | | | | | ----OVERALL RESULTS IF SOLD AT YEAR END---- | | | | | |
|---|---|---|---|---|---|---|---|---|---|---|---|---|---|---|---|---|---|
| YR | GROSS INCOME | OPERATE EXPENSE | INTR | AMORT | CASH FLOW | % RE TURN | DEPREC IATION | TAXABLE INCOME | TAXES DUE | CASH FLOW | % RE TURN | SALE PRICE | DEBT REPAY | TAXES DUE | CASH FLOW | TOTAL PROFIT | % IRR |
| 1 | 200 | 80 | 60 | 6 | 55 | 13.6 | 93 | -33 | -17 | 71 | 17.8 | 940 | 594 | 17 | 329 | 0 | 0.0 |
| 2 | 200 | 80 | 59 | 6 | 55 | 13.6 | 82 | -22 | -11 | 65 | 16.3 | 940 | 588 | 44 | 308 | 45 | 5.9 |
| 3 | 200 | 80 | 58 | 7 | 55 | 13.6 | 73 | -11 | -6 | 60 | 15.1 | 940 | 581 | 64 | 295 | 91 | 8.4 |
| 4 | 200 | 80 | 58 | 8 | 55 | 13.6 | 64 | -2 | -1 | 56 | 13.9 | 940 | 573 | 80 | 286 | 138 | 9.8 |
| 5 | 200 | 80 | 57 | 8 | 55 | 13.6 | 57 | 6 | 3 | 51 | 12.9 | 940 | 565 | 93 | 282 | 186 | 10.7 |

Reprinted with the permission of The Mader Group, Inc., Narberth, PA.

# TABLE 14.2 (concluded)

## INFLATION OF SALE PRICE, INCOME, AND EXPENSE AT 5-10-15% ANNUALLY

OPERATING RESULTS ---

| YR | GROSS INCOME | OPERATE EXPENSE | MORTGAGE-- INTR | AMORT | HOLDING RESULTS BEFORE INCOME TAXES CASH FLOW | % RE TURN | HOLDING RESULTS AFTER TAXES DEPREC IATION | TAXABLE INCOME | TAXES DUE | CASH FLOW | % RE TURN | OVERALL RESULTS IF SOLD AT YEAR END SALE PRICE | DEBT REPAY | TAXES DUE | CASH FLOW | TOTAL PROFIT | % IRR |
|---|---|---|---|---|---|---|---|---|---|---|---|---|---|---|---|---|---|
| 1 | 200 | 80 | 60 | 6 | 55 | 13.6 | 93 | -33 | -17 | 71 | 17.8 | 987 | 594 | 28 | 365 | 36 | 8.9 |
| 2 | 220 | 92 | 59 | 6 | 63 | 15.6 | 82 | -14 | -7 | 69 | 17.3 | 1036 | 588 | 63 | 385 | 126 | 15.9 |
| 3 | 242 | 106 | 58 | 7 | 71 | 17.7 | 73 | 5 | 2 | 68 | 17.1 | 1088 | 581 | 94 | 413 | 222 | 18.4 |
| 4 | 266 | 122 | 58 | 8 | 79 | 19.8 | 64 | 22 | 11 | 68 | 17.0 | 1143 | 573 | 121 | 448 | 325 | 19.6 |
| 5 | 293 | 140 | 57 | 8 | 87 | 21.9 | 57 | 39 | 20 | 68 | 17.0 | 1200 | 565 | 145 | 490 | 435 | 20.3 |

## INFLATION OF SALE PRICE, INCOME, AND EXPENSE AT 10% ANNUALLY

OPERATING RESULTS ---

| YR | GROSS INCOME | OPERATE EXPENSE | MORTGAGE-- INTR | AMORT | HOLDING RESULTS BEFORE INCOME TAXES CASH FLOW | % RE TURN | HOLDING RESULTS AFTER TAXES DEPREC IATION | TAXABLE INCOME | TAXES DUE | CASH FLOW | % RE TURN | OVERALL RESULTS IF SOLD AT YEAR END SALE PRICE | DEBT REPAY | TAXES DUE | CASH FLOW | TOTAL PROFIT | % IRR |
|---|---|---|---|---|---|---|---|---|---|---|---|---|---|---|---|---|---|
| 1 | 200 | 80 | 60 | 6 | 55 | 13.6 | 93 | -33 | -17 | 71 | 17.8 | 1034 | 594 | 37 | 402 | 73 | 18.3 |
| 2 | 220 | 88 | 59 | 6 | 67 | 16.6 | 82 | -10 | -5 | 71 | 17.8 | 1137 | 588 | 83 | 466 | 208 | 25.1 |
| 3 | 242 | 97 | 58 | 7 | 80 | 19.9 | 73 | 14 | 7 | 73 | 18.2 | 1251 | 581 | 127 | 544 | 359 | 27.1 |
| 4 | 266 | 106 | 58 | 8 | 94 | 23.6 | 64 | 38 | 19 | 75 | 18.9 | 1376 | 573 | 168 | 635 | 526 | 27.9 |
| 5 | 293 | 117 | 57 | 8 | 110 | 27.6 | 57 | 62 | 31 | 79 | 19.8 | 1514 | 565 | 208 | 741 | 711 | 28.1 |

Reprinted with the permission of The Mader Group, Inc., Narberth, PA.

## TABLE 14.3
Residential—175 percent of straight line depreciation (per $1,000)

KEY OPERATING FACTORS ARE ---

| TOTAL PROJECT COST | ---MORTGAGE TERMS--- | | | ----OPERATING & INFLATION ASSUMPTIONS------ | | | | | | ----DEPRECIATION--- | | | ----TAX RATES--- | |
|---|---|---|---|---|---|---|---|---|---|---|---|---|---|---|
| | AMOUNT | % INTR | LIFE | NET RESALE PRICE | % INFL | GROSS INCOME | % INFL | OPERATING EXPENSE | % INFL | AMOUNT | LIFE | RATE | INCOME | CAP GAIN |
| 1000 | 600 | 15.00 | 25 | 940 | 0 | 150 | 0 | 60 | 0 | 800 | 15 | 175% | 50% | 20% |

PRE-OPERATING SUMMARY ---

| EQUITY AMOUNT | ---MORTGAGE TERMS---- | | | % NET RESALE TO COST | % INCOME TO COST | GROSS RENT MULT | % EXPENSE TO INCOME | % NOI TO COST | % DEPREC TO COST |
|---|---|---|---|---|---|---|---|---|---|
| | % DEBT | MONTHLY | YEARLY | | | | | | |
| 400 | 60.00 | 8 | 92 | 94.0 | 15.0 | 6.7 | 40.0 | 9.0 | 80.0 |

OPERATING RESULTS ---

| | ----HOLDING RESULTS BEFORE INCOME TAXES---- | | | | | | ----HOLDING RESULTS AFTER TAXES--- | | | | | ----OVERALL RESULTS IF SOLD AT YEAR END---- | | | | | |
|---|---|---|---|---|---|---|---|---|---|---|---|---|---|---|---|---|---|
| YR | GROSS INCOME | OPERATE EXPENSE | --MORTGAGE-- INTR | AMORT | CASH FLOW | % RE TURN | DEPREC IATION | TAXABLE INCOME | TAXES DUE | CASH FLOW | % RE TURN | SALE PRICE | DEBT REPAY | TAXES DUE | CASH FLOW | TOTAL PROFIT | % IRR |
| 1 | 150 | 60 | 90 | 2 | -2 | -0.6 | 93 | -93 | -47 | 44 | 11.1 | 940 | 598 | 17 | 326 | -30 | -7.5 |
| 2 | 150 | 60 | 89 | 3 | -2 | -0.6 | 82 | -82 | -41 | 39 | 9.7 | 940 | 595 | 44 | 301 | -16 | -2.1 |
| 3 | 150 | 60 | 89 | 3 | -2 | -0.6 | 73 | -72 | -36 | 34 | 8.4 | 940 | 592 | 64 | 284 | 1 | 0.1 |
| 4 | 150 | 60 | 88 | 4 | -2 | -0.6 | 64 | -63 | -31 | 29 | 7.3 | 940 | 588 | 80 | 272 | 18 | 1.3 |
| 5 | 150 | 60 | 88 | 4 | -2 | -0.6 | 57 | -55 | -27 | 25 | 6.3 | 940 | 584 | 93 | 264 | 35 | 2.1 |

Reprinted with the permission of The Mader Group, Inc., Narberth, PA.

TABLE 14.3 (concluded)

## INFLATION OF SALE PRICE, INCOME, AND EXPENSE AT 5-10-15% ANNUALLY

| YR | ---HOLDING RESULTS BEFORE INCOME TAXES--- GROSS INCOME | OPERATE EXPENSE | --MORTGAGE-- INTR | AMORT | CASH FLOW | % RE TURN | ---HOLDING RESULTS AFTER TAXES--- DEPRECIATION | TAXABLE INCOME | TAXES DUE | CASH FLOW | % RE TURN | ---OVERALL RESULTS IF SOLD AT YEAR END---- SALE PRICE | DEBT REPAY | TAXES DUE | CASH FLOW | TOTAL PROFIT | % IRR |
|---|---|---|---|---|---|---|---|---|---|---|---|---|---|---|---|---|---|
| 1 | 150 | 60 | 90 | 2 | -2 | -0.6 | 93 | -93 | -47 | 44 | 11.1 | 987 | 598 | 28 | 361 | 6 | 1.4 |
| 2 | 165 | 69 | 89 | 3 | 4 | 0.9 | 82 | -76 | -38 | 42 | 10.4 | 1036 | 595 | 63 | 378 | 64 | 8.2 |
| 3 | 181 | 79 | 89 | 3 | 10 | 2.5 | 73 | -60 | -30 | 40 | 9.9 | 1088 | 592 | 94 | 403 | 128 | 10.7 |
| 4 | 200 | 91 | 88 | 4 | 16 | 4.0 | 64 | -44 | -22 | 38 | 9.6 | 1143 | 588 | 121 | 434 | 198 | 12.1 |
| 5 | 220 | 105 | 88 | 4 | 22 | 5.6 | 57 | -30 | -15 | 37 | 9.4 | 1200 | 584 | 145 | 471 | 273 | 12.9 |

## INFLATION OF SALE PRICE, INCOME, AND EXPENSE AT 10% ANNUALLY

| YR | ---HOLDING RESULTS BEFORE INCOME TAXES--- GROSS INCOME | OPERATE EXPENSE | --MORTGAGE-- INTR | AMORT | CASH FLOW | % RE TURN | ---HOLDING RESULTS AFTER TAXES--- DEPRECIATION | TAXABLE INCOME | TAXES DUE | CASH FLOW | % RE TURN | ---OVERALL RESULTS IF SOLD AT YEAR END---- SALE PRICE | DEBT REPAY | TAXES DUE | CASH FLOW | TOTAL PROFIT | % IRR |
|---|---|---|---|---|---|---|---|---|---|---|---|---|---|---|---|---|---|
| 1 | 150 | 60 | 90 | 2 | -2 | -0.6 | 93 | -93 | -47 | 44 | 11.1 | 1034 | 598 | 37 | 399 | 43 | 10.8 |
| 2 | 165 | 66 | 89 | 3 | 7 | 1.7 | 82 | -73 | -36 | 43 | 10.8 | 1137 | 595 | 83 | 459 | 147 | 17.8 |
| 3 | 181 | 73 | 89 | 3 | 17 | 4.2 | 73 | -53 | -26 | 43 | 10.8 | 1251 | 592 | 127 | 533 | 264 | 20.0 |
| 4 | 200 | 80 | 88 | 4 | 28 | 6.9 | 64 | -33 | -17 | 44 | 11.0 | 1376 | 588 | 168 | 621 | 395 | 21.1 |
| 5 | 220 | 88 | 88 | 4 | 40 | 9.9 | 57 | -13 | -6 | 46 | 11.5 | 1514 | 584 | 208 | 723 | 543 | 21.5 |

Reprinted with the permission of The Mader Group, Inc., Narberth, PA.

## TABLE 14.4
Residential—175 percent of straight line depreciation (per $1,000)

KEY OPERATING FACTORS ARE ---

| TOTAL PROJECT COST | ---MORTGAGE TERMS--- AMOUNT | % INTR | LIFE | ----OPERATING & INFLATION ASSUMPTIONS----- NET RESALE PRICE | % INFL | GROSS INCOME | % INFL | OPERATING EXPENSE | % INFL | ----DEPRECIATION--- AMOUNT | LIFE | RATE | ----TAX RATES--- INCOME | CAP GAIN |
|---|---|---|---|---|---|---|---|---|---|---|---|---|---|---|
| 1000 | 600 | 15.00 | 25 | 940 | 0 | 200 | 0 | 80 | 0 | 800 | 15 | 175% | 50% | 20% |

PRE-OPERATING SUMMARY ---

| EQUITY AMOUNT | ---MORTGAGE TERMS--- % DEBT | MONTHLY | YEARLY | % NET RESALE TO COST | % INCOME TO COST | GROSS RENT MULT | % EXPENSE TO INCOME | % NOI TO COST | % DEPREC TO COST |
|---|---|---|---|---|---|---|---|---|---|
| 400 | 60.00 | 8 | 92 | 94.0 | 20.0 | 5.0 | 40.0 | 12.0 | 80.0 |

OPERATING RESULTS ---

| YR | ----HOLDING RESULTS BEFORE INCOME TAXES---- GROSS INCOME | OPERATE EXPENSE | --MORTGAGE-- INTR | AMORT | CASH FLOW | % RE TURN | ----HOLDING RESULTS AFTER TAXES-- DEPREC IATION | TAXABLE INCOME | TAXES DUE | CASH FLOW | % RE TURN | ----OVERALL RESULTS IF SOLD AT YEAR END---- SALE PRICE | DEBT REPAY | TAXES DUE | CASH FLOW | TOTAL PROFIT | % IRR |
|---|---|---|---|---|---|---|---|---|---|---|---|---|---|---|---|---|---|
| 1 | 200 | 80 | 90 | 2 | 28 | 6.9 | 93 | -63 | -32 | 59 | 14.8 | 940 | 598 | 17 | 326 | -15 | -3.7 |
| 2 | 200 | 80 | 89 | 3 | 28 | 6.9 | 82 | -52 | -26 | 54 | 13.4 | 940 | 595 | 44 | 301 | 14 | 1.9 |
| 3 | 200 | 80 | 89 | 3 | 28 | 6.9 | 73 | -42 | -21 | 49 | 12.2 | 940 | 592 | 64 | 284 | 46 | 4.3 |
| 4 | 200 | 80 | 88 | 4 | 28 | 6.9 | 64 | -33 | -16 | 44 | 11.0 | 940 | 588 | 80 | 272 | 78 | 5.6 |
| 5 | 200 | 80 | 88 | 4 | 28 | 6.9 | 57 | -25 | -12 | 40 | 10.0 | 940 | 584 | 93 | 264 | 110 | 6.5 |

Reprinted with the permission of The Mader Group, Inc., Narberth, PA.

TABLE 14.4 (concluded)

## INFLATION OF SALE PRICE, INCOME, AND EXPENSE AT 5-10-15% ANNUALLY

| YR | GROSS INCOME | OPERATE EXPENSE | MORTGAGE INTR | MORTGAGE AMORT | CASH FLOW | % RE TURN | DEPREC IATION | TAXABLE INCOME | TAXES DUE | CASH FLOW | % RE TURN | SALE PRICE | DEBT REPAY | TAXES DUE | CASH FLOW | TOTAL PROFIT | % IRR |
|----|------|------|------|------|------|------|------|------|------|------|------|------|------|------|------|------|------|
| 1 | 200 | 80 | 90 | 2 | 28 | 6.9 | 93 | -63 | -32 | 59 | 14.8 | 987 | 598 | 28 | 361 | 21 | 5.2 |
| 2 | 220 | 92 | 89 | 3 | 36 | 8.9 | 82 | -44 | -22 | 58 | 14.4 | 1036 | 595 | 63 | 378 | 95 | 12.1 |
| 3 | 242 | 106 | 89 | 3 | 44 | 11.0 | 73 | -26 | -13 | 57 | 14.2 | 1088 | 592 | 94 | 403 | 176 | 14.7 |
| 4 | 266 | 122 | 88 | 4 | 52 | 13.1 | 64 | -8 | -4 | 56 | 14.1 | 1143 | 588 | 121 | 434 | 264 | 16.1 |
| 5 | 293 | 140 | 88 | 4 | 61 | 15.2 | 57 | 8 | 4 | 57 | 14.1 | 1200 | 584 | 145 | 471 | 358 | 16.9 |

## INFLATION OF SALE PRICE, INCOME, AND EXPENSE AT 10% ANNUALLY

| YR | GROSS INCOME | OPERATE EXPENSE | MORTGAGE INTR | MORTGAGE AMORT | CASH FLOW | % RE TURN | DEPREC IATION | TAXABLE INCOME | TAXES DUE | CASH FLOW | % RE TURN | SALE PRICE | DEBT REPAY | TAXES DUE | CASH FLOW | TOTAL PROFIT | % IRR |
|----|------|------|------|------|------|------|------|------|------|------|------|------|------|------|------|------|------|
| 1 | 200 | 80 | 90 | 2 | 28 | 6.9 | 93 | -63 | -32 | 59 | 14.8 | 1034 | 598 | 37 | 399 | 58 | 14.6 |
| 2 | 220 | 88 | 89 | 3 | 40 | 9.9 | 82 | -40 | -20 | 60 | 14.9 | 1137 | 595 | 83 | 459 | 178 | 21.6 |
| 3 | 242 | 97 | 89 | 3 | 53 | 13.2 | 73 | -17 | -8 | 61 | 15.3 | 1251 | 592 | 127 | 533 | 313 | 23.8 |
| 4 | 266 | 106 | 88 | 4 | 68 | 16.9 | 64 | 7 | 3 | 64 | 16.0 | 1376 | 588 | 168 | 621 | 465 | 24.8 |
| 5 | 293 | 117 | 88 | 4 | 83 | 20.9 | 57 | 31 | 15 | 68 | 17.0 | 1514 | 584 | 208 | 723 | 635 | 25.2 |

Reprinted with the permission of The Mader Group, Inc., Narberth, PA.

TABLE 14.5
Residential—175 percent of straight line depreciation (per $1,000)

KEY OPERATING FACTORS ARE ---

| TOTAL PROJECT COST | MORTGAGE TERMS AMOUNT | % INTR | LIFE | NET RESALE PRICE | % INFL | GROSS INCOME | % INFL | OPERATING EXPENSE | % INFL | DEPRECIATION AMOUNT | LIFE | RATE | TAX RATES INCOME | CAP GAIN |
|---|---|---|---|---|---|---|---|---|---|---|---|---|---|---|
| 1000 | 800 | 10.00 | 25 | 940 | 0 | 150 | 0 | 60 | 0 | 800 | 15 | 175% | 50% | 20% |

PRE-OPERATING SUMMARY ---

| EQUITY AMOUNT | MORTGAGE TERMS % DEBT | MONTHLY | YEARLY | % NET RESALE TO COST | % INCOME TO COST | GROSS RENT MULT | % EXPENSE TO INCOME | % NOI TO COST | % DEPREC TO COST |
|---|---|---|---|---|---|---|---|---|---|
| 200 | 80.00 | 7 | 87 | 94.0 | 15.0 | 6.7 | 40.0 | 9.0 | 80.0 |

OPERATING RESULTS ---

| | HOLDING RESULTS BEFORE INCOME TAXES | | | | | HOLDING RESULTS AFTER TAXES | | | | | OVERALL RESULTS IF SOLD AT YEAR END | | | | | |
|---|---|---|---|---|---|---|---|---|---|---|---|---|---|---|---|---|---|
| YR | GROSS INCOME | OPERATE EXPENSE | MORTGAGE INTR | AMORT | CASH FLOW | % RE TURN | DEPREC IATION | TAXABLE INCOME | TAXES DUE | CASH FLOW | % RE TURN | SALE PRICE | DEBT REPAY | TAXES DUE | CASH FLOW | TOTAL PROFIT | % IRR |
| 1 | 150 | 60 | 80 | 8 | 3 | 1.4 | 93 | -83 | -41 | 44 | 22.1 | 940 | 792 | 17 | 131 | -25 | -12.4 |
| 2 | 150 | 60 | 79 | 8 | 3 | 1.4 | 82 | -71 | -36 | 38 | 19.2 | 940 | 784 | 44 | 112 | -5 | -1.5 |
| 3 | 150 | 60 | 78 | 9 | 3 | 1.4 | 73 | -61 | -30 | 33 | 16.6 | 940 | 775 | 64 | 101 | 17 | 3.4 |
| 4 | 150 | 60 | 77 | 10 | 3 | 1.4 | 64 | -51 | -26 | 28 | 14.2 | 940 | 765 | 80 | 95 | 39 | 6.3 |
| 5 | 150 | 60 | 76 | 11 | 3 | 1.4 | 57 | -43 | -21 | 24 | 12.1 | 940 | 753 | 93 | 94 | 62 | 8.2 |

Reprinted with the permission of The Mader Group, Inc., Narberth, PA.

TABLE 14.5 (concluded)

## INFLATION OF SALE PRICE, INCOME, AND EXPENSE AT 5-10-15% ANNUALLY

| YR | ----HOLDING RESULTS BEFORE INCOME TAXES---- GROSS INCOME | OPERATE EXPENSE | --MORTGAGE-- INTR | AMORT | CASH FLOW | % RE TURN | ----HOLDING RESULTS AFTER TAXES-- DEPREC IATION | TAXABLE INCOME | TAXES DUE | CASH FLOW | % RE TURN | ----OVERALL RESULTS IF SOLD AT YEAR END---- SALE PRICE | DEBT REPAY | TAXES DUE | CASH FLOW | TOTAL PROFIT | % IRR |
|---|---|---|---|---|---|---|---|---|---|---|---|---|---|---|---|---|---|
| 1 | 150 | 60 | 80 | 8 | 3 | 1.4 | 93 | -83 | -41 | 44 | 22.1 | 987 | 792 | 28 | 167 | 11 | 5.4 |
| 2 | 165 | 69 | 79 | 8 | 9 | 4.4 | 82 | -65 | -33 | 41 | 20.7 | 1036 | 784 | 63 | 189 | 75 | 19.0 |
| 3 | 181 | 79 | 78 | 9 | 15 | 7.5 | 73 | -49 | -24 | 39 | 19.6 | 1088 | 775 | 94 | 219 | 144 | 23.6 |
| 4 | 200 | 91 | 77 | 10 | 21 | 10.6 | 64 | -33 | -16 | 38 | 18.8 | 1143 | 765 | 121 | 257 | 220 | 25.5 |
| 5 | 220 | 105 | 76 | 11 | 27 | 13.7 | 57 | -18 | -9 | 36 | 18.2 | 1200 | 753 | 145 | 302 | 301 | 26.4 |

## INFLATION OF SALE PRICE, INCOME, AND EXPENSE AT 10% ANNUALLY

| YR | ----HOLDING RESULTS BEFORE INCOME TAXES---- GROSS INCOME | OPERATE EXPENSE | --MORTGAGE-- INTR | AMORT | CASH FLOW | % RE TURN | ----HOLDING RESULTS AFTER TAXES-- DEPREC IATION | TAXABLE INCOME | TAXES DUE | CASH FLOW | % RE TURN | ----OVERALL RESULTS IF SOLD AT YEAR END---- SALE PRICE | DEBT REPAY | TAXES DUE | CASH FLOW | TOTAL PROFIT | % IRR |
|---|---|---|---|---|---|---|---|---|---|---|---|---|---|---|---|---|---|
| 1 | 150 | 60 | 80 | 8 | 3 | 1.4 | 93 | -83 | -41 | 44 | 22.1 | 1034 | 792 | 37 | 204 | 48 | 24.2 |
| 2 | 165 | 66 | 79 | 8 | 12 | 5.9 | 82 | -62 | -31 | 43 | 21.5 | 1137 | 784 | 83 | 270 | 157 | 36.6 |
| 3 | 181 | 73 | 78 | 9 | 22 | 10.8 | 73 | -42 | -21 | 43 | 21.3 | 1251 | 775 | 127 | 350 | 280 | 39.0 |
| 4 | 200 | 80 | 77 | 10 | 33 | 16.3 | 64 | -22 | -11 | 43 | 21.7 | 1376 | 765 | 168 | 444 | 417 | 39.1 |
| 5 | 220 | 88 | 76 | 11 | 45 | 22.3 | 57 | -1 | -1 | 45 | 22.5 | 1514 | 753 | 208 | 553 | 571 | 38.4 |

Reprinted with the permission of The Mader Group, Inc., Narberth, PA.

TABLE 14.6
Residential—175 percent of straight line depreciation (per $1,000)

KEY OPERATING FACTORS ARE ---

| TOTAL PROJECT COST | --MORTGAGE TERMS--- AMOUNT | % INTR | LIFE | -----OPERATING & INFLATION ASSUMPTIONS------ NET RESALE PRICE | % INFL | GROSS INCOME | % INFL | OPERATING EXPENSE | % INFL | ----DEPRECIATION---- AMOUNT | LIFE | RATE | ----TAX RATES--- INCOME | CAP GAIN |
|---|---|---|---|---|---|---|---|---|---|---|---|---|---|---|
| 1000 | 800 | 10.00 | 25 | 940 | 0 | 200 | 0 | 80 | 0 | 800 | 15 | 175% | 50% | 20% |

PRE-OPERATING SUMMARY ---

| EQUITY AMOUNT | ----MORTGAGE TERMS---- % DEBT | MONTHLY | YEARLY | % NET RESALE TO COST | % INCOME TO COST | GROSS RENT MULT | % EXPENSE TO INCOME | % NOI TO COST | % DEPREC TO COST |
|---|---|---|---|---|---|---|---|---|---|
| 200 | 80.00 | 7 | 87 | 94.0 | 20.0 | 5.0 | 40.0 | 12.0 | 80.0 |

OPERATING RESULTS ---

| YR | ----HOLDING RESULTS BEFORE INCOME TAXES---- GROSS INCOME | OPERATE EXPENSE | --MORTGAGE-- INTR | AMORT | CASH FLOW | % RE TURN | ----HOLDING RESULTS AFTER TAXES---- DEPREC IATION | TAXABLE INCOME | TAXES DUE | CASH FLOW | % RE TURN | ----OVERALL RESULTS IF SOLD AT YEAR END---- SALE PRICE | DEBT REPAY | TAXES DUE | CASH FLOW | TOTAL PROFIT | % IRR |
|---|---|---|---|---|---|---|---|---|---|---|---|---|---|---|---|---|---|
| 1 | 200 | 80 | 80 | 8 | 33 | 16.4 | 93 | -53 | -26 | 59 | 29.6 | 940 | 792 | 17 | 131 | -10 | -4.9 |
| 2 | 200 | 80 | 79 | 8 | 33 | 16.4 | 82 | -41 | -21 | 53 | 26.7 | 940 | 784 | 44 | 112 | 25 | 7.0 |
| 3 | 200 | 80 | 78 | 9 | 33 | 16.4 | 73 | -31 | -15 | 48 | 24.1 | 940 | 775 | 64 | 101 | 62 | 12.4 |
| 4 | 200 | 80 | 77 | 10 | 33 | 16.4 | 64 | -21 | -11 | 43 | 21.7 | 940 | 765 | 80 | 95 | 99 | 15.6 |
| 5 | 200 | 80 | 76 | 11 | 33 | 16.4 | 57 | -13 | -6 | 39 | 19.6 | 940 | 753 | 93 | 94 | 137 | 17.7 |

Reprinted with the permission of The Mader Group, Inc., Narberth, PA.

TABLE 14.6 (concluded)

## INFLATION OF SALE PRICE, INCOME, AND EXPENSE AT 5-10-15% ANNUALLY

| YR | ----HOLDING RESULTS BEFORE INCOME TAXES---- | | | | | | ----HOLDING RESULTS AFTER TAXES---- | | | | | ----OVERALL RESULTS IF SOLD AT YEAR END---- | | | | | |
|---|---|---|---|---|---|---|---|---|---|---|---|---|---|---|---|---|---|
| | GROSS INCOME | OPERATE EXPENSE | --MORTGAGE-- INTR | AMORT | CASH FLOW | % RE TURN | DEPREC IATION | TAXABLE INCOME | TAXES DUE | CASH FLOW | % RE TURN | SALE PRICE | DEBT REPAY | TAXES DUE | CASH FLOW | TOTAL PROFIT | % IRR |
| 1 | 200 | 80 | 80 | 8 | 33 | 16.4 | 93 | -53 | -26 | 59 | 29.6 | 987 | 792 | 28 | 167 | 26 | 12.9 |
| 2 | 220 | 92 | 79 | 8 | 41 | 20.4 | 82 | -33 | -17 | 57 | 28.7 | 1036 | 784 | 63 | 189 | 106 | 26.8 |
| 3 | 242 | 106 | 78 | 9 | 49 | 24.5 | 73 | -15 | -7 | 56 | 28.1 | 1088 | 775 | 94 | 219 | 192 | 31.4 |
| 4 | 266 | 122 | 77 | 10 | 57 | 28.6 | 64 | 3 | 2 | 56 | 27.9 | 1143 | 765 | 121 | 257 | 286 | 33.2 |
| 5 | 293 | 140 | 76 | 11 | 66 | 32.8 | 57 | 20 | 10 | 56 | 27.8 | 1200 | 753 | 145 | 302 | 386 | 33.9 |

TABLE 14-6: RESIDENTIAL - 175 PERCENT OF STRAIGHT LINE OF DEPRECIATION (PER $1000)

## INFLATION OF SALE PRICE, INCOME, AND EXPENSE AT 10% ANNUALLY

| YR | ----HOLDING RESULTS BEFORE INCOME TAXES---- | | | | | | ----HOLDING RESULTS AFTER TAXES---- | | | | | ----OVERALL RESULTS IF SOLD AT YEAR END---- | | | | | |
|---|---|---|---|---|---|---|---|---|---|---|---|---|---|---|---|---|---|
| | GROSS INCOME | OPERATE EXPENSE | --MORTGAGE-- INTR | AMORT | CASH FLOW | % RE TURN | DEPREC IATION | TAXABLE INCOME | TAXES DUE | CASH FLOW | % RE TURN | SALE PRICE | DEBT REPAY | TAXES DUE | CASH FLOW | TOTAL PROFIT | % IRR |
| 1 | 200 | 80 | 80 | 8 | 33 | 16.4 | 93 | -53 | -26 | 59 | 29.6 | 1034 | 792 | 37 | 204 | 63 | 31.7 |
| 2 | 220 | 88 | 79 | 8 | 45 | 22.4 | 82 | -29 | -15 | 59 | 29.7 | 1137 | 784 | 83 | 270 | 189 | 44.0 |
| 3 | 242 | 97 | 78 | 9 | 58 | 29.0 | 73 | -6 | -3 | 61 | 30.4 | 1251 | 775 | 127 | 350 | 329 | 46.1 |
| 4 | 266 | 106 | 77 | 10 | 72 | 36.2 | 64 | 18 | 9 | 63 | 31.6 | 1376 | 765 | 168 | 444 | 487 | 45.9 |
| 5 | 293 | 117 | 76 | 11 | 88 | 44.2 | 57 | 43 | 21 | 67 | 33.5 | 1514 | 753 | 208 | 553 | 663 | 45.0 |

Reprinted with the permission of The Mader Group, Inc., Narberth, PA.

## TABLE 14.7
### Residential—175 percent of straight line depreciation (per $1,000)

KEY OPERATING FACTORS ARE ---

| TOTAL PROJECT COST | --MORTGAGE TERMS--- AMOUNT | % INTR | LIFE | NET RESALE PRICE | % INFL | GROSS INCOME | % INCOME INFL | % OPERATING EXPENSE | % EXPENSE INFL | --DEPRECIATION-- AMOUNT | LIFE | RATE | --TAX RATES-- INCOME | CAP GAIN |
|---|---|---|---|---|---|---|---|---|---|---|---|---|---|---|
| 1000 | 800 | 15.00 | 25 | 940 | 0 | 150 | 0 | 60 | 0 | 800 | 15 | 175% | 50% | 20% |

PRE-OPERATING SUMMARY ---

| EQUITY AMOUNT | --MORTGAGE TERMS-- % DEBT | MONTHLY | YEARLY | % NET RESALE TO COST | % INCOME TO COST | GROSS RENT MULT | % EXPENSE TO INCOME | % NOI TO COST | % DEPREC TO COST |
|---|---|---|---|---|---|---|---|---|---|
| 200 | 80.00 | 10 | 123 | 94.0 | 15.0 | 6.7 | 40.0 | 9.0 | 80.0 |

OPERATING RESULTS ---

| | --HOLDING RESULTS BEFORE INCOME TAXES-- | | | | | --HOLDING RESULTS AFTER TAXES-- | | | | | --OVERALL RESULTS IF SOLD AT YEAR END-- | | | | | |
|---|---|---|---|---|---|---|---|---|---|---|---|---|---|---|---|---|---|
| YR | GROSS INCOME | OPERATE EXPENSE | MORTGAGE INTR | AMORT | CASH FLOW | % RE TURN | DEPREC IATION | TAXABLE INCOME | TAXES DUE | CASH FLOW | % RE TURN | SALE PRICE | DEBT REPAY | TAXES DUE | CASH FLOW | TOTAL PROFIT | % IRR |
| 1 | 150 | 60 | 120 | 3 | -33 | -16.5 | 93 | -123 | -62 | 29 | 14.3 | 940 | 797 | 17 | 127 | -45 | -22.4 |
| 2 | 150 | 60 | 119 | 4 | -33 | -16.5 | 82 | -112 | -56 | 23 | 11.5 | 940 | 793 | 44 | 103 | -46 | -13.2 |
| 3 | 150 | 60 | 119 | 4 | -33 | -16.5 | 73 | -102 | -51 | 18 | 8.9 | 940 | 789 | 64 | 87 | -44 | -9.4 |
| 4 | 150 | 60 | 118 | 5 | -33 | -16.5 | 64 | -92 | -46 | 13 | 6.6 | 940 | 784 | 80 | 76 | -42 | -7.3 |
| 5 | 150 | 60 | 117 | 6 | -33 | -16.5 | 57 | -84 | -42 | 9 | 4.5 | 940 | 778 | 93 | 69 | -39 | -5.9 |

Reprinted with the permission of The Mader Group, Inc., Narberth, PA.

TABLE 14.7 (concluded)

## INFLATION OF SALE PRICE, INCOME, AND EXPENSE AT 5-10-15% ANNUALLY

| | | | ----HOLDING RESULTS BEFORE INCOME TAXES---- | | | | ----HOLDING RESULTS AFTER TAXES--- | | | | | ----OVERALL RESULTS IF SOLD AT YEAR END---- | | | | | |
| | | | --MORTGAGE-- | | | | | | | | | | | | | | |
| YR | GROSS INCOME | OPERATE EXPENSE | INTR | AMORT | CASH FLOW | % RE TURN | DEPREC IATION | TAXABLE INCOME | TAXES DUE | CASH FLOW | % RE TURN | SALE PRICE | DEBT REPAY | TAXES DUE | CASH FLOW | TOTAL PROFIT | % IRR |
|---|---|---|---|---|---|---|---|---|---|---|---|---|---|---|---|---|---|
| 1 | 150 | 60 | 120 | 3 | -33 | -16.5 | 93 | -123 | -62 | 29 | 14.3 | 987 | 797 | 28 | 162 | -9 | -4.6 |
| 2 | 165 | 69 | 119 | 4 | -27 | -13.5 | 82 | -106 | -53 | 26 | 13.0 | 1036 | 793 | 63 | 180 | 35 | 8.9 |
| 3 | 181 | 79 | 119 | 4 | -21 | -10.4 | 73 | -89 | -45 | 24 | 11.9 | 1088 | 789 | 94 | 205 | 84 | 13.9 |
| 4 | 200 | 91 | 118 | 5 | -15 | -7.3 | 64 | -74 | -37 | 22 | 11.2 | 1143 | 784 | 121 | 238 | 138 | 16.5 |
| 5 | 220 | 105 | 117 | 6 | -8 | -4.1 | 57 | -59 | -30 | 21 | 10.7 | 1200 | 778 | 145 | 277 | 199 | 17.9 |

## INFLATION OF SALE PRICE, INCOME, AND EXPENSE AT 10% ANNUALLY

| | | | ----HOLDING RESULTS BEFORE INCOME TAXES---- | | | | ----HOLDING RESULTS AFTER TAXES-- | | | | | ----OVERALL RESULTS IF SOLD AT YEAR END---- | | | | | |
| | | | --MORTGAGE-- | | | | | | | | | | | | | | |
| YR | GROSS INCOME | OPERATE EXPENSE | INTR | AMORT | CASH FLOW | % RE TURN | DEPREC IATION | TAXABLE INCOME | TAXES DUE | CASH FLOW | % RE TURN | SALE PRICE | DEBT REPAY | TAXES DUE | CASH FLOW | TOTAL PROFIT | % IRR |
|---|---|---|---|---|---|---|---|---|---|---|---|---|---|---|---|---|---|
| 1 | 150 | 60 | 120 | 3 | -33 | -16.5 | 93 | -123 | -62 | 29 | 14.3 | 1034 | 797 | 37 | 200 | 28 | 14.1 |
| 2 | 165 | 66 | 119 | 4 | -24 | -12.0 | 82 | -103 | -51 | 27 | 13.7 | 1137 | 793 | 83 | 261 | 117 | 27.4 |
| 3 | 181 | 73 | 119 | 4 | -14 | -7.0 | 73 | -83 | -41 | 27 | 13.6 | 1251 | 789 | 127 | 336 | 219 | 30.8 |
| 4 | 200 | 80 | 118 | 5 | -3 | -1.6 | 64 | -63 | -31 | 28 | 14.0 | 1376 | 784 | 168 | 425 | 336 | 31.7 |
| 5 | 220 | 88 | 117 | 6 | 9 | 4.4 | 57 | -42 | -21 | 30 | 15.0 | 1514 | 778 | 208 | 528 | 469 | 31.6 |

Reprinted with the permission of The Mader Group, Inc., Narberth, PA.

## TABLE 14.8
### Residential—175 percent of straight line depreciation (per $1,000)

KEY OPERATING FACTORS ARE ---

| TOTAL PROJECT COST | ---MORTGAGE TERMS--- AMOUNT | % INTR | LIFE | ---OPERATING & INFLATION ASSUMPTIONS--- NET RESALE PRICE | % INFL | GROSS INCOME | % INFL | GROSS RENT MULT | OPERATING EXPENSE | % INFL | ---DEPRECIATION--- AMOUNT | LIFE | RATE | ---TAX RATES--- INCOME | CAP GAIN |
|---|---|---|---|---|---|---|---|---|---|---|---|---|---|---|---|
| 1000 | 800 | 15.00 | 25 | 940 | 0 | 200 | 0 | 0 | 80 | 0 | 800 | 15 | 175% | 50% | 20% |

PRE-OPERATING SUMMARY ---

| EQUITY AMOUNT | ---MORTGAGE TERMS--- % DEBT | MONTHLY | YEARLY | % NET RESALE TO COST | % INCOME TO COST | GROSS RENT MULT | % EXPENSE TO INCOME | % NOI TO COST | % DEPREC TO COST |
|---|---|---|---|---|---|---|---|---|---|
| 200 | 80.00 | 10 | 123 | 94.0 | 20.0 | 5.0 | 40.0 | 12.0 | 80.0 |

OPERATING RESULTS ---

| YR | GROSS INCOME | OPERATE EXPENSE | ---MORTGAGE--- INTR | AMORT | ---HOLDING RESULTS BEFORE INCOME TAXES--- CASH FLOW | % RE TURN | ---HOLDING RESULTS AFTER TAXES--- DEPRECIATION | TAXABLE INCOME | TAXES DUE | CASH FLOW | % RE TURN | ---OVERALL RESULTS IF SOLD AT YEAR END--- SALE PRICE | DEBT REPAY | TAXES DUE | CASH FLOW | TOTAL PROFIT | % IRR |
|---|---|---|---|---|---|---|---|---|---|---|---|---|---|---|---|---|---|
| 1 | 200 | 80 | 120 | 3 | -3 | -1.5 | 93 | -93 | -47 | 44 | 21.8 | 940 | 797 | 17 | 127 | -30 | -14.9 |
| 2 | 200 | 80 | 119 | 4 | -3 | -1.5 | 82 | -82 | -41 | 38 | 19.0 | 940 | 793 | 44 | 103 | -16 | -4.5 |
| 3 | 200 | 80 | 119 | 4 | -3 | -1.5 | 73 | -72 | -36 | 33 | 16.4 | 940 | 789 | 64 | 87 | 1 | 0.2 |
| 4 | 200 | 80 | 118 | 5 | -3 | -1.5 | 64 | -62 | -31 | 28 | 14.1 | 940 | 784 | 80 | 76 | 18 | 3.1 |
| 5 | 200 | 80 | 117 | 6 | -3 | -1.5 | 57 | -54 | -27 | 24 | 12.0 | 940 | 778 | 93 | 69 | 36 | 5.1 |

Reprinted with the permission of The Mader Group, Inc., Narberth, PA.

TABLE 14.8 (concluded)

## INFLATION OF SALE PRICE, INCOME, AND EXPENSE AT 5-10-15% ANNUALLY

| | ----HOLDING RESULTS BEFORE INCOME TAXES---- | | | | | | ----HOLDING RESULTS AFTER TAXES---- | | | | | ----OVERALL RESULTS IF SOLD AT YEAR END---- | | | | | |
|---|---|---|---|---|---|---|---|---|---|---|---|---|---|---|---|---|---|
| | GROSS | OPERATE | --MORTGAGE-- | | CASH | % RE | DEPREC | TAXABLE | TAXES | CASH | % RE | SALE | DEBT | TAXES | CASH | TOTAL | % |
| YR | INCOME | EXPENSE | INTR | AMORT | FLOW | TURN | IATION | INCOME | DUE | FLOW | TURN | PRICE | REPAY | DUE | FLOW | PROFIT | IRR |
| 1 | 200 | 80 | 120 | 3 | -3 | -1.5 | 93 | -93 | -47 | 44 | 21.8 | 987 | 797 | 28 | 162 | 6 | 2.8 |
| 2 | 220 | 92 | 119 | 4 | 5 | 2.5 | 82 | -74 | -37 | 42 | 21.0 | 1036 | 793 | 63 | 180 | 66 | 16.8 |
| 3 | 242 | 106 | 119 | 4 | 13 | 6.6 | 73 | -55 | -28 | 41 | 20.4 | 1088 | 789 | 94 | 205 | 132 | 21.9 |
| 4 | 266 | 122 | 118 | 5 | 22 | 10.8 | 64 | -38 | -19 | 40 | 20.2 | 1143 | 784 | 121 | 238 | 205 | 24.3 |
| 5 | 293 | 140 | 117 | 6 | 30 | 15.0 | 57 | -21 | -11 | 41 | 20.3 | 1200 | 778 | 145 | 277 | 284 | 25.5 |

## INFLATION OF SALE PRICE, INCOME, AND EXPENSE AT 10% ANNUALLY

| | ----HOLDING RESULTS BEFORE INCOME TAXES---- | | | | | | ----HOLDING RESULTS AFTER TAXES---- | | | | | ----OVERALL RESULTS IF SOLD AT YEAR END---- | | | | | |
|---|---|---|---|---|---|---|---|---|---|---|---|---|---|---|---|---|---|
| | GROSS | OPERATE | --MORTGAGE-- | | CASH | % RE | DEPREC | TAXABLE | TAXES | CASH | % RE | SALE | DEBT | TAXES | CASH | TOTAL | % |
| YR | INCOME | EXPENSE | INTR | AMORT | FLOW | TURN | IATION | INCOME | DUE | FLOW | TURN | PRICE | REPAY | DUE | FLOW | PROFIT | IRR |
| 1 | 200 | 80 | 120 | 3 | -3 | -1.5 | 93 | -93 | -47 | 44 | 21.8 | 1034 | 797 | 37 | 200 | 43 | 21.6 |
| 2 | 220 | 88 | 119 | 4 | 9 | 4.5 | 82 | -70 | -35 | -44 | 22.0 | 1137 | 793 | 83 | 261 | 148 | 34.8 |
| 3 | 242 | 97 | 119 | 4 | 22 | 11.1 | 73 | -46 | -23 | 45 | 22.7 | 1251 | 789 | 127 | 336 | 269 | 37.9 |
| 4 | 266 | 106 | 118 | 5 | 37 | 18.4 | 64 | -23 | -11 | 48 | 24.0 | 1376 | 784 | 168 | 425 | 406 | 38.5 |
| 5 | 293 | 117 | 117 | 6 | 53 | 26.4 | 57 | 2 | 1 | 52 | 25.9 | 1514 | 778 | 208 | 528 | 561 | 38.2 |

Reprinted with the permission of The Mader Group, Inc., Narberth, PA.

# 15 Commerical Property

This chapter presents eight reference tables. It covers the profitability of *commercial property* (or residential property where straight-line is chosen). Such property qualifies for *100 percent of straight-line depreciation.* Below is an index to this chapter's specific tables, showing the key factors varied and summarized results.

| Table | Percent Mortgaged | Percent Mortgage Interest Rate | Percent Net Operating Income (NOI) to Total Project Cost | Percent Year 5 Rates of Return | | |
|---|---|---|---|---|---|---|
| | | | | 0% Inflation | 5-10-15% Inflation | 10% Inflation |
| 15.1 | 60 | 10 | 9 | 5.9 | 15.4 | 23.2 |
| 15.2 | 60 | 10 | 12 | 9.9 | 19.2 | 26.7 |
| 15.3 | 60 | 15 | 9 | 1.9 | 12.2 | 20.5 |
| 15.4 | 60 | 15 | 12 | 6.0 | 16.0 | 24.0 |
| 15.5 | 80 | 10 | 9 | 7.0 | 23.8 | 35.4 |
| 15.6 | 80 | 10 | 12 | 15.2 | 30.7 | 41.6 |
| 15.7 | 80 | 15 | 9 | −4.8 | 16.0 | 29.1 |
| 15.8 | 80 | 15 | 12 | 4.2 | 22.9 | 35.2 |

TABLE 15.1
Commercial—100 percent of straight line depreciation (per $1,000)

KEY OPERATING FACTORS ARE ---

| TOTAL PROJECT COST | ---MORTGAGE TERMS--- | | | ---OPERATING & INFLATION ASSUMPTIONS--- | | | | | | ---DEPRECIATION--- | | | ----TAX RATES--- | |
|---|---|---|---|---|---|---|---|---|---|---|---|---|---|---|
| | AMOUNT | % INTR | LIFE | NET RESALE PRICE | % INFL | GROSS INCOME | % INCOME INFL | % OPERATING EXPENSE | % EXPENSE INFL | AMOUNT | LIFE | RATE | INCOME | CAP GAIN |
| 1000 | 600 | 10.00 | 25 | 940 | 0 | 150 | 0 | 60 | 0 | 800 | 15 | 100% | 50% | 20% |

PRE-OPERATING SUMMARY ---

| EQUITY AMOUNT | ---MORTGAGE TERMS---- | | | % NET RESALE TO COST | % INCOME TO COST | GROSS RENT MULT | % NOI TO COST | % DEPREC TO COST |
|---|---|---|---|---|---|---|---|---|
| | % DEBT | MONTHLY | YEARLY | | | | | |
| 400 | 60.00 | 5 | 65 | 94.0 | 15.0 | 6.7 | 9.0 | 80.0 |

OPERATING RESULTS ---

| YR | ---HOLDING RESULTS BEFORE INCOME TAXES--- | | | | | | ---HOLDING RESULTS AFTER TAXES--- | | | | | ---OVERALL RESULTS IF SOLD AT YEAR END---- | | | | | |
|---|---|---|---|---|---|---|---|---|---|---|---|---|---|---|---|---|---|
| | GROSS INCOME | OPERATE EXPENSE | --MORTGAGE-- INTR | AMORT | CASH FLOW | % RE TURN | DEPREC IATION | TAXABLE INCOME | TAXES DUE | CASH FLOW | % RE TURN | SALE PRICE | DEBT REPAY | TAXES DUE | CASH FLOW | TOTAL PROFIT | % IRR |
| 1 | 150 | 60 | 60 | 6 | 25 | 6.1 | 53 | -23 | -12 | 36 | 9.0 | 940 | 594 | -1 | 347 | -17 | -4.2 |
| 2 | 150 | 60 | 59 | 6 | 25 | 6.1 | 53 | -22 | -11 | 36 | 9.0 | 940 | 588 | 9 | 343 | 15 | 1.9 |
| 3 | 150 | 60 | 58 | 7 | 25 | 6.1 | 53 | -22 | -11 | 35 | 8.9 | 940 | 581 | 20 | 339 | 46 | 4.1 |
| 4 | 150 | 60 | 58 | 8 | 25 | 6.1 | 53 | -21 | -11 | 35 | 8.8 | 940 | 573 | 31 | 336 | 78 | 5.2 |
| 5 | 150 | 60 | 57 | 8 | 25 | 6.1 | 53 | -20 | -10 | 35 | 8.7 | 940 | 565 | 41 | 334 | 111 | 5.9 |

Reprinted with the permission of The Mader Group, Inc., Narberth, PA.

TABLE 15.1 (concluded)

## INFLATION OF SALE PRICE, INCOME, AND EXPENSE AT 5-10-15% ANNUALLY

| | HOLDING RESULTS BEFORE INCOME TAXES | | | | | | HOLDING RESULTS AFTER TAXES | | | | | OVERALL RESULTS IF SOLD AT YEAR END | | | | | |
|---|---|---|---|---|---|---|---|---|---|---|---|---|---|---|---|---|---|
| | | | MORTGAGE | | | | | | | | | | | | | | |
| YR | GROSS INCOME | OPERATE EXPENSE | INTR | AMORT | CASH FLOW | % RE TURN | DEPREC IATION | TAXABLE INCOME | TAXES DUE | CASH FLOW | % RE TURN | SALE PRICE | DEBT REPAY | TAXES DUE | CASH FLOW | TOTAL PROFIT | % IRR |
| 1 | 150 | 60 | 60 | 6 | 25 | 6.1 | 53 | -23 | -12 | 36 | 9.0 | 987 | 594 | 8 | 385 | 21 | 5.2 |
| 2 | 165 | 69 | 59 | 6 | 31 | 7.6 | 53 | -16 | -8 | 39 | 9.7 | 1036 | 588 | 29 | 420 | 95 | 11.7 |
| 3 | 181 | 79 | 58 | 7 | 37 | 9.2 | 53 | -10 | -5 | 42 | 10.4 | 1088 | 581 | 50 | 457 | 174 | 13.8 |
| 4 | 200 | 91 | 58 | 8 | 43 | 10.7 | 53 | -3 | -1 | 44 | 11.1 | 1143 | 573 | 71 | 498 | 259 | 14.8 |
| 5 | 220 | 105 | 57 | 8 | 49 | 12.3 | 53 | 4 | 2 | 47 | 11.8 | 1200 | 565 | 93 | 541 | 349 | 15.4 |

## INFLATION OF SALE PRICE, INCOME, AND EXPENSE AT 10% ANNUALLY

| | HOLDING RESULTS BEFORE INCOME TAXES | | | | | | HOLDING RESULTS AFTER TAXES | | | | | OVERALL RESULTS IF SOLD AT YEAR END | | | | | |
|---|---|---|---|---|---|---|---|---|---|---|---|---|---|---|---|---|---|
| | | | MORTGAGE | | | | | | | | | | | | | | |
| YR | GROSS INCOME | OPERATE EXPENSE | INTR | AMORT | CASH FLOW | % RE TURN | DEPREC IATION | TAXABLE INCOME | TAXES DUE | CASH FLOW | % RE TURN | SALE PRICE | DEBT REPAY | TAXES DUE | CASH FLOW | TOTAL PROFIT | % IRR |
| 1 | 150 | 60 | 60 | 6 | 25 | 6.1 | 53 | -23 | -12 | 36 | 9.0 | 1034 | 594 | 17 | 422 | 58 | 14.6 |
| 2 | 165 | 66 | 59 | 6 | 34 | 8.4 | 53 | -13 | -7 | 40 | 10.1 | 1137 | 588 | 49 | 501 | 177 | 20.9 |
| 3 | 181 | 73 | 58 | 7 | 43 | 10.9 | 53 | -3 | -1 | 45 | 11.2 | 1251 | 581 | 82 | 588 | 309 | 22.6 |
| 4 | 200 | 80 | 58 | 8 | 54 | 13.6 | 53 | 9 | 4 | 50 | 12.5 | 1376 | 573 | 118 | 685 | 456 | 23.1 |
| 5 | 220 | 88 | 57 | 8 | 66 | 16.6 | 53 | 21 | 11 | 56 | 13.9 | 1514 | 565 | 156 | 793 | 620 | 23.2 |

Reprinted with the permission of The Mader Group, Inc., Narberth, PA.

## TABLE 15.2
Commercial—100 percent of straight line depreciation (per $1,000)

### KEY OPERATING FACTORS ARE ---

| TOTAL PROJECT COST | ---MORTGAGE TERMS--- | | | ---OPERATING & INFLATION ASSUMPTIONS--- | | | | | | | ---DEPRECIATION--- | | | ---TAX RATES--- | |
|---|---|---|---|---|---|---|---|---|---|---|---|---|---|---|---|
| | AMOUNT | % INTR | LIFE | NET RESALE PRICE | % INFL | GROSS INCOME | % INFL | OPERATING EXPENSE | % INFL | | AMOUNT | LIFE | RATE | INCOME | CAP GAIN |
| 1000 | 600 | 10.00 | 25 | 940 | 0 | 200 | 0 | 80 | 0 | | 800 | 15 | 100% | 50% | 20% |

### PRE-OPERATING SUMMARY ---

| EQUITY AMOUNT | ---MORTGAGE TERMS--- | | | % NET RESALE TO COST | % INCOME TO COST | GROSS RENT MULT | % EXPENSE TO INCOME | % NOI TO COST | % DEPREC TO COST |
|---|---|---|---|---|---|---|---|---|---|
| | % DEBT | MONTHLY | YEARLY | | | | | | |
| 400 | 60.00 | 5 | 65 | 94.0 | 20.0 | 5.0 | 40.0 | 12.0 | 80.0 |

### OPERATING RESULTS ---

| | ---HOLDING RESULTS BEFORE INCOME TAXES--- | | | | | | ---HOLDING RESULTS AFTER TAXES--- | | | | | ---OVERALL RESULTS IF SOLD AT YEAR END--- | | | | | |
|---|---|---|---|---|---|---|---|---|---|---|---|---|---|---|---|---|---|
| YR | GROSS INCOME | OPERATE EXPENSE | ----MORTGAGE-- INTR | AMORT | CASH FLOW | % RE TURN | DEPREC IATION | TAXABLE INCOME | TAXES DUE | CASH FLOW | % RE TURN | SALE PRICE | DEBT REPAY | TAXES DUE | CASH FLOW | TOTAL PROFIT | % IRR |
| 1 | 200 | 80 | 60 | 6 | 55 | 13.6 | 53 | 7 | 3 | 51 | 12.8 | 940 | 594 | -1 | 347 | -2 | -0.5 |
| 2 | 200 | 80 | 59 | 6 | 55 | 13.6 | 53 | 8 | 4 | 51 | 12.7 | 940 | 588 | 9 | 343 | 45 | 5.8 |
| 3 | 200 | 80 | 58 | 7 | 55 | 13.6 | 53 | 8 | 4 | 50 | 12.6 | 940 | 581 | 20 | 339 | 91 | 8.0 |
| 4 | 200 | 80 | 58 | 8 | 55 | 13.6 | 53 | 9 | 4 | 50 | 12.5 | 940 | 573 | 31 | 336 | 138 | 9.2 |
| 5 | 200 | 80 | 57 | 8 | 55 | 13.6 | 53 | 10 | 5 | 50 | 12.4 | 940 | 565 | 41 | 334 | 186 | 9.9 |

Reprinted with the permission of The Mader Group, Inc., Narberth, PA.

TABLE 15.2 (concluded)

## INFLATION OF SALE PRICE, INCOME, AND EXPENSE AT 5-10-15% ANNUALLY

| | ----HOLDING RESULTS BEFORE INCOME TAXES---- | | --MORTGAGE-- | | | | ----HOLDING RESULTS AFTER TAXES-- | | | | | ----OVERALL RESULTS IF SOLD AT YEAR END----- | | | | | |
|---|---|---|---|---|---|---|---|---|---|---|---|---|---|---|---|---|---|
| YR | GROSS INCOME | OPERATE EXPENSE | INTR | AMORT | CASH FLOW | % RE TURN | DEPREC IATION | TAXABLE INCOME | TAXES DUE | CASH FLOW | % RE TURN | SALE PRICE | DEBT REPAY | TAXES DUE | CASH FLOW | TOTAL PROFIT | % IRR |
| 1 | 200 | 80 | 60 | 6 | 55 | 13.6 | 53 | 7 | 3 | 51 | 12.8 | 987 | 594 | 8 | 385 | 36 | 8.9 |
| 2 | 220 | 92 | 59 | 6 | 63 | 15.6 | 53 | 16 | 8 | 55 | 13.7 | 1036 | 588 | 29 | 420 | 126 | 15.5 |
| 3 | 242 | 106 | 58 | 7 | 71 | 17.7 | 53 | 24 | 12 | 59 | 14.6 | 1088 | 581 | 50 | 457 | 222 | 17.6 |
| 4 | 266 | 122 | 58 | 8 | 79 | 19.8 | 53 | 33 | 17 | 62 | 15.6 | 1143 | 573 | 71 | 498 | 325 | 18.6 |
| 5 | 293 | 140 | 57 | 8 | 87 | 21.9 | 53 | 43 | 21 | 66 | 16.5 | 1200 | 565 | 93 | 541 | 435 | 19.2 |

## INFLATION OF SALE PRICE, INCOME, AND EXPENSE AT 10% ANNUALLY

| | ---HOLDING RESULTS BEFORE INCOME TAXES-- | | --MORTGAGE-- | | | | ---HOLDING RESULTS AFTER TAXES-- | | | | | ----OVERALL RESULTS IF SOLD AT YEAR END----- | | | | | |
|---|---|---|---|---|---|---|---|---|---|---|---|---|---|---|---|---|---|
| YR | GROSS INCOME | OPERATE EXPENSE | INTR | AMORT | CASH FLOW | % RE TURN | DEPREC IATION | TAXABLE INCOME | TAXES DUE | CASH FLOW | % RE TURN | SALE PRICE | DEBT REPAY | TAXES DUE | CASH FLOW | TOTAL PROFIT | % IRR |
| 1 | 200 | 80 | 60 | 6 | 55 | 13.6 | 53 | 7 | 3 | 51 | 12.8 | 1034 | 594 | 17 | 422 | 73 | 18.3 |
| 2 | 220 | 88 | 59 | 6 | 67 | 16.6 | 53 | 20 | 10 | 57 | 14.2 | 1137 | 588 | 49 | 501 | 208 | 24.6 |
| 3 | 242 | 97 | 58 | 7 | 80 | 19.9 | 53 | 33 | 17 | 63 | 15.8 | 1251 | 581 | 82 | 588 | 359 | 26.2 |
| 4 | 266 | 106 | 58 | 8 | 94 | 23.6 | 53 | 49 | 24 | 70 | 17.5 | 1376 | 573 | 118 | 685 | 526 | 26.7 |
| 5 | 293 | 117 | 57 | 8 | 110 | 27.6 | 53 | 65 | 33 | 78 | 19.4 | 1514 | 565 | 156 | 793 | 711 | 26.7 |

Reprinted with the permission of The Mader Group, Inc., Narberth, PA.

**TABLE 15.3**
Commercial—100 percent of straight line depreciation (per $1,000)

**KEY OPERATING FACTORS ARE ---**

| TOTAL PROJECT COST | ---MORTGAGE TERMS--- | | | ---OPERATING & INFLATION ASSUMPTIONS--- | | | | | | ---DEPRECIATION--- | | | ---TAX RATES--- | |
|---|---|---|---|---|---|---|---|---|---|---|---|---|---|---|
| | AMOUNT | %INTR | LIFE | NET RESALE PRICE | %INFL | GROSS INCOME | %INFL | OPERATING EXPENSE | %INFL | AMOUNT | LIFE | RATE | INCOME | CAP GAIN |
| 1000 | 600 | 15.00 | 25 | 940 | 0 | 150 | 0 | 60 | 0 | 800 | 15 | 100% | 50% | 20% |

**PRE-OPERATING SUMMARY ---**

| EQUITY AMOUNT | ---MORTGAGE TERMS--- | | | %NET RESALE TO COST | %INCOME TO COST | GROSS RENT MULT | %EXPENSE TO INCOME | %NOI TO COST | %DEPREC TO COST |
|---|---|---|---|---|---|---|---|---|---|
| | %DEBT | MONTHLY | YEARLY | | | | | | |
| 400 | 60.00 | 8 | 92 | 94.0 | 15.0 | 6.7 | 40.0 | 9.0 | 80.0 |

**OPERATING RESULTS ---**

| YR | ---HOLDING RESULTS BEFORE INCOME TAXES--- | | | | | ---HOLDING RESULTS AFTER TAXES-- | | | | | ---OVERALL RESULTS IF SOLD AT YEAR END---- | | | | | |
|---|---|---|---|---|---|---|---|---|---|---|---|---|---|---|---|---|
| | GROSS INCOME | OPERATE EXPENSE | --MORTGAGE-- INTR | AMORT | CASH FLOW | %RE TURN | DEPREC IATION | TAXABLE INCOME | TAXES DUE | CASH FLOW | %RE TURN | SALE PRICE | DEBT REPAY | TAXES DUE | CASH FLOW | TOTAL PROFIT | %IRR |
| 1 | 150 | 60 | 90 | 2 | -2 | -0.6 | 53 | -53 | -27 | 24 | 6.1 | 940 | 598 | -1 | 344 | -32 | -8.0 |
| 2 | 150 | 60 | 89 | 3 | -2 | -0.6 | 53 | -53 | -26 | 24 | 6.0 | 940 | 595 | 9 | 336 | -16 | -2.0 |
| 3 | 150 | 60 | 89 | 3 | -2 | -0.6 | 53 | -52 | -26 | 24 | 6.0 | 940 | 592 | 20 | 328 | 1 | 0.1 |
| 4 | 150 | 60 | 88 | 4 | -2 | -0.6 | 53 | -52 | -26 | 24 | 5.9 | 940 | 588 | 31 | 321 | 18 | 1.2 |
| 5 | 150 | 60 | 88 | 4 | -2 | -0.6 | 53 | -51 | -26 | 23 | 5.8 | 940 | 584 | 41 | 315 | 35 | 1.9 |

Reprinted with the permission of The Mader Group, Inc., Narberth, PA.

TABLE 15.3 (concluded)

## INFLATION OF SALE PRICE, INCOME, AND EXPENSE AT 5-10-15% ANNUALLY

| YR | ----HOLDING RESULTS BEFORE INCOME TAXES---- GROSS INCOME | OPERATE EXPENSE | --MORTGAGE-- INTR | AMORT | CASH FLOW | % RE TURN | ---HOLDING RESULTS AFTER TAXES--- DEPREC IATION | TAXABLE INCOME | TAXES DUE | CASH FLOW | % RE TURN | ----OVERALL RESULTS IF SOLD AT YEAR END---- SALE PRICE | DEBT REPAY | TAXES DUE | CASH FLOW | TOTAL PROFIT | % IRR |
|---|---|---|---|---|---|---|---|---|---|---|---|---|---|---|---|---|---|
| 1 | 150 | 60 | 90 | 2 | -2 | -0.6 | 53 | -53 | -27 | 24 | 6.1 | 987 | 598 | 8 | 381 | 6 | 1.4 |
| 2 | 165 | 69 | 89 | 3 | 4 | 0.9 | 53 | -47 | -23 | 27 | 6.8 | 1036 | 595 | 29 | 413 | 64 | 8.0 |
| 3 | 181 | 79 | 89 | 3 | 10 | 2.5 | 53 | -40 | -20 | 30 | 7.5 | 1088 | 592 | 50 | 447 | 128 | 10.3 |
| 4 | 200 | 91 | 88 | 4 | 16 | 4.0 | 53 | -33 | -17 | 33 | 8.2 | 1143 | 588 | 71 | 483 | 198 | 11.5 |
| 5 | 220 | 105 | 88 | 4 | 22 | 5.6 | 53 | -27 | -13 | 36 | 8.9 | 1200 | 584 | 93 | 523 | 273 | 12.2 |

## INFLATION OF SALE PRICE, INCOME, AND EXPENSE AT 10% ANNUALLY

| YR | ----HOLDING RESULTS BEFORE INCOME TAXES---- GROSS INCOME | OPERATE EXPENSE | --MORTGAGE-- INTR | AMORT | CASH FLOW | % RE TURN | ---HOLDING RESULTS AFTER TAXES--- DEPREC IATION | TAXABLE INCOME | TAXES DUE | CASH FLOW | % RE TURN | ----OVERALL RESULTS IF SOLD AT YEAR END---- SALE PRICE | DEBT REPAY | TAXES DUE | CASH FLOW | TOTAL PROFIT | % IRR |
|---|---|---|---|---|---|---|---|---|---|---|---|---|---|---|---|---|---|
| 1 | 150 | 60 | 90 | 2 | -2 | -0.6 | 53 | -53 | -27 | 24 | 6.1 | 1034 | 598 | 17 | 419 | 43 | 10.8 |
| 2 | 165 | 66 | 89 | 3 | 7 | 1.7 | 53 | -44 | -22 | 29 | 7.2 | 1137 | 595 | 49 | 494 | 147 | 17.4 |
| 3 | 181 | 73 | 89 | 3 | 17 | 4.2 | 53 | -33 | -17 | 33 | 8.4 | 1251 | 592 | 82 | 577 | 264 | 19.3 |
| 4 | 200 | 80 | 88 | 4 | 28 | 6.9 | 53 | -22 | -11 | 39 | 9.6 | 1376 | 588 | 118 | 670 | 395 | 20.1 |
| 5 | 220 | 88 | 88 | 4 | 40 | 9.9 | 53 | -9 | -5 | 44 | 11.1 | 1514 | 584 | 156 | 774 | 543 | 20.5 |

Reprinted with the permission of The Mader Group, Inc., Narberth, PA.

## TABLE 15.4
Commercial—100 percent of straight line depreciation (per $1,000)

KEY OPERATING FACTORS ARE ---

| TOTAL PROJECT COST | ---MORTGAGE TERMS--- AMOUNT | %INTR | LIFE | ----OPERATING & INFLATION ASSUMPTIONS---- NET RESALE PRICE | %INFL | GROSS INCOME | %INFL | %OPERATING EXPENSE | %INFL | ----DEPRECIATION--- AMOUNT | LIFE | RATE | ----TAX RATES--- INCOME | CAP GAIN |
|---|---|---|---|---|---|---|---|---|---|---|---|---|---|---|
| 1000 | 600 | 15.00 | 25 | 940 | 0 | 200 | 0 | 80 | 0 | 800 | 15 | 100% | 50% | 20% |

PRE-OPERATING SUMMARY ---

| EQUITY AMOUNT | ---MORTGAGE TERMS--- %DEBT | MONTHLY | YEARLY | %NET RESALE TO COST | %INCOME TO COST | GROSS RENT MULT | %EXPENSE TO INCOME | %NOI TO COST | %DEPREC TO COST |
|---|---|---|---|---|---|---|---|---|---|
| 400 | 60.00 | 8 | 92 | 94.0 | 20.0 | 5.0 | 40.0 | 12.0 | 80.0 |

OPERATING RESULTS ---

| YR | ---HOLDING RESULTS BEFORE INCOME TAXES--- GROSS INCOME | OPERATE EXPENSE | ---MORTGAGE--- IMTR | AMORT | CASH FLOW | %RE TURN | ---HOLDING RESULTS AFTER TAXES--- DEPRECIATION | TAXABLE INCOME | TAXES DUE | CASH FLOW | %RE TURN | ---OVERALL RESULTS IF SOLD AT YEAR END--- SALE PRICE | DEBT REPAY | TAXES DUE | CASH FLOW | TOTAL PROFIT | %IRR |
|---|---|---|---|---|---|---|---|---|---|---|---|---|---|---|---|---|---|
| 1 | 200 | 80 | 90 | 2 | 28 | 6.9 | 53 | -23 | -12 | 39 | 9.8 | 940 | 598 | -1 | 344 | -17 | -4.2 |
| 2 | 200 | 80 | 89 | 3 | 28 | 6.9 | 53 | -23 | -11 | 39 | 9.8 | 940 | 595 | 9 | 336 | 14 | 1.9 |
| 3 | 200 | 80 | 89 | 3 | 28 | 6.9 | 53 | -22 | -11 | 39 | 9.7 | 940 | 592 | 20 | 328 | 46 | 4.1 |
| 4 | 200 | 80 | 88 | 4 | 28 | 6.9 | 53 | -22 | -11 | 39 | 9.7 | 940 | 588 | 31 | 321 | 78 | 5.2 |
| 5 | 200 | 80 | 88 | 4 | 28 | 6.9 | 53 | -21 | -11 | 38 | 9.6 | 940 | 584 | 41 | 315 | 110 | 6.0 |

Reprinted with the permission of The Mader Group, Inc., Narberth, PA.

TABLE 15.4 *(concluded)*

## INFLATION OF SALE PRICE, INCOME, AND EXPENSE AT 5-10-15% ANNUALLY

| | ----HOLDING RESULTS BEFORE INCOME TAXES---- | | | | | | ----HOLDING RESULTS AFTER TAXES---- | | | | | ----OVERALL RESULTS IF SOLD AT YEAR END---- | | | | | |
| | GROSS | OPERATE | --MORTGAGE-- | | CASH | % RE | DEPREC | TAXABLE | TAXES | CASH | % RE | SALE | DEBT | TAXES | CASH | TOTAL | % |
| YR | INCOME | EXPENSE | INTR | AMORT | FLOW | TURN | IATION | INCOME | DUE | FLOW | TURN | PRICE | REPAY | DUE | FLOW | PROFIT | IRR |
|---|---|---|---|---|---|---|---|---|---|---|---|---|---|---|---|---|---|
| 1 | 200 | 80 | 90 | 2 | 28 | 6.9 | 53 | -23 | -12 | 39 | 9.8 | 987 | 598 | 8 | 381 | 21 | 5.2 |
| 2 | 220 | 92 | 89 | 3 | 36 | 8.9 | 53 | -15 | -7 | 43 | 10.8 | 1036 | 595 | 29 | 413 | 95 | 11.8 |
| 3 | 242 | 106 | 89 | 3 | 44 | 11.0 | 53 | -6 | -3 | 47 | 11.8 | 1088 | 592 | 50 | 447 | 176 | 14.1 |
| 4 | 266 | 122 | 88 | 4 | 52 | 13.1 | 53 | 3 | 1 | 51 | 12.7 | 1143 | 588 | 71 | 483 | 264 | 15.3 |
| 5 | 293 | 140 | 88 | 4 | 61 | 15.2 | 53 | 12 | 6 | 55 | 13.7 | 1200 | 584 | 93 | 523 | 358 | 16.0 |

## INFLATION OF SALE PRICE, INCOME, AND EXPENSE AT 10% ANNUALLY

| | ----HOLDING RESULTS BEFORE INCOME TAXES---- | | | | | | ----HOLDING RESULTS AFTER TAXES---- | | | | | ----OVERALL RESULTS IF SOLD AT YEAR END---- | | | | | |
| | GROSS | OPERATE | --MORTGAGE-- | | CASH | % RE | DEPREC | TAXABLE | TAXES | CASH | % RE | SALE | DEBT | TAXES | CASH | TOTAL | % |
| YR | INCOME | EXPENSE | INTR | AMORT | FLOW | TURN | IATION | INCOME | DUE | FLOW | TURN | PRICE | REPAY | DUE | FLOW | PROFIT | IRR |
|---|---|---|---|---|---|---|---|---|---|---|---|---|---|---|---|---|---|
| 1 | 200 | 80 | 90 | 2 | 28 | 6.9 | 53 | -23 | -12 | 39 | 9.8 | 1034 | 598 | 17 | 419 | 58 | 14.6 |
| 2 | 220 | 88 | 89 | 3 | 40 | 9.9 | 53 | -11 | -5 | 45 | 11.3 | 1137 | 595 | 49 | 494 | 178 | 21.1 |
| 3 | 242 | 97 | 89 | 3 | 53 | 13.2 | 53 | 3 | 1 | 52 | 12.9 | 1251 | 592 | 82 | 577 | 313 | 23.0 |
| 4 | 266 | 106 | 88 | 4 | 68 | 16.9 | 53 | 18 | 9 | 59 | 14.6 | 1376 | 588 | 118 | 670 | 465 | 23.7 |
| 5 | 293 | 117 | 88 | 4 | 83 | 20.9 | 53 | 34 | 17 | 66 | 16.6 | 1514 | 584 | 156 | 774 | 635 | 24.0 |

Reprinted with the permission of The Mader Group, Inc., Narberth, PA.

**TABLE 15.5**
Commercial—100 percent of straight line depreciation (per $1,000)

### KEY OPERATING FACTORS ARE ---

| TOTAL PROJECT COST | ---MORTGAGE TERMS--- | | | ----OPERATING & INFLATION ASSUMPTIONS------ | | | | | | ----DEPRECIATION--- | | | ----TAX RATES--- | |
| | AMOUNT | % INTR | LIFE | NET RESALE PRICE | % INFL | GROSS INCOME | % INFL | OPERATING EXPENSE | % INFL | AMOUNT | LIFE | RATE | INCOME | CAP GAIN |
|---|---|---|---|---|---|---|---|---|---|---|---|---|---|---|
| 1000 | 800 | 10.00 | 25 | 940 | 0 | 150 | 0 | 60 | 0 | 800 | 15 | 100% | 50% | 20% |

### PRE-OPERATING SUMMARY ---

| EQUITY AMOUNT | ---MORTGAGE TERMS---- | | | % NET RESALE TO COST | % INCOME TO COST | GROSS RENT MULT | % EXPENSE TO INCOME | % NOI TO COST | % DEPREC TO COST |
| | % DEBT | MONTHLY | YEARLY | | | | | | |
|---|---|---|---|---|---|---|---|---|---|
| 200 | 80.00 | 7 | 87 | 94.0 | 15.0 | 6.7 | 40.0 | 9.0 | 80.0 |

### OPERATING RESULTS ---

| | ----HOLDING RESULTS BEFORE INCOME TAXES--- | | | | | | ----HOLDING RESULTS AFTER TAXES-- | | | | | ----OVERALL RESULTS IF SOLD AT YEAR END----- | | | | | |
| YR | GROSS INCOME | OPERATE EXPENSE | INTR | AMORT | CASH FLOW | % RE TURN | DEPREC IATION | TAXABLE INCOME | TAXES DUE | CASH FLOW | % RE TURN | SALE PRICE | DEBT REPAY | TAXES DUE | CASH FLOW | TOTAL PROFIT | % IRR |
|---|---|---|---|---|---|---|---|---|---|---|---|---|---|---|---|---|---|
| 1 | 150 | 60 | 80 | 8 | 3 | 1.4 | 53 | -43 | -21 | 24 | 12.1 | 940 | 792 | -1 | 149 | -27 | -13.4 |
| 2 | 150 | 60 | 79 | 8 | 3 | 1.4 | 53 | -42 | -21 | 24 | 11.9 | 940 | 784 | 9 | 147 | -5 | -1.4 |
| 3 | 150 | 60 | 78 | 9 | 3 | 1.4 | 53 | -41 | -21 | 23 | 11.7 | 940 | 775 | 20 | 145 | 17 | 3.1 |
| 4 | 150 | 60 | 77 | 10 | 3 | 1.4 | 53 | -40 | -20 | 23 | 11.5 | 940 | 765 | 31 | 145 | 39 | 5.5 |
| 5 | 150 | 60 | 76 | 11 | 3 | 1.4 | 53 | -39 | -20 | 22 | 11.2 | 940 | 753 | 41 | 145 | 62 | 7.0 |

TABLE 15.5 (concluded)

INFLATION OF SALE PRICE, INCOME, AND EXPENSE AT 5-10-15% ANNUALLY

| | | | ---HOLDING RESULTS BEFORE INCOME TAXES--- | | | | ---HOLDING RESULTS AFTER TAXES--- | | | | | ---OVERALL RESULTS IF SOLD AT YEAR END--- | | | | | |
|---|---|---|---|---|---|---|---|---|---|---|---|---|---|---|---|---|---|
| YR | GROSS INCOME | OPERATE EXPENSE | MORTGAGE INTR | AMORT | CASH FLOW | % RE TURN | DEPREC IATION | TAXABLE INCOME | TAXES DUE | CASH FLOW | % RE TURN | SALE PRICE | DEBT REPAY | TAXES DUE | CASH FLOW | TOTAL PROFIT | % IRR |
| 1 | 150 | 60 | 80 | 8 | 3 | 1.4 | 53 | -43 | -21 | 24 | 12.1 | 987 | 792 | 8 | 187 | 11 | 5.4 |
| 2 | 165 | 69 | 79 | 8 | 9 | 4.4 | 53 | -36 | -18 | 27 | 13.4 | 1036 | 784 | 29 | 224 | 75 | 18.2 |
| 3 | 181 | 79 | 78 | 9 | 15 | 7.5 | 53 | -29 | -15 | 30 | 14.8 | 1088 | 775 | 50 | 264 | 144 | 21.9 |
| 4 | 200 | 91 | 77 | 10 | 21 | 10.6 | 53 | -22 | -11 | 32 | 16.1 | 1143 | 765 | 71 | 307 | 220 | 23.2 |
| 5 | 220 | 105 | 76 | 11 | 27 | 13.7 | 53 | -15 | -7 | 35 | 17.4 | 1200 | 753 | 93 | 353 | 301 | 23.8 |

INFLATION OF SALE PRICE, INCOME, AND EXPENSE AT 10% ANNUALLY

| | | | ---HOLDING RESULTS BEFORE INCOME TAXES--- | | | | ---HOLDING RESULTS AFTER TAXES--- | | | | | ---OVERALL RESULTS IF SOLD AT YEAR END--- | | | | | |
|---|---|---|---|---|---|---|---|---|---|---|---|---|---|---|---|---|---|
| YR | GROSS INCOME | OPERATE EXPENSE | MORTGAGE INTR | AMORT | CASH FLOW | % RE TURN | DEPREC IATION | TAXABLE INCOME | TAXES DUE | CASH FLOW | % RE TURN | SALE PRICE | DEBT REPAY | TAXES DUE | CASH FLOW | TOTAL PROFIT | % IRR |
| 1 | 150 | 60 | 80 | 8 | 3 | 1.4 | 53 | -43 | -21 | 24 | 12.1 | 1034 | 792 | 17 | 224 | 48 | 24.2 |
| 2 | 165 | 66 | 79 | 8 | 12 | 5.9 | 53 | -33 | -17 | 28 | 14.2 | 1137 | 784 | 49 | 305 | 157 | 35.2 |
| 3 | 181 | 73 | 78 | 9 | 22 | 10.8 | 53 | -22 | -11 | 33 | 16.4 | 1251 | 775 | 82 | 394 | 280 | 36.7 |
| 4 | 200 | 80 | 77 | 10 | 33 | 16.3 | 53 | -11 | -5 | 38 | 18.9 | 1376 | 765 | 118 | 494 | 417 | 36.3 |
| 5 | 220 | 88 | 76 | 11 | 45 | 22.3 | 53 | 2 | 1 | 43 | 21.6 | 1514 | 753 | 156 | 604 | 571 | 35.4 |

Reprinted with the permission of The Mader Group, Inc., Narberth, PA.

## TABLE 15.6
Commercial—100 percent of straight line depreciation (per $1,000)

### KEY OPERATING FACTORS ARE ---

| TOTAL PROJECT COST | MORTGAGE TERMS--- | | | OPERATING & INFLATION ASSUMPTIONS--- | | | | | | DEPRECIATION--- | | | TAX RATES--- | |
|---|---|---|---|---|---|---|---|---|---|---|---|---|---|---|
| | AMOUNT | % INTR | LIFE | NET RESALE PRICE | % RESALE INFL | GROSS INCOME | % INCOME INFL | OPERATING EXPENSE | % EXPENSE INFL | AMOUNT | LIFE | RATE | INCOME | CAP GAIN |
| 1000 | 800 | 10.00 | 25 | 940 | 0 | 200 | 0 | 80 | 0 | 800 | 15 | 100% | 50% | 20% |

### PRE-OPERATING SUMMARY ---

| EQUITY AMOUNT | MORTGAGE TERMS--- | | | % NET RESALE TO COST | % INCOME TO COST | GROSS RENT MULT | % EXPENSE TO INCOME | % NOI TO COST | % DEPREC TO COST |
|---|---|---|---|---|---|---|---|---|---|
| | % DEBT | MONTHLY | YEARLY | | | | | | |
| 200 | 80.00 | 7 | 87 | 94.0 | 20.0 | 5.0 | 40.0 | 12.0 | 80.0 |

### OPERATING RESULTS ---

| YR | HOLDING RESULTS BEFORE INCOME TAXES---- | | | | | | HOLDING RESULTS AFTER TAXES--- | | | | | OVERALL RESULTS IF SOLD AT YEAR END----- | | | | | |
|---|---|---|---|---|---|---|---|---|---|---|---|---|---|---|---|---|---|
| | GROSS INCOME | OPERATE EXPENSE | MORTGAGE INTR | AMORT | CASH FLOW | % RE TURN | DEPREC IATION | TAXABLE INCOME | TAXES DUE | CASH FLOW | % RE TURN | SALE PRICE | DEBT REPAY | TAXES DUE | CASH FLOW | TOTAL PROFIT | % IRR |
| 1 | 200 | 80 | 80 | 8 | 33 | 16.4 | 53 | -13 | -6 | 39 | 19.6 | 940 | 792 | -1 | 149 | -12 | -5.9 |
| 2 | 200 | 80 | 79 | 8 | 33 | 16.4 | 53 | -12 | -6 | 39 | 19.4 | 940 | 784 | 9 | 147 | 25 | 6.6 |
| 3 | 200 | 80 | 78 | 9 | 33 | 16.4 | 53 | -11 | -6 | 38 | 19.2 | 940 | 775 | 20 | 145 | 62 | 11.3 |
| 4 | 200 | 80 | 77 | 10 | 33 | 16.4 | 53 | -10 | -5 | 38 | 19.0 | 940 | 765 | 31 | 145 | 99 | 13.7 |
| 5 | 200 | 80 | 76 | 11 | 33 | 16.4 | 53 | -9 | -5 | 37 | 18.7 | 940 | 753 | 41 | 145 | 137 | 15.2 |

Reprinted with the permission of The Mader Group, Inc., Narberth, PA.

TABLE 15.6 (concluded)

INFLATION OF SALE PRICE, INCOME, AND EXPENSE AT 5-10-15% ANNUALLY

| | ----HOLDING RESULTS BEFORE INCOME TAXES---- | | | | | | ----HOLDING RESULTS AFTER TAXES---- | | | | | ----OVERALL RESULTS IF SOLD AT YEAR END---- | | | | | |
|---|---|---|---|---|---|---|---|---|---|---|---|---|---|---|---|---|---|
| YR | GROSS INCOME | OPERATE EXPENSE | MORTGAGE-- INTR | AMORT | CASH FLOW | % RETURN | DEPRECIATION | TAXABLE INCOME | TAXES DUE | CASH FLOW | % RETURN | SALE PRICE | DEBT REPAY | TAXES DUE | CASH FLOW | TOTAL PROFIT | % IRR |
| 1 | 200 | 80 | 80 | 8 | 33 | 16.4 | 53 | -13 | -6 | 39 | 19.6 | 987 | 792 | 8 | 187 | 26 | 12.9 |
| 2 | 220 | 92 | 79 | 8 | 41 | 20.4 | 53 | -4 | -2 | 43 | 21.4 | 1036 | 784 | 29 | 224 | 106 | 25.7 |
| 3 | 242 | 106 | 78 | 9 | 49 | 24.5 | 53 | 5 | 2 | 47 | 23.3 | 1088 | 775 | 50 | 264 | 192 | 29.2 |
| 4 | 266 | 122 | 77 | 10 | 57 | 28.6 | 53 | 14 | 7 | 50 | 25.1 | 1143 | 765 | 71 | 307 | 286 | 30.4 |
| 5 | 293 | 140 | 76 | 11 | 66 | 32.8 | 53 | 24 | 12 | 54 | 26.9 | 1200 | 753 | 93 | 353 | 386 | 30.7 |

INFLATION OF SALE PRICE, INCOME, AND EXPENSE AT 10% ANNUALLY

| | ----HOLDING RESULTS BEFORE INCOME TAXES---- | | | | | | ----HOLDING RESULTS AFTER TAXES---- | | | | | ----OVERALL RESULTS IF SOLD AT YEAR END---- | | | | | |
|---|---|---|---|---|---|---|---|---|---|---|---|---|---|---|---|---|---|
| YR | GROSS INCOME | OPERATE EXPENSE | MORTGAGE-- INTR | AMORT | CASH FLOW | % RETURN | DEPRECIATION | TAXABLE INCOME | TAXES DUE | CASH FLOW | % RETURN | SALE PRICE | DEBT REPAY | TAXES DUE | CASH FLOW | TOTAL PROFIT | % IRR |
| 1 | 200 | 80 | 80 | 8 | 33 | 16.4 | 53 | -13 | -6 | 39 | 19.6 | 1034 | 792 | 17 | 224 | 63 | 31.7 |
| 2 | 220 | 88 | 79 | 8 | 45 | 22.4 | 53 | 0 | 0 | 45 | 22.4 | 1137 | 784 | 49 | 305 | 189 | 42.4 |
| 3 | 242 | 97 | 78 | 9 | 58 | 29.0 | 53 | 14 | 7 | 51 | 25.5 | 1251 | 775 | 82 | 394 | 329 | 43.4 |
| 4 | 266 | 106 | 77 | 10 | 72 | 36.2 | 53 | 29 | 15 | 58 | 28.9 | 1376 | 765 | 118 | 494 | 487 | 42.7 |
| 5 | 293 | 117 | 76 | 11 | 88 | 44.2 | 53 | 46 | 23 | 65 | 32.6 | 1514 | 753 | 156 | 604 | 663 | 41.6 |

Reprinted with the permission of The Mader Group, Inc., Narberth, PA.

## TABLE 15.7
Commercial—100 percent of straight line depreciation (per $1,000)

**KEY OPERATING FACTORS ARE ---**

| TOTAL PROJECT COST | ---MORTGAGE TERMS--- AMOUNT | %INTR | LIFE | ---OPERATING & INFLATION ASSUMPTIONS--- NET RESALE PRICE | %INFL | GROSS INCOME | %INFL | OPERATING EXPENSE | %INFL | ---DEPRECIATION--- AMOUNT | LIFE | RATE | ---TAX RATES--- INCOME | CAP GAIN |
|---|---|---|---|---|---|---|---|---|---|---|---|---|---|---|
| 1000 | 800 | 15.00 | 25 | 940 | 0 | 150 | 0 | 60 | 0 | 800 | 15 | 100% | 50% | 20% |

**PRE-OPERATING SUMMARY ---**

| EQUITY AMOUNT | ---MORTGAGE TERMS--- %DEBT | MONTHLY | YEARLY | %NET RESALE TO COST | %INCOME TO COST | GROSS RENT MULT | %EXPENSE TO INCOME | %NOI TO COST | %DEPREC TO COST |
|---|---|---|---|---|---|---|---|---|---|
| 200 | 80.00 | 10 | 123 | 94.0 | 15.0 | 6.7 | 40.0 | 9.0 | 80.0 |

**OPERATING RESULTS ---**

| YR | GROSS INCOME | OPERATE EXPENSE | ---MORTGAGE-- INTR | AMORT | CASH FLOW | %RE TURN | DEPREC IATION | TAXABLE INCOME | TAXES DUE | CASH FLOW | %RE TURN | SALE PRICE | DEBT REPAY | TAXES DUE | CASH FLOW | TOTAL PROFIT | %IRR |
|---|---|---|---|---|---|---|---|---|---|---|---|---|---|---|---|---|---|
| 1 | 150 | 60 | 120 | 3 | -33 | -16.5 | 53 | -83 | -42 | 9 | 4.3 | 940 | 797 | -1 | 145 | -47 | -23.4 |
| 2 | 150 | 60 | 119 | 4 | -33 | -16.5 | 53 | -83 | -41 | 8 | 4.2 | 940 | 793 | 9 | 138 | -46 | -12.4 |
| 3 | 150 | 60 | 119 | 4 | -33 | -16.5 | 53 | -82 | -41 | 8 | 4.0 | 940 | 789 | 20 | 131 | -44 | -8.3 |
| 4 | 150 | 60 | 118 | 5 | -33 | -16.5 | 53 | -81 | -41 | 8 | 3.9 | 940 | 784 | 31 | 125 | -42 | -6.2 |
| 5 | 150 | 60 | 117 | 6 | -33 | -16.5 | 53 | -81 | -40 | 7 | 3.7 | 940 | 778 | 41 | 121 | -39 | -4.8 |

Reprinted with the permission of The Mader Group, Inc., Narberth, PA.

TABLE 15.7 (concluded)

## INFLATION OF SALE PRICE, INCOME, AND EXPENSE AT 5-10-15% ANNUALLY

| | | | ----HOLDING RESULTS BEFORE INCOME TAXES---- | | | | ----HOLDING RESULTS AFTER TAXES---- | | | | | ----OVERALL RESULTS IF SOLD AT YEAR END---- | | | | | |
|---|---|---|---|---|---|---|---|---|---|---|---|---|---|---|---|---|---|
| | GROSS | OPERATE | --MORTGAGE-- | | CASH | % RE | DEPREC | TAXABLE | TAXES | CASH | % RE | SALE | DEBT | TAXES | CASH | TOTAL | % |
| YR | INCOME | EXPENSE | INTR | AMORT | FLOW | TURN | IATION | INCOME | DUE | FLOW | TURN | PRICE | REPAY | DUE | FLOW | PROFIT | IRR |
| 1 | 150 | 60 | 120 | 3 | -33 | -16.5 | 53 | -83 | -42 | 9 | 4.3 | 987 | 797 | 8 | 182 | -9 | -4.6 |
| 2 | 165 | 69 | 119 | 4 | -27 | -13.5 | 53 | -77 | -38 | 11 | 5.7 | 1036 | 793 | 29 | 215 | 35 | 8.5 |
| 3 | 181 | 79 | 119 | 4 | -21 | -10.4 | 53 | -70 | -35 | 14 | 7.1 | 1088 | 789 | 50 | 250 | 84 | 12.9 |
| 4 | 200 | 91 | 118 | 5 | -15 | -7.3 | 53 | -63 | -31 | 17 | 8.5 | 1143 | 784 | 71 | 287 | 138 | 14.9 |
| 5 | 220 | 105 | 117 | 6 | -8 | -4.1 | 53 | -56 | -28 | 20 | 9.8 | 1200 | 778 | 93 | 328 | 199 | 16.0 |

## INFLATION OF SALE PRICE, INCOME, AND EXPENSE AT 10% ANNUALLY

| | | | ----HOLDING RESULTS BEFORE INCOME TAXES---- | | | | ----HOLDING RESULTS AFTER TAXES---- | | | | | ----OVERALL RESULTS IF SOLD AT YEAR END---- | | | | | |
|---|---|---|---|---|---|---|---|---|---|---|---|---|---|---|---|---|---|
| | GROSS | OPERATE | --MORTGAGE-- | | CASH | % RE | DEPREC | TAXABLE | TAXES | CASH | % RE | SALE | DEBT | TAXES | CASH | TOTAL | % |
| YR | INCOME | EXPENSE | INTR | AMORT | FLOW | TURN | IATION | INCOME | DUE | FLOW | TURN | PRICE | REPAY | DUE | FLOW | PROFIT | IRR |
| 1 | 150 | 60 | 120 | 3 | -33 | -16.5 | 53 | -83 | -42 | 9 | 4.3 | 1034 | 797 | 17 | 220 | 28 | 14.1 |
| 2 | 165 | 66 | 119 | 4 | -24 | -12.0 | 53 | -74 | -37 | 13 | 6.4 | 1137 | 793 | 49 | 295 | 117 | 26.3 |
| 3 | 181 | 73 | 119 | 4 | -14 | -7.0 | 53 | -63 | -32 | 17 | 8.7 | 1251 | 789 | 82 | 380 | 219 | 28.9 |
| 4 | 200 | 80 | 118 | 5 | -3 | -1.6 | 53 | -52 | -26 | 23 | 11.3 | 1376 | 784 | 118 | 474 | 336 | 29.3 |
| 5 | 220 | 88 | 117 | 6 | 9 | 4.4 | 53 | -39 | -19 | 28 | 14.1 | 1514 | 778 | 156 | 580 | 469 | 29.1 |

Reprinted with the permission of The Mader Group, Inc., Narberth, PA.

TABLE 15.8
Commercial—100 percent of straight line depreciation (per $1,000)

KEY OPERATING FACTORS ARE ---

| TOTAL PROJECT COST | ---MORTGAGE TERMS--- | | | ----OPERATING & INFLATION ASSUMPTIONS---- | | | | | | ----DEPRECIATION--- | | | ----TAX RATES--- | |
|---|---|---|---|---|---|---|---|---|---|---|---|---|---|---|
| | AMOUNT | %INTR | LIFE | NET RESALE PRICE | %INFL | GROSS INCOME | %INFL | OPERATING EXPENSE | %INFL | AMOUNT | LIFE | RATE | INCOME | CAP GAIN |
| 1000 | 800 | 15.00 | 25 | 940 | 0 | 200 | 0 | 80 | 0 | 800 | 15 | 100% | 50% | 20% |

PRE-OPERATING SUMMARY ---

| EQUITY AMOUNT | ---MORTGAGE TERMS--- | | | %NET RESALE TO COST | %INCOME TO COST | GROSS RENT MULT | %EXPENSE TO INCOME | %NOI TO COST | %DEPREC TO COST |
|---|---|---|---|---|---|---|---|---|---|
| | %DEBT | MONTHLY | YEARLY | | | | | | |
| 200 | 80.00 | 10 | 123 | 94.0 | 20.0 | 5.0 | 40.0 | 12.0 | 80.0 |

OPERATING RESULTS ---

| | ---HOLDING RESULTS BEFORE INCOME TAXES--- | | | | | | ---HOLDING RESULTS AFTER TAXES--- | | | | | ----OVERALL RESULTS IF SOLD AT YEAR END---- | | | | | |
|---|---|---|---|---|---|---|---|---|---|---|---|---|---|---|---|---|---|
| YR | GROSS INCOME | OPERATE EXPENSE | MORTGAGE-- INTR | AMORT | CASH FLOW | %RE TURN | DEPREC IATION | TAXABLE INCOME | TAXES DUE | CASH FLOW | %RE TURN | SALE PRICE | DEBT REPAY | TAXES DUE | CASH FLOW | TOTAL PROFIT | %IRR |
| 1 | 200 | 80 | 120 | 3 | -3 | -1.5 | 53 | -53 | -27 | 24 | 11.8 | 940 | 797 | -1 | 145 | -32 | -15.9 |
| 2 | 200 | 80 | 119 | 4 | -3 | -1.5 | 53 | -53 | -26 | 23 | 11.7 | 940 | 793 | 9 | 138 | -16 | -4.2 |
| 3 | 200 | 80 | 119 | 4 | -3 | -1.5 | 53 | -52 | -26 | 23 | 11.5 | 940 | 789 | 20 | 131 | 1 | 0.2 |
| 4 | 200 | 80 | 118 | 5 | -3 | -1.5 | 53 | -51 | -26 | 23 | 11.4 | 940 | 784 | 31 | 125 | 18 | 2.6 |
| 5 | 200 | 80 | 117 | 6 | -3 | -1.5 | 53 | -51 | -25 | 22 | 11.2 | 940 | 778 | 41 | 121 | 36 | 4.2 |

Reprinted with the permission of The Mader Group, Inc., Narberth, PA.

TABLE 15.8 *(concluded)*

## INFLATION OF SALE PRICE, INCOME, AND EXPENSE AT 5-10-15% ANNUALLY

| YR | GROSS INCOME | OPERATE EXPENSE | MORTGAGE-- INTR | MORTGAGE-- AMORT | CASH FLOW | % RE TURN | DEPREC IATION | TAXABLE INCOME | TAXES DUE | CASH FLOW | % RE TURN | SALE PRICE | DEBT REPAY | TAXES DUE | CASH FLOW | TOTAL PROFIT | % IRR |
|---|---|---|---|---|---|---|---|---|---|---|---|---|---|---|---|---|---|
| | | | HOLDING RESULTS BEFORE INCOME TAXES | | | | | HOLDING RESULTS AFTER TAXES | | | | | OVERALL RESULTS IF SOLD AT YEAR END | | | | |
| 1 | 200 | 80 | 120 | 3 | -3 | -1.5 | 53 | -53 | -27 | 24 | 11.8 | 987 | 797 | 8 | 182 | 6 | 2.8 |
| 2 | 220 | 92 | 119 | 4 | 5 | 2.5 | 53 | -45 | -22 | 27 | 13.7 | 1036 | 793 | 29 | 215 | 66 | 16.0 |
| 3 | 242 | 106 | 119 | 4 | 13 | 6.6 | 53 | -36 | -18 | 31 | 15.6 | 1088 | 789 | 50 | 250 | 132 | 20.3 |
| 4 | 266 | 122 | 118 | 5 | 22 | 10.8 | 53 | -27 | -13 | 35 | 17.5 | 1143 | 784 | 71 | 287 | 205 | 22.1 |
| 5 | 293 | 140 | 117 | 6 | 30 | 15.0 | 53 | -18 | -9 | 39 | 19.4 | 1200 | 778 | 93 | 328 | 284 | 22.9 |

## INFLATION OF SALE PRICE, INCOME, AND EXPENSE AT 10% ANNUALLY

| YR | GROSS INCOME | OPERATE EXPENSE | MORTGAGE-- INTR | MORTGAGE-- AMORT | CASH FLOW | % RE TURN | DEPREC IATION | TAXABLE INCOME | TAXES DUE | CASH FLOW | % RE TURN | SALE PRICE | DEBT REPAY | TAXES DUE | CASH FLOW | TOTAL PROFIT | % IRR |
|---|---|---|---|---|---|---|---|---|---|---|---|---|---|---|---|---|---|
| | | | HOLDING RESULTS BEFORE INCOME TAXES | | | | | HOLDING RESULTS AFTER TAXES | | | | | OVERALL RESULTS IF SOLD AT YEAR END | | | | |
| 1 | 200 | 80 | 120 | 3 | -3 | -1.5 | 53 | -53 | -27 | 24 | 11.8 | 1034 | 797 | 17 | 220 | 43 | 21.6 |
| 2 | 220 | 88 | 119 | 4 | 9 | 4.5 | 53 | -41 | -20 | 29 | 14.7 | 1137 | 793 | 49 | 295 | 148 | 33.5 |
| 3 | 242 | 97 | 119 | 4 | 22 | 11.1 | 53 | -27 | -13 | 36 | 17.8 | 1251 | 789 | 82 | 380 | 269 | 35.6 |
| 4 | 266 | 106 | 118 | 5 | 37 | 18.4 | 53 | -12 | -6 | 43 | 21.3 | 1376 | 784 | 118 | 474 | 406 | 35.7 |
| 5 | 293 | 117 | 117 | 6 | 53 | 26.4 | 53 | 5 | 3 | 50 | 25.1 | 1514 | 778 | 156 | 580 | 561 | 35.2 |

Reprinted with the permission of The Mader Group, Inc., Narberth, PA.

# 16 Land and Development Property

This chapter presents six reference tables detailing the profitability of non-income-generating *land and development property that is non-depreciable*. Below is an index to this chapter's specific tables, showing the key factors varied and summarized results.

| Table | Percent Mortgaged | Percent Mortgage Interest Rate | Percent Year 5 Rates of Return | | |
|-------|-------------------|-------------------------------|--------------------------------|--------------------------------|--------------------------------|
| | | | 5–0–10% Inflation | 15-0-10% Inflation | 25–0–10% Inflation |
| 16.1 | 60 | 10 | − 2.5 | 13.2 | 27.2 |
| 16.2 | 60 | 15 | − 5.2 | 11.3 | 25.8 |
| 16.3 | 60 | 20 | − 8.1 | 9.3 | 24.2 |
| 16.4 | 80 | 10 | − 5.8 | 16.3 | 34.5 |
| 16.5 | 80 | 15 | − 11.2 | 12.9 | 31.9 |
| 16.6 | 80 | 20 | − 17.2 | 9.2 | 29.0 |

## TABLE 16.1
## Land and development property—no depreciation (per $1,000)

KEY OPERATING FACTORS ARE ---

| TOTAL PROJECT COST | ---MORTGAGE TERMS--- AMOUNT | % INTR | LIFE | ----OPERATING & INFLATION ASSUMPTIONS---- NET RESALE PRICE | % INFL | GROSS INCOME | % INFL | OPERATING EXPENSE | % INFL | ----DEPRECIATION--- AMOUNT | LIFE | RATE | ---TAX RATES--- INCOME | CAP GAIN |
|---|---|---|---|---|---|---|---|---|---|---|---|---|---|---|
| 1000 | 600 | 10.00 | 10 | 900 | 5 | 0 | 0 | 20 | 10 | | | | 50% | 20% |

PRE-OPERATING SUMMARY ---

| EQUITY AMOUNT | ---MORTGAGE TERMS--- % DEBT | MONTHLY | YEARLY | % NET RESALE TO COST | GROSS RENT MULT | % INCOME TO COST | % NOI TO COST | % DEPREC TO COST |
|---|---|---|---|---|---|---|---|---|
| 400 | 60.00 | 8 | 95 | 90.0 | 0.0 | 0.0 | -2.0 | 0.0 |

OPERATING RESULTS ---

| YR | ---HOLDING RESULTS BEFORE INCOME TAXES--- GROSS INCOME | OPERATE EXPENSE | --MORTGAGE-- INTR | AMORT | CASH FLOW | % RE TURN | ---HOLDING RESULTS AFTER TAXES-- DEPREC IATION | TAXABLE INCOME | TAXES DUE | CASH FLOW | % RE TURN | ----OVERALL RESULTS IF SOLD AT YEAR END---- SALE PRICE | DEBT REPAY | TAXES DUE | CASH FLOW | TOTAL PROFIT | % IRR |
|---|---|---|---|---|---|---|---|---|---|---|---|---|---|---|---|---|---|
| 1 | 0 | 20 | 58 | 37 | -115 | -28.8 | 0 | -78 | -39 | -76 | -19.0 | 945 | 563 | -11 | 393 | -83 | -20.8 |
| 2 | 0 | 22 | 54 | 41 | -117 | -29.3 | 0 | -76 | -38 | -79 | -19.7 | 992 | 523 | -2 | 471 | -84 | -10.0 |
| 3 | 0 | 24 | 50 | 45 | -119 | -29.8 | 0 | -74 | -37 | -82 | -20.5 | 1042 | 478 | 8 | 556 | -81 | -6.0 |
| 4 | 0 | 27 | 46 | 50 | -122 | -30.4 | 0 | -72 | -36 | -86 | -21.4 | 1094 | 428 | 19 | 647 | -76 | -3.8 |
| 5 | 0 | 29 | 40 | 55 | -124 | -31.1 | 0 | -70 | -35 | -90 | -22.4 | 1149 | 373 | 30 | 746 | -67 | -2.5 |

# TABLE 16.1 (concluded)

## INFLATION OF SALE PRICE, INCOME, AND EXPENSE AT 15-0-10% ANNUALLY

OPERATING RESULTS ---

| | ---HOLDING RESULTS BEFORE INCOME TAXES--- | | | | | ---HOLDING RESULTS AFTER TAXES-- | | | | | ---OVERALL RESULTS IF SOLD AT YEAR END---- | | | | | |
|---|---|---|---|---|---|---|---|---|---|---|---|---|---|---|---|---|
| YR | GROSS INCOME | OPERATE EXPENSE | MORTGAGE-- INTR | AMORT | CASH FLOW | % RE TURN | DEPREC IATION | TAXABLE INCOME | TAXES DUE | CASH FLOW | % RE TURN | SALE PRICE | DEBT REPAY | TAXES DUE | CASH FLOW | TOTAL PROFIT | % IRR |
| 1 | 20 | 58 | 37 | -115 | -28.8 | 0 | -78 | -39 | -76 | -19.0 | 1035 | 563 | 7 | 465 | -11 | -2.8 |
| 2 | 22 | 54 | 41 | -117 | -29.3 | 0 | -76 | -38 | -79 | -19.7 | 1190 | 523 | 38 | 630 | 75 | 8.2 |
| 3 | 24 | 50 | 45 | -119 | -29.8 | 0 | -74 | -37 | -82 | -20.5 | 1369 | 478 | 74 | 817 | 180 | 11.4 |
| 4 | 27 | 46 | 50 | -122 | -30.4 | 0 | -72 | -36 | -86 | -21.4 | 1574 | 428 | 115 | 1031 | 309 | 12.7 |
| 5 | 29 | 40 | 55 | -124 | -31.1 | 0 | -70 | -35 | -90 | -22.4 | 1810 | 373 | 162 | 1275 | 463 | 13.2 |

## INFLATION OF SALE PRICE, INCOME, AND EXPENSE AT 25-0-10% ANNUALLY

OPERATING RESULTS ---

| | ---HOLDING RESULTS BEFORE INCOME TAXES--- | | | | | ---HOLDING RESULTS AFTER TAXES-- | | | | | ---OVERALL RESULTS IF SOLD AT YEAR END---- | | | | | |
|---|---|---|---|---|---|---|---|---|---|---|---|---|---|---|---|---|
| YR | GROSS INCOME | OPERATE EXPENSE | MORTGAGE-- INTR | AMORT | CASH FLOW | % RE TURN | DEPREC IATION | TAXABLE INCOME | TAXES DUE | CASH FLOW | % RE TURN | SALE PRICE | DEBT REPAY | TAXES DUE | CASH FLOW | TOTAL PROFIT | % IRR |
| 1 | 20 | 58 | 37 | -115 | -28.8 | 0 | -78 | -39 | -76 | -19.0 | 1125 | 563 | 25 | 537 | 61 | 15.2 |
| 2 | 22 | 54 | 41 | -117 | -29.3 | 0 | -76 | -38 | -79 | -19.7 | 1406 | 523 | 81 | 802 | 248 | 25.3 |
| 3 | 24 | 50 | 45 | -119 | -29.8 | 0 | -74 | -37 | -82 | -20.5 | 1758 | 478 | 152 | 1129 | 492 | 27.2 |
| 4 | 27 | 46 | 50 | -122 | -30.4 | 0 | -72 | -36 | -86 | -21.4 | 2197 | 428 | 239 | 1530 | 807 | 27.4 |
| 5 | 29 | 40 | 55 | -124 | -31.1 | 0 | -70 | -35 | -90 | -22.4 | 2747 | 373 | 349 | 2024 | 1212 | 27.2 |

Reprinted with the permission of The Mader Group, Inc., Narberth, PA.

## TABLE 16.2
### Land and development property—no depreciation (per $1,000)

KEY OPERATING FACTORS ARE ---

| TOTAL PROJECT COST | ---MORTGAGE TERMS--- | | | ----OPERATING & INFLATION ASSUMPTIONS---- | | | | | | ---TAX RATES--- | |
|---|---|---|---|---|---|---|---|---|---|---|---|
| | AMOUNT | % INTR | LIFE | NET RESALE PRICE | % INFL | GROSS INCOME | % INFL | OPERATING EXPENSE | % INFL | INCOME | CAP GAIN |
| 1000 | 600 | 15.00 | 10 | 900 | 5 | 0 | 0 | 20 | 10 | 50% | 20% |

PRE-OPERATING SUMMARY ---

| EQUITY AMOUNT | ---MORTGAGE TERMS--- | | | % NET RESALE TO COST | % INCOME TO COST | GROSS RENT MULT | % EXPENSE TO INCOME | ----DEPRECIATION--- | | % NOI TO COST | % DEPREC TO COST |
|---|---|---|---|---|---|---|---|---|---|---|---|
| | % DEBT | MONTHLY | YEARLY | | | | | AMOUNT LIFE | RATE | | |
| 400 | 60.00 | 10 | 116 | 90.0 | 0.0 | 0.0 | 0.0 | | | -2.0 | 0.0 |

OPERATING RESULTS ---

| YR | ---HOLDING RESULTS BEFORE INCOME TAXES--- | | | | | | ---HOLDING RESULTS AFTER TAXES--- | | | | | ---OVERALL RESULTS IF SOLD AT YEAR END---- | | | | | |
|---|---|---|---|---|---|---|---|---|---|---|---|---|---|---|---|---|---|
| | GROSS INCOME | OPERATE EXPENSE | --MORTGAGE-- INTR | AMORT | CASH FLOW | % RE TURN | DEPREC IATION | TAXABLE INCOME | TAXES DUE | CASH FLOW | % RE TURN | SALE PRICE | DEBT REPAY | TAXES DUE | CASH FLOW | TOTAL PROFIT | % IRR |
| 1 | 0 | 20 | 88 | 28 | -136 | -34.0 | 0 | -108 | -54 | -82 | -20.5 | 945 | 572 | -11 | 384 | -98 | -24.5 |
| 2 | 0 | 22 | 84 | 33 | -138 | -34.5 | 0 | -106 | -53 | -85 | -21.3 | 992 | 539 | -2 | 454 | -113 | -13.7 |
| 3 | 0 | 24 | 78 | 38 | -140 | -35.1 | 0 | -103 | -51 | -89 | -22.3 | 1042 | 502 | 8 | 532 | -125 | -9.4 |
| 4 | 0 | 27 | 72 | 44 | -143 | -35.7 | 0 | -99 | -49 | -93 | -23.3 | 1094 | 458 | 19 | 617 | -132 | -6.9 |
| 5 | 0 | 29 | 65 | 51 | -145 | -36.4 | 0 | -95 | -47 | -98 | -24.5 | 1149 | 407 | 30 | 712 | -136 | -5.2 |

Reprinted with the permission of The Mader Group, Inc., Narberth, PA.

TABLE 16.2 (concluded)

## INFLATION OF SALE PRICE, INCOME, AND EXPENSE AT 15-0-10% ANNUALLY

OPERATING RESULTS ---

| YR | GROSS INCOME | OPERATE EXPENSE | MORTGAGE INTR | MORTGAGE AMORT | CASH FLOW | % RE TURN | DEPREC IATION | TAXABLE INCOME | TAXES DUE | CASH FLOW | % RE TURN | SALE PRICE | DEBT REPAY | TAXES DUE | CASH FLOW | TOTAL PROFIT | % IRR |
|---|---|---|---|---|---|---|---|---|---|---|---|---|---|---|---|---|---|
| 1 | 0 | 20 | 88 | 28 | -136 | -34.0 | 0 | -108 | -54 | -82 | -20.5 | 1035 | 572 | 7 | 456 | -26 | -6.5 |
| 2 | 0 | 22 | 84 | 33 | -138 | -34.5 | 0 | -106 | -53 | -85 | -21.3 | 1190 | 539 | 38 | 613 | 45 | 5.0 |
| 3 | 0 | 24 | 78 | 38 | -140 | -35.1 | 0 | -103 | -51 | -89 | -22.3 | 1369 | 502 | 74 | 793 | 137 | 8.7 |
| 4 | 0 | 27 | 72 | 44 | -143 | -35.7 | 0 | -99 | -49 | -93 | -23.3 | 1574 | 458 | 115 | 1001 | 252 | 10.4 |
| 5 | 0 | 29 | 65 | 51 | -145 | -36.4 | 0 | -95 | -47 | -98 | -24.5 | 1810 | 407 | 162 | 1241 | 393 | 11.3 |

## INFLATION OF SALE PRICE, INCOME, AND EXPENSE AT 25-0-10% ANNUALLY

OPERATING RESULTS ---

| YR | GROSS INCOME | OPERATE EXPENSE | MORTGAGE INTR | MORTGAGE AMORT | CASH FLOW | % RE TURN | DEPREC IATION | TAXABLE INCOME | TAXES DUE | CASH FLOW | % RE TURN | SALE PRICE | DEBT REPAY | TAXES DUE | CASH FLOW | TOTAL PROFIT | % IRR |
|---|---|---|---|---|---|---|---|---|---|---|---|---|---|---|---|---|---|
| 1 | 0 | 20 | 88 | 28 | -136 | -34.0 | 0 | -108 | -54 | -82 | -20.5 | 1125 | 572 | 25 | 528 | 46 | 11.5 |
| 2 | 0 | 22 | 84 | 33 | -138 | -34.5 | 0 | -106 | -53 | -85 | -21.3 | 1406 | 539 | 81 | 786 | 218 | 22.4 |
| 3 | 0 | 24 | 78 | 38 | -140 | -35.1 | 0 | -103 | -51 | -89 | -22.3 | 1758 | 502 | 152 | 1105 | 448 | 25.0 |
| 4 | 0 | 27 | 72 | 44 | -143 | -35.7 | 0 | -99 | -49 | -93 | -23.3 | 2197 | 458 | 239 | 1500 | 750 | 25.7 |
| 5 | 0 | 29 | 65 | 51 | -145 | -36.4 | 0 | -95 | -47 | -98 | -24.5 | 2747 | 407 | 349 | 1990 | 1142 | 25.8 |

Reprinted with the permission of The Mader Group, Inc., Narberth, PA.

# TABLE 16.3
## Land and development property—no depreciation (per $1,000)

KEY OPERATING FACTORS ARE ---

| TOTAL PROJECT COST | ---MORTGAGE TERMS--- | | | NET RESALE PRICE | ----OPERATING & INFLATION ASSUMPTIONS---- | | | | | ----DEPRECIATION---- | | | ---TAX RATES--- | |
|---|---|---|---|---|---|---|---|---|---|---|---|---|---|---|
| | AMOUNT | % INTR | LIFE | | % RESALE INFL | GROSS INCOME | % INCOME INFL | % OPERATING EXPENSE | EXPENSE INFL | AMOUNT | LIFE | RATE | INCOME | CAP GAIN |
| 1000 | 600 | 20.00 | 10 | 900 | 5 | 0 | 0 | 20 | 10 | | | | 50% | 20% |

PRE-OPERATING SUMMARY ---

| EQUITY AMOUNT | ---MORTGAGE TERMS--- | | | % NET RESALE TO COST | % INCOME TO COST | GROSS RENT MULT | % EXPENSE TO INCOME | % NOI TO COST | % DEPREC TO COST |
|---|---|---|---|---|---|---|---|---|---|
| | % DEBT | MONTHLY | YEARLY | | | | | | |
| 400 | 60.00 | 12 | 139 | 90.0 | 0.0 | 0.0 | 0.0 | -2.0 | 0.0 |

OPERATING RESULTS ---

| YR | ---HOLDING RESULTS BEFORE INCOME TAXES--- | | | | | | ---HOLDING RESULTS AFTER TAXES--- | | | | | ---OVERALL RESULTS IF SOLD AT YEAR END--- | | | | | |
|---|---|---|---|---|---|---|---|---|---|---|---|---|---|---|---|---|---|
| | GROSS INCOME | OPERATE EXPENSE | MORTGAGE INTR | MORTGAGE AMORT | CASH FLOW | % RE TURN | DEPREC IATION | TAXABLE INCOME | TAXES DUE | CASH FLOW | % RE TURN | SALE PRICE | DEBT REPAY | TAXES DUE | CASH FLOW | TOTAL PROFIT | % IRR |
| 1 | 0 | 20 | 118 | 21 | -159 | -39.8 | 0 | -138 | -69 | -90 | -22.5 | 945 | 579 | -11 | 377 | -113 | -28.3 |
| 2 | 0 | 22 | 114 | 26 | -161 | -40.3 | 0 | -136 | -68 | -93 | -23.3 | 992 | 553 | -2 | 440 | -143 | -17.4 |
| 3 | 0 | 24 | 108 | 31 | -163 | -40.8 | 0 | -132 | -66 | -97 | -24.3 | 1042 | 522 | 8 | 511 | -169 | -12.9 |
| 4 | 0 | 27 | 101 | 38 | -166 | -41.4 | 0 | -128 | -64 | -102 | -25.5 | 1094 | 484 | 19 | 591 | -192 | -10.1 |
| 5 | 0 | 29 | 93 | 46 | -168 | -42.1 | 0 | -122 | -61 | -107 | -26.9 | 1149 | 438 | 30 | 681 | -209 | -8.1 |

Reprinted with the permission of The Mader Group, Inc., Narberth, PA.

# TABLE 16.3 (concluded)

## INFLATION OF SALE PRICE, INCOME, AND EXPENSE AT 15-0-10% ANNUALLY

OPERATING RESULTS ---

| YR | ---HOLDING RESULTS BEFORE INCOME TAXES---- GROSS INCOME | OPERATE EXPENSE | --MORTGAGE-- INTR | AMORT | CASH FLOW | % RE TURN | ---HOLDING RESULTS AFTER TAXES-- DEPREC IATION | TAXABLE INCOME | TAXES DUE | CASH FLOW | % RE TURN | ---OVERALL RESULTS IF SOLD AT YEAR END----- SALE PRICE | DEBT REPAY | TAXES DUE | CASH FLOW | TOTAL PROFIT | % IRR |
|---|---|---|---|---|---|---|---|---|---|---|---|---|---|---|---|---|---|
| 1 | 0 | 20 | 118 | 21 | -159 | -39.8 | 0 | -138 | -69 | -90 | -22.5 | 1035 | 579 | 7 | 449 | -41 | -10.3 |
| 2 | 0 | 22 | 114 | 26 | -161 | -40.3 | 0 | -136 | -68 | -93 | -23.3 | 1190 | 553 | 38 | 599 | 15 | 1.7 |
| 3 | 0 | 24 | 108 | 31 | -163 | -40.8 | 0 | -132 | -66 | -97 | -24.3 | 1369 | 522 | 74 | 773 | 92 | 5.9 |
| 4 | 0 | 27 | 101 | 38 | -166 | -41.4 | 0 | -128 | -64 | -102 | -25.5 | 1574 | 484 | 115 | 975 | 193 | 8.1 |
| 5 | 0 | 29 | 93 | 46 | -168 | -42.1 | 0 | -122 | -61 | -107 | -26.9 | 1810 | 438 | 162 | 1211 | 320 | 9.3 |

## INFLATION OF SALE PRICE, INCOME, AND EXPENSE AT 25-0-10% ANNUALLY

OPERATING RESULTS ---

| YR | ---HOLDING RESULTS BEFORE INCOME TAXES---- GROSS INCOME | OPERATE EXPENSE | --MORTGAGE-- INTR | AMORT | CASH FLOW | % RE TURN | ---HOLDING RESULTS AFTER TAXES-- DEPREC IATION | TAXABLE INCOME | TAXES DUE | CASH FLOW | % RE TURN | ---OVERALL RESULTS IF SOLD AT YEAR END----- SALE PRICE | DEBT REPAY | TAXES DUE | CASH FLOW | TOTAL PROFIT | % IRR |
|---|---|---|---|---|---|---|---|---|---|---|---|---|---|---|---|---|---|
| 1 | 0 | 20 | 118 | 21 | -159 | -39.8 | 0 | -138 | -69 | -90 | -22.5 | 1125 | 579 | 25 | 521 | 31 | 7.7 |
| 2 | 0 | 22 | 114 | 26 | -161 | -40.3 | 0 | -136 | -68 | -93 | -23.3 | 1406 | 553 | 81 | 772 | 188 | 19.4 |
| 3 | 0 | 24 | 108 | 31 | -163 | -40.8 | 0 | -132 | -66 | -97 | -24.3 | 1758 | 522 | 152 | 1084 | 403 | 22.6 |
| 4 | 0 | 27 | 101 | 38 | -166 | -41.4 | 0 | -128 | -64 | -102 | -25.5 | 2197 | 484 | 239 | 1474 | 691 | 23.7 |
| 5 | 0 | 29 | 93 | 46 | -168 | -42.1 | 0 | -122 | -61 | -107 | -26.9 | 2747 | 438 | 349 | 1960 | 1070 | 24.2 |

Reprinted with the permission of The Mader Group, Inc., Narberth, PA.

## TABLE 16.4
### Land and development property—no depreciation (per $1,000)

KEY OPERATING FACTORS ARE ---

| TOTAL PROJECT COST | --MORTGAGE TERMS--- | | | -----OPERATING & INFLATION ASSUMPTIONS----- | | | | | | ----DEPRECIATION--- | | | ----TAX RATES--- | |
|---|---|---|---|---|---|---|---|---|---|---|---|---|---|---|
| | AMOUNT | % INTR | LIFE | NET RESALE PRICE | % INFL | GROSS INCOME | % INFL | OPERATING EXPENSE | % INFL | AMOUNT | LIFE | RATE | INCOME | CAP GAIN |
| 1000 | 800 | 10.00 | 10 | 900 | 5 | 0 | 0 | 20 | 10 | | | | 50% | 20% |

PRE-OPERATING SUMMARY ---

| EQUITY AMOUNT | --MORTGAGE TERMS--- | | | % NET RESALE TO COST | % INCOME TO COST | GROSS RENT MULT | % EXPENSE TO INCOME | % NOI TO COST | % DEPREC TO COST |
|---|---|---|---|---|---|---|---|---|---|
| | % DEBT | MONTHLY | YEARLY | | | | | | |
| 200 | 80.00 | 11 | 127 | 90.0 | 0.0 | 0.0 | 0.0 | -2.0 | 0.0 |

OPERATING RESULTS ---

| YR | ---HOLDING RESULTS BEFORE INCOME TAXES--- | | | | | | ---HOLDING RESULTS AFTER TAXES-- | | | | | ----OVERALL RESULTS IF SOLD AT YEAR END---- | | | | | |
|---|---|---|---|---|---|---|---|---|---|---|---|---|---|---|---|---|---|
| | GROSS INCOME | OPERATE EXPENSE | --MORTGAGE-- INTR | AMORT | CASH FLOW | % RE TURN | DEPREC IATION | TAXABLE INCOME | TAXES DUE | CASH FLOW | % RE TURN | SALE PRICE | DEBT REPAY | TAXES DUE | CASH FLOW | TOTAL PROFIT | % IRR |
| 1 | 0 | 20 | 78 | 49 | -147 | -73.4 | 0 | -98 | -49 | -98 | -49.0 | 945 | 751 | -11 | 205 | -93 | -46.4 |
| 2 | 0 | 22 | 73 | 54 | -149 | -74.4 | 0 | -95 | -47 | -102 | -50.8 | 992 | 697 | -2 | 297 | -102 | -22.6 |
| 3 | 0 | 24 | 67 | 60 | -151 | -75.5 | 0 | -91 | -46 | -105 | -52.7 | 1042 | 637 | 8 | 397 | -108 | -13.4 |
| 4 | 0 | 27 | 61 | 66 | -153 | -76.7 | 0 | -87 | -44 | -110 | -54.9 | 1094 | 571 | 19 | 504 | -110 | -8.7 |
| 5 | 0 | 29 | 54 | 73 | -156 | -78.1 | 0 | -83 | -42 | -115 | -57.3 | 1149 | 498 | 30 | 621 | -108 | -5.8 |

Reprinted with the permission of The Mader Group, Inc., Narberth, PA.

TABLE 16.4 (concluded)

## INFLATION OF SALE PRICE, INCOME, AND EXPENSE AT 15-0-10% ANNUALLY

OPERATING RESULTS ---

| | | | | | | | | | | | | | | | | | |
|---|---|---|---|---|---|---|---|---|---|---|---|---|---|---|---|---|---|
| | ---HOLDING RESULTS BEFORE INCOME TAXES--- | | --MORTGAGE-- | | | | ---HOLDING RESULTS AFTER TAXES-- | | | | | ---OVERALL RESULTS IF SOLD AT YEAR END--- | | | | | |
| YR | GROSS INCOME | OPERATE EXPENSE | INTR | AMORT | CASH FLOW | % RE TURN | DEPREC IATION | TAXABLE INCOME | TAXES DUE | CASH FLOW | % RE TURN | SALE PRICE | DEBT REPAY | TAXES DUE | CASH FLOW | TOTAL PROFIT | % IRR |
| 1 | 0 | 20 | 78 | 49 | -147 | -73.4 | 0 | -98 | -49 | -98 | -49.0 | 1035 | 751 | 7 | 277 | -21 | -10.4 |
| 2 | 0 | 22 | 73 | 54 | -149 | -74.4 | 0 | -95 | -47 | -102 | -50.8 | 1190 | 697 | 38 | 455 | 56 | 10.8 |
| 3 | 0 | 24 | 67 | 60 | -151 | -75.5 | 0 | -91 | -46 | -105 | -52.7 | 1369 | 637 | 74 | 658 | 153 | 15.2 |
| 4 | 0 | 27 | 61 | 66 | -153 | -76.7 | 0 | -87 | -44 | -110 | -54.9 | 1574 | 571 | 115 | 889 | 274 | 16.2 |
| 5 | 0 | 29 | 54 | 73 | -156 | -78.1 | 0 | -83 | -42 | -115 | -57.3 | 1810 | 498 | 162 | 1151 | 421 | 16.3 |

## INFLATION OF SALE PRICE, INCOME, AND EXPENSE AT 25-0-10% ANNUALLY

OPERATING RESULTS ---

| | | | | | | | | | | | | | | | | | |
|---|---|---|---|---|---|---|---|---|---|---|---|---|---|---|---|---|---|
| | ---HOLDING RESULTS BEFORE INCOME TAXES--- | | --MORTGAGE-- | | | | ---HOLDING RESULTS AFTER TAXES-- | | | | | ---OVERALL RESULTS IF SOLD AT YEAR END--- | | | | | |
| YR | GROSS INCOME | OPERATE EXPENSE | INTR | AMORT | CASH FLOW | % RE TURN | DEPREC IATION | TAXABLE INCOME | TAXES DUE | CASH FLOW | % RE TURN | SALE PRICE | DEBT REPAY | TAXES DUE | CASH FLOW | TOTAL PROFIT | % IRR |
| 1 | 0 | 20 | 78 | 49 | -147 | -73.4 | 0 | -98 | -49 | -98 | -49.0 | 1125 | 751 | 25 | 349 | 51 | 25.5 |
| 2 | 0 | 22 | 73 | 54 | -149 | -74.4 | 0 | -95 | -47 | -102 | -50.8 | 1406 | 697 | 81 | 628 | 229 | 39.6 |
| 3 | 0 | 24 | 67 | 60 | -151 | -75.5 | 0 | -91 | -46 | -105 | -52.7 | 1758 | 637 | 152 | 969 | 464 | 38.8 |
| 4 | 0 | 27 | 61 | 66 | -153 | -76.7 | 0 | -87 | -44 | -110 | -54.9 | 2197 | 571 | 239 | 1387 | 772 | 36.5 |
| 5 | 0 | 29 | 54 | 73 | -156 | -78.1 | 0 | -83 | -42 | -115 | -57.3 | 2747 | 498 | 349 | 1900 | 1170 | 34.5 |

Reprinted with the permission of The Mader Group, Inc., Narberth, PA.

## TABLE 16.5
### Land and development property—no depreciation (per $1,000)

KEY OPERATING FACTORS ARE ---

| TOTAL PROJECT COST | ---MORTGAGE TERMS--- | | | ----OPERATING & INFLATION ASSUMPTIONS------ | | | | | | ----TAX RATES--- | |
|---|---|---|---|---|---|---|---|---|---|---|---|
| | AMOUNT | % INTR | LIFE | NET RESALE PRICE | % INFL | GROSS INCOME | % INFL | % OPERATING EXPENSE | % INFL | INCOME | CAP GAIN |
| 1000 | 800 | 15.00 | 10 | 900 | 5 | 0 | 0 | 20 | 10 | 50% | 20% |

| ----DEPRECIATION--- | | |
|---|---|---|
| AMOUNT | LIFE | RATE |
| | | |

PRE-OPERATING SUMMARY ---

| EQUITY AMOUNT | ----MORTGAGE TERMS---- | | | % NET RESALE TO COST | % INCOME TO COST | GROSS RENT MULT | % EXPENSE TO INCOME | % NOI TO COST | % DEPREC TO COST |
|---|---|---|---|---|---|---|---|---|---|
| | % DEBT | MONTHLY | YEARLY | | | | | | |
| 200 | 80.00 | 13 | 155 | 90.0 | 0.0 | 0.0 | 0.0 | -2.0 | 0.0 |

OPERATING RESULTS ---

| | ---HOLDING RESULTS BEFORE INCOME TAXES--- | | | | | | ---HOLDING RESULTS AFTER TAXES--- | | | | | ---OVERALL RESULTS IF SOLD AT YEAR END---- | | | | | |
|---|---|---|---|---|---|---|---|---|---|---|---|---|---|---|---|---|---|
| YR | GROSS INCOME | OPERATE EXPENSE | MORTGAGE INTR | MORTGAGE AMORT | CASH FLOW | % RE TURN | DEPREC IATION | TAXABLE INCOME | TAXES DUE | CASH FLOW | % RE TURN | SALE PRICE | DEBT REPAY | TAXES DUE | CASH FLOW | TOTAL PROFIT | % IRR |
| 1 | 0 | 20 | 117 | 37 | -175 | -87.4 | 0 | -137 | -69 | -106 | -53.1 | 945 | 763 | -11 | 193 | -113 | -56.4 |
| 2 | 0 | 22 | 111 | 43 | -177 | -88.4 | 0 | -133 | -67 | -110 | -55.1 | 992 | 719 | -2 | 275 | -142 | -32.1 |
| 3 | 0 | 24 | 105 | 50 | -179 | -89.5 | 0 | -129 | -64 | -115 | -57.4 | 1042 | 669 | 8 | 365 | -166 | -21.3 |
| 4 | 0 | 27 | 96 | 58 | -182 | -90.8 | 0 | -123 | -62 | -120 | -60.0 | 1094 | 610 | 19 | 465 | -186 | -15.2 |
| 5 | 0 | 29 | 87 | 68 | -184 | -92.1 | 0 | -116 | -58 | -126 | -63.0 | 1149 | 543 | 30 | 576 | -201 | -11.2 |

Reprinted with the permission of The Mader Group, Inc., Narberth, PA.

# TABLE 16.5 (concluded)

## INFLATION OF SALE PRICE, INCOME, AND EXPENSE AT 15-0-10% ANNUALLY

OPERATING RESULTS ---

| YR | GROSS INCOME | OPERATE EXPENSE | MORTGAGE-- INTR | AMORT | CASH FLOW | % RE TURN | DEPREC IATION | TAXABLE INCOME | TAXES DUE | CASH FLOW | % RE TURN | SALE PRICE | DEBT REPAY | TAXES DUE | CASH FLOW | TOTAL PROFIT | IRR |
|----|----|----|----|----|----|----|----|----|----|----|----|----|----|----|----|----|----|
| | | | | | HOLDING RESULTS BEFORE INCOME TAXES--- | | | HOLDING RESULTS AFTER TAXES-- | | | | OVERALL RESULTS IF SOLD AT YEAR END---- | | | | | |
| 1 | 0 | 20 | 117 | 37 | -175 | -87.4 | 0 | -137 | -69 | -106 | -53.1 | 1035 | 763 | 7 | 265 | -41 | -20.4 |
| 2 | 0 | 22 | 111 | 43 | -177 | -88.4 | 0 | -133 | -67 | -110 | -55.1 | 1190 | 719 | 38 | 433 | 17 | 3.3 |
| 3 | 0 | 24 | 105 | 50 | -179 | -89.5 | 0 | -129 | -64 | -115 | -57.4 | 1369 | 669 | 74 | 626 | 95 | 9.6 |
| 4 | 0 | 27 | 96 | 58 | -182 | -90.8 | 0 | -123 | -62 | -120 | -60.0 | 1574 | 610 | 115 | 849 | 198 | 11.9 |
| 5 | 0 | 29 | 87 | 68 | -184 | -92.1 | 0 | -116 | -58 | -126 | -63.0 | 1810 | 543 | 162 | 1106 | 329 | 12.9 |

## INFLATION OF SALE PRICE, INCOME, AND EXPENSE AT 25-0-10% ANNUALLY

OPERATING RESULTS ---

| YR | GROSS INCOME | OPERATE EXPENSE | MORTGAGE-- INTR | AMORT | CASH FLOW | % RE TURN | DEPREC IATION | TAXABLE INCOME | TAXES DUE | CASH FLOW | % RE TURN | SALE PRICE | DEBT REPAY | TAXES DUE | CASH FLOW | TOTAL PROFIT | IRR |
|----|----|----|----|----|----|----|----|----|----|----|----|----|----|----|----|----|----|
| | | | | | HOLDING RESULTS BEFORE INCOME TAXES--- | | | HOLDING RESULTS AFTER TAXES-- | | | | OVERALL RESULTS IF SOLD AT YEAR END---- | | | | | |
| 1 | 0 | 20 | 117 | 37 | -175 | -87.4 | 0 | -137 | -69 | -106 | -53.1 | 1125 | 763 | 25 | 337 | 31 | 15.6 |
| 2 | 0 | 22 | 111 | 43 | -177 | -88.4 | 0 | -133 | -67 | -110 | -55.1 | 1406 | 719 | 81 | 606 | 190 | 33.1 |
| 3 | 0 | 24 | 105 | 50 | -179 | -89.5 | 0 | -129 | -64 | -115 | -57.4 | 1758 | 669 | 152 | 937 | 406 | 34.2 |
| 4 | 0 | 27 | 96 | 58 | -182 | -90.8 | 0 | -123 | -62 | -120 | -60.0 | 2197 | 610 | 239 | 1347 | 696 | 33.2 |
| 5 | 0 | 29 | 87 | 68 | -184 | -92.1 | 0 | -116 | -58 | -126 | -63.0 | 2747 | 543 | 349 | 1855 | 1078 | 31.9 |

Reprinted with the permission of The Mader Group, Inc., Narberth, PA.

## TABLE 16.6
## Land and development property—no depreciation (per $1,000)

KEY OPERATING FACTORS ARE ---

| TOTAL PROJECT COST | --MORTGAGE TERMS--- AMOUNT | % INTR | LIFE | ----OPERATING & INFLATION ASSUMPTIONS----- NET RESALE PRICE | % INFL | GROSS INCOME | % INFL | % OPERATING EXPENSE | INFL | ----DEPRECIATION--- AMOUNT | LIFE | RATE | ---TAX RATES--- INCOME | CAP GAIN |
|---|---|---|---|---|---|---|---|---|---|---|---|---|---|---|
| 1000 | 800 | 20.00 | 10 | 900 | 5 | 0 | 0 | 20 | 10 | | | | 50% | 20% |

PRE-OPERATING SUMMARY ---

| EQUITY AMOUNT | ---MORTGAGE TERMS---- % DEBT | MONTHLY | YEARLY | % NET RESALE TO COST | % INCOME TO COST | GROSS RENT MULT | % EXPENSE TO INCOME | % NOI TO COST | % DEPREC TO COST |
|---|---|---|---|---|---|---|---|---|---|
| 200 | 80.00 | 15 | 186 | 90.0 | 0.0 | 0.0 | 0.0 | -2.0 | 0.0 |

OPERATING RESULTS ---

| YR | ---HOLDING RESULTS BEFORE INCOME TAXES--- GROSS INCOME | OPERATE EXPENSE | --MORTGAGE-- INTR | AMORT | CASH FLOW | % RE TURN | ---HOLDING RESULTS AFTER TAXES--- DEPREC IATION | TAXABLE INCOME | TAXES DUE | CASH FLOW | % RE TURN | ---OVERALL RESULTS IF SOLD AT YEAR END---- SALE PRICE | DEBT REPAY | TAXES DUE | CASH FLOW | TOTAL PROFIT | % IRR |
|---|---|---|---|---|---|---|---|---|---|---|---|---|---|---|---|---|---|
| 1 | 0 | 20 | 158 | 28 | -206 | -102.8 | 0 | -178 | -89 | -117 | -58.4 | 945 | 772 | -11 | 184 | -133 | -66.4 |
| 2 | 0 | 22 | 151 | 34 | -208 | -103.8 | 0 | -173 | -87 | -121 | -60.4 | 992 | 738 | -2 | 256 | -182 | -42.0 |
| 3 | 0 | 24 | 144 | 42 | -210 | -104.9 | 0 | -168 | -84 | -126 | -62.8 | 1042 | 696 | 8 | 337 | -226 | -29.9 |
| 4 | 0 | 27 | 135 | 51 | -212 | -106.1 | 0 | -161 | -81 | -131 | -65.7 | 1094 | 645 | 19 | 430 | -265 | -22.3 |
| 5 | 0 | 29 | 124 | 62 | -215 | -107.4 | 0 | -153 | -76 | -138 | -69.2 | 1149 | 584 | 30 | 535 | -298 | -17.2 |

Reprinted with the permission of The Mader Group, Inc., Narberth, PA.

# TABLE 16.6 (concluded)

## INFLATION OF SALE PRICE, INCOME, AND EXPENSE AT 15-0-10% ANNUALLY

OPERATING RESULTS ---

| YR | GROSS INCOME | OPERATE EXPENSE | INTR | AMORT | CASH FLOW | % RE TURN | DEPREC IATION | TAXABLE INCOME | TAXES DUE | CASH FLOW | % RE TURN | SALE PRICE | DEBT REPAY | TAXES DUE | CASH FLOW | TOTAL PROFIT | % IRR |
|---|---|---|---|---|---|---|---|---|---|---|---|---|---|---|---|---|---|
| | | | ---HOLDING RESULTS BEFORE INCOME TAXES--- | | | | ---HOLDING RESULTS AFTER TAXES--- | | | | | ----OVERALL RESULTS IF SOLD AT YEAR END---- | | | | | |
| 1 | 0 | 20 | 158 | 28 | -206 | -102.8 | 0 | -178 | -89 | -117 | -58.4 | 1035 | 772 | 7 | 256 | -61 | -30.4 |
| 2 | 0 | 22 | 151 | 34 | -208 | -103.8 | 0 | -173 | -87 | -121 | -60.4 | 1190 | 738 | 38 | 414 | -23 | -4.6 |
| 3 | 0 | 24 | 144 | 42 | -210 | -104.9 | 0 | -168 | -84 | -126 | -62.8 | 1369 | 696 | 74 | 599 | 36 | 3.6 |
| 4 | 0 | 27 | 135 | 51 | -212 | -106.1 | 0 | -161 | -81 | -131 | -65.7 | 1574 | 645 | 115 | 814 | 119 | 7.2 |
| 5 | 0 | 29 | 124 | 62 | -215 | -107.4 | 0 | -153 | -76 | -138 | -69.2 | 1810 | 584 | 162 | 1065 | 232 | 9.2 |

## INFLATION OF SALE PRICE, INCOME, AND EXPENSE AT 25-0-10% ANNUALLY

OPERATING RESULTS ---

| YR | GROSS INCOME | OPERATE EXPENSE | INTR | AMORT | CASH FLOW | % RE TURN | DEPREC IATION | TAXABLE INCOME | TAXES DUE | CASH FLOW | % RE TURN | SALE PRICE | DEBT REPAY | TAXES DUE | CASH FLOW | TOTAL PROFIT | % IRR |
|---|---|---|---|---|---|---|---|---|---|---|---|---|---|---|---|---|---|
| | | | ---HOLDING RESULTS BEFORE INCOME TAXES--- | | | | ---HOLDING RESULTS AFTER TAXES--- | | | | | ----OVERALL RESULTS IF SOLD AT YEAR END---- | | | | | |
| 1 | 0 | 20 | 158 | 28 | -206 | -102.8 | 0 | -178 | -89 | -117 | -58.4 | 1125 | 772 | 25 | 328 | 11 | 5.6 |
| 2 | 0 | 22 | 151 | 34 | -208 | -103.8 | 0 | -173 | -87 | -121 | -60.4 | 1406 | 738 | 81 | 587 | 150 | 26.3 |
| 3 | 0 | 24 | 144 | 42 | -210 | -104.9 | 0 | -168 | -84 | -126 | -62.8 | 1758 | 696 | 152 | 910 | 347 | 29.3 |
| 4 | 0 | 27 | 135 | 51 | -212 | -106.1 | 0 | -161 | -81 | -131 | -65.7 | 2197 | 645 | 239 | 1312 | 618 | 29.5 |
| 5 | 0 | 29 | 124 | 62 | -215 | -107.4 | 0 | -153 | -76 | -138 | -69.2 | 2747 | 584 | 349 | 1814 | 981 | 29.0 |

Reprinted with the permission of The Mader Group, Inc., Narberth, PA.

# Index